The Administrator's Guide to School–Community Relations

Second Edition

George E. Pawlas

EYE ON EDUCATION
6 DEPOT WAY WEST, SUITE 106
LARCHMONT, NY 10538
(914) 833–0551
(914) 833–0761 fax
www.eyeoneducation.com

Library of Congress Cataloging-in-Publication Data

Pawlas, George.
The administrator's guide to school–community relations / George Pawlas. —2nd ed.
        p. cm.
ISBN 1-59667-005-3
    1. Community and school—United States. 2. School principals—United States. 3. Educational leadership—United States. I. Title.
LC221.P38 2005
371.19—dc22

                                                          2005002236

10 9 8 7 6 5 4 3

Editorial and production services provided by
Freelance Editorial Services
52 Oakwood Blvd., Poughkeepsie, NY 12603-4112
(845-471-3566)

Acknowledgments

This second edition, like the original, has been a collaborative effort. Many educators shared their ideas, strategies, examples, and artifacts as I developed the book. Their contributions are a large part of what you will experience as you work your way through the chapters.

Special thanks to my wife Sharon for her words of encouragement during the writing phase and to Bob Sickles for his support during the process.

TABLE OF CONTENTS

About the Author

George E. Pawlas, PhD, has spent 37 years in education. During his career, he has been an elementary school teacher, an elementary school principal, a district-level administrator, a state department consultant, and a coordinator of educational programs at an area campus. He is currently a professor in the educational leadership program at the University of Central Florida. In addition to working with students in the master's and doctoral degree programs, he has developed three courses at the master's level, including one on community school administration. Pawlas has authored more than 30 articles on education topics, coauthored three editions of a book on educational supervision, coauthored a book on adjunct teaching, and authored the second edition of this book. He has also conducted seminars and workshops and made presentations on relevant topics in education.

Preface

The responsibilities of a school principal continue to be expanded, reviewed, and scrutinized. Anyone who has ever served in that capacity will testify to that. One of the main tasks of the principalship centers on the communication that occurs within the school and what comes forth from the school. As the number of citizens who have school-age children continues to decrease, the need for sharing information with them about the school has increased.

Some school principals have taken a course on school–community relations as part of their preparation program. Others received little or no information about the topic as they prepared to become school principals. This book has been developed to help both groups as they meet the challenges of communicating with the school's publics—both internal and external.

The first edition of the *Administrator's Guide to School–Community Relations*, published in 1995, was the result of my personal experiences as a school principal. The examples and strategies of many of my principal colleagues were a major part of that edition. Some of these examples remain a part of the second edition, along with many new examples from today's practitioners.

I designed and teach a community school relations course as part of the educational leadership program at the University of Central Florida. Some examples of materials that were developed by students in the course have been included, too. The examples of some high-achieving "wannabe" school principals are part of a resource file that each student must prepare as a requirement of the course.

Years ago, I had the wonderful opportunity to meet and learn from Laurel Pennock. At the time, he was retired from a successful career as an elementary principal in Rochester, Minnesota. The importance of developing and maintaining positive school–community relations was an integral part of his message. He stressed paying attention to people and the details that others often overlook. I still remember two important messages he shared with me and others who were fortunate enough to meet him. First, "Smile until 11 a.m. and the rest of the day will take care of itself." And, a second message he emphasized was, "Be open and honest in your communications with all of the audiences associated with your school. Effective communications will gain support for the school's programs, curricula, and discipline which reflect an effective school." From my work with students in our program and the principals with whom they work, Mr. Pennock's words remain relevant today and should become part of a principal's standard operating procedures.

Although a principal can be effective in developing the mission of a school, the principal cannot carry the entire responsibility of the task. The perceptions people have about organizations, including schools, are the result of what those involved with the organization have about it. So the leadership of the principal is vital in setting the proper tone of all messages.

This second edition has been written to help school principals in providing leadership in developing an effective school–community relations plan. The focus of the book centers on providing the rationale for a school–community relations plan, along with actual strategies and examples used by practitioners and others. Readers are encouraged to use the information and examples of what worked for other principals—but each reader should consider how the idea or example can be modified for use in his or her own school.

Best wishes to each of you as you work in one of the best jobs in education: the principalship. The work you do each day is vital to our country's future and the success and well-being of all of the children and adults in your school. Please share your comments, successes, and ideas with me (gpawlas@pegasus.cc.ucf.edu). Together, we can continue to learn from each other while also helping those who will follow us.

George E. Pawlas

1
Uncommon Ideas for Uncommon Principals

Why Use Uncommon Ideas?

♦ The uncommon ideas used at a school will help to gain support for the school and the learning program at the school.

♦ The extra effort needed to implement these uncommon ideas is often very little in comparison to the impact they will bring.

♦ It is better to be proactive than reactive. Why not be the principal who does what others agree is good but that they never do?

Although schools have their own uniqueness and similarities, there are specific ways the school principal can provide the leadership to make a school very special in the community. Through the use of some tried-and-true strategies that other successful principals have used, they can make their mark and put the school in the forefront of the community. To be effective, a well-developed school–community relations plan must be developed. The 10 components of such a plan are the following:

♦ Provide the people with information about their schools.

♦ Provide the school with information about the community.

♦ Establish and maintain public confidence in the schools.

♦ Secure community support for the school and its program.

♦ Develop a commonality of purpose, effort, and achievement.

♦ Develop in the community a recognition of the vital importance of education in our social and economic life.

♦ Keep the community informed of new trends and developments in education.

♦ Develop an atmosphere of cooperation between the school and other social institutions of the community.

♦ Secure an evaluation of the school's program in terms of educational needs as the community sees them.

♦ Develop public goodwill toward the school.

The National School Public Relations Association (NSPRA) defines the efforts school principals must make as a planned, systematic, two-way process of communication between a school and its internal and external community through the use of interpersonal communication and mass media.

Goodwill Ambassadors for the Schools

Teachers, staff members, and students who are satisfied with their work and studies can be ambassadors of the school's mission in their community.

The interactions the teachers, staff members, and students have through their interpersonal communications with members of the external public associated with a school. One-to-one communication is often the best way to convey messages and help to change opinions people may have.

For more than 30 years, the Phi Delta Kappa/Gallup Poll of the Public's Attitudes Toward the Public Schools has revealed what Americans feel about public education. The 36th Annual Poll, which was released to the public in September 2004, contained the responses of 1,003 surveyed adults. One of the questions asked of those being surveyed was to grade the schools in their communities. The following chart reflects those responses:

Grading the Public Schools

	National Totals		No. of Children in School		Public School Parents	
	2004 %	2003 %	2004 %	2003 %	2004 %	2003 %
A & B	47	48	42	45	61	55
A	13	11	11	8	17	17
B	34	37	31	37	44	38
C	33	31	37	30	24	31
D	10	10	9	10	10	10
Fail	4	5	3	7	5	3
Don't know	6	6	9	8	0*	1

*Less than 0.05%

Source: *Phi Delta Kappan*, September 2004, Vol. 86, No. 1

Common Ideas to Put Your Plan in Action

Getting started with your school–community relations plan is the next step that needs to be taken. There are a number of tried-and-proven strategies, activities, and events that will support the school's mission while impacting the image of the school in the community. The following ideas have been implemented by schools around the country.

Getting Your School Identified and Noticed

School Marquee

The marquee is an effective tool to use to convey important messages to everyone passing by the school. Lori Kinney, principal at Mark Twain Elementary School in Littleton, Colorado, uses the school's marquee to announce the "Night of the Arts" as well as the school's "Field Days." She has developed a form for anyone who wants a message to be displayed, to be given to her before the message is displayed. Principal Ken Winn of Herbert C. Hoover Middle School in Indialantic, Florida, announced his school's achievement as a Florida "A" school with this message: "Congratulations: Hoover is an A School." Meanwhile, Cindy Van Meter, principal of Suntree Elementary School in Melbourne, Florida, told the community, "We need tennis balls." A call to the school revealed the need for the tennis balls to help the students' chairs glide across the tiled floors better. Scott Hollinger, principal of Christa McAuliffe Elementary School in McAllen, Texas, was actively involved in the installation of the school's new marquee, which has an electronic message sending capability. Joe Loffek, principal of Port Malabar Elementary School in Palm Bay, Florida, used the school's prominently displayed marquee (p. 4), on the school's roof, to announce an evening event, "Strings–Chorus Concert," and another event, "Young Authors Day." Other marquees have been seen that had messages recognizing teachers and students who accomplished something very special, such as National Board Certification for the teachers or a science fair or other competition for students.

School Profile Brochure

Some school principals have realized the value of having a colorful trifold brochure to share with interested people who might move into their school district. Julie Sharpe, a teacher at Oak Park Elementary School in Titusville, Florida, who is preparing to become an administrator, designed a trifold brochure for her school as a project when she was a student in a school–community relations course I taught. She used her color printer to develop the brochure, which included important information about the school's academic program course offerings. In addition, the fact the school was a Florida A+ School was included along

Port Malabar Elementary Marquee

with the school's vision and mission statements. (Julie's creation is shown opposite.) Mark Twain Elementary School shares important details about the school's Peak Performance School Program (p. 6) and the Kindergarten Extended Day Program (p. 7) through professionally developed trifold brochures. Principal Jim Hoogheem of Fernbrook Elementary School in Maple Grove, Minnesota, worked with members of his school to develop their "Let's Get Ready for Kindergarten" brochure (p. 8). Parents whose children might be involved in the Title I program at Port Malabar Elementary School benefit from the informative trifold brochure the school's principal, Joe Loffek, has available for them. Anne Young, principal at Clark Elementary School in Franklin, Indiana, has developed a trifold brochure with the personal information, professional preparation, and educational philosophies of each faculty member (p. 9). These are sent home with the children at the start of the school year. Each brochure has the person's voice mail and e-mail information. When developing a brochure or card about a school, plan for the unique programs or features of the school to be part of the contents. Some principals use the data and information gathered for the school's annual report in their brochure. There are limitless uses for such brochures—for example, distributing them to prospective home buyers, real estate agents, church leaders, and other community members.

(Text continues on page 10.)

Oak Park Elementary School Brochure

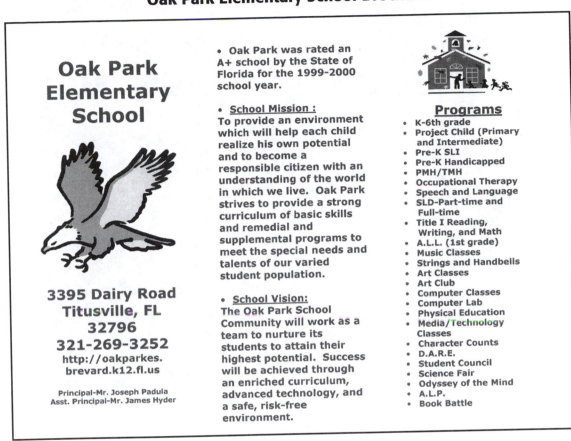

Oak Park Elementary School

3395 Dairy Road
Titusville, FL
32796
321-269-3252
http://oakparkes.
brevard.k12.fl.us

Principal-Mr. Joseph Padula
Asst. Principal-Mr. James Hyder

- Oak Park was rated an A+ school by the State of Florida for the 1999-2000 school year.

- **School Mission :**
To provide an environment which will help each child realize his own potential and to become a responsible citizen with an understanding of the world in which we live. Oak Park strives to provide a strong curriculum of basic skills and remedial and supplemental programs to meet the special needs and talents of our varied student population.

- **School Vision:**
The Oak Park School Community will work as a team to nurture its students to attain their highest potential. Success will be achieved through an enriched curriculum, advanced technology, and a safe, risk-free environment.

Programs
- K-6th grade
- Project Child (Primary and Intermediate)
- Pre-K SLI
- Pre-K Handicapped
- PMH/TMH
- Occupational Therapy
- Speech and Language
- SLD-Part-time and Full-time
- Title I Reading, Writing, and Math
- A.L.L. (1st grade)
- Music Classes
- Strings and Handbells
- Art Classes
- Art Club
- Computer Classes
- Computer Lab
- Physical Education
- Media/Technology Classes
- Character Counts
- D.A.R.E.
- Student Council
- Science Fair
- Odyssey of the Mind
- A.L.P.
- Book Battle

Mark Twain Elementary School Peak Performance Brochure

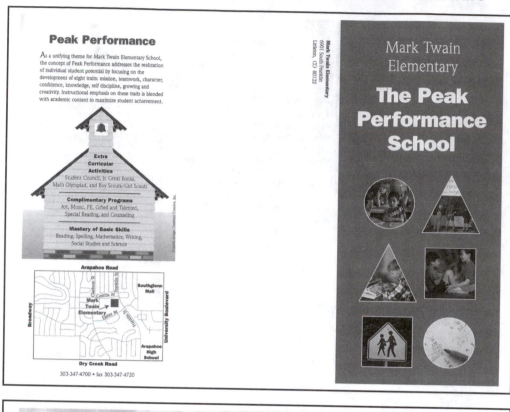

Peak Performance

As a unifying theme for Mark Twain Elementary School, the concept of Peak Performance addresses the realization of individual student potential by focusing on the development of eight traits: mission, teamwork, character, confidence, knowledge, self discipline, growing and creativity. Instructional emphasis on these traits is blended with academic content to maximize student achievement.

Extra Curricular Activities
Student Council, Jr. Great Books, Math Olympiad, and Boy Scouts/Girl Scouts

Complimentary Programs
Art, Music, PE, Gifted and Talented, Special Reading, and Counseling

Mastery of Basic Skills
Reading, Spelling, Mathematics, Writing, Social Studies and Science

303-347-4700 • fax 303-347-4720

Mark Twain Elementary
6901 South Franklin
Littleton, CO 80122

Mark Twain Elementary

The Peak Performance School

Curriculum

Mark Twain Elementary School offers students a full curriculum of both core academic subjects and special supplementary courses designed to strengthen and enrich the education process.

Along with daily instruction in essential subjects such as reading, spelling, mathematics, writing, social studies and science, all students attend regular classes in art, music, physical education, computer use and library skills, as well as periodic enrichment programs on a variety of topics. When appropriate, individual Twain students are also offered additional opportunities in gifted and talented, special reading, counseling, and other targeted areas.

Instruction

The instructional system employed at Twain Elementary is derived from a carefully planned mixture of traditional and progressive techniques.

It encourages a love for learning among students while requiring them to demonstrate a mastery of basic skills. It is directed by the teachers but fashioned to the individual needs of students. Social as well as academic prowess is emphasized. Extra-curricular activities (including Odyssey of the Mind, chess and Spanish clubs, Student Council, Boy Scouts/Girl Scouts, Junior Great Books, Math Olympiad, Room to Grow before and after-school care, and access to South Suburban Metropolitan Recreation and Park District) further enhance the overall program.

Teamwork

Twain teachers and staff work closely with each other and members of the community in a manner that is almost unprecedented today.

The well-regarded faculty, noted for their low turnover rate and high level of professional development, is also active in numerous district-wide committees organized by Littleton Public Schools. True school-centered decision making is achieved by staff and parental involvement in two advisory groups: the Twain Management Council (TMC) and Accountability Committee for School Improvement (ACSI). Also, Twain's Parent Teacher Organization (PTO) works to enrich the student experience through fundraising, communication, and special projects ranging from family reading night to the annual school yearbook.

Assessment

Multiple assessment methods are employed at Twain, enabling faculty and parents to closely monitor the academic progress of all students — and fine-tune the curriculum, when necessary, to meet their individual needs.

Mark Twain provides five opportunities during the school year for feedback concerning student progress. Highly detailed report cards are issued to all students at the end of each trimester, along with two individual parent-teacher conferences. An extensive research project is required annually of all older students, and assessed for both depth of information obtained and delivery of an oral presentation. Standardized national examinations, such as the Iowa Test of Basic Skills, are also given each year to students in grades 2-5.

Technology

Mark Twain Elementary School, home to one of Colorado's showplace computer labs, has long prided itself on the use of high-tech tools to broaden the educational experience of all its students.

Twain's WICAT computer lab, which is installed in its own special wing of the building, allows students in all grades to participate regularly and at their own pace in appropriate skill-building drills and specialized academic exercises. Additional electronic programs are planned by the school's Technology Committee. These include the availability of up-to-date computers in every classroom and the location of a state-of-the-art centralized multimedia work station in the Media Center. The school also has been readied for staff and student Internet access.

Behavior

The creation of a safe, well-disciplined and caring environment has always been one of Mark Twain Elementary's primary goals.

The school's well-defined and widely understood behavioral policies — along with the procedures for dealing with infractions — are intended to promote the safety and general welfare of all students, encourage respect and courtesy for all individuals, and create an atmosphere that encourages learning. Special services for students and families in need of additional assistance are available, as are periodic school-wide programs on topics like self-control and conflict resolution.

Mark Twain Elementary School Kindergarten Brochure

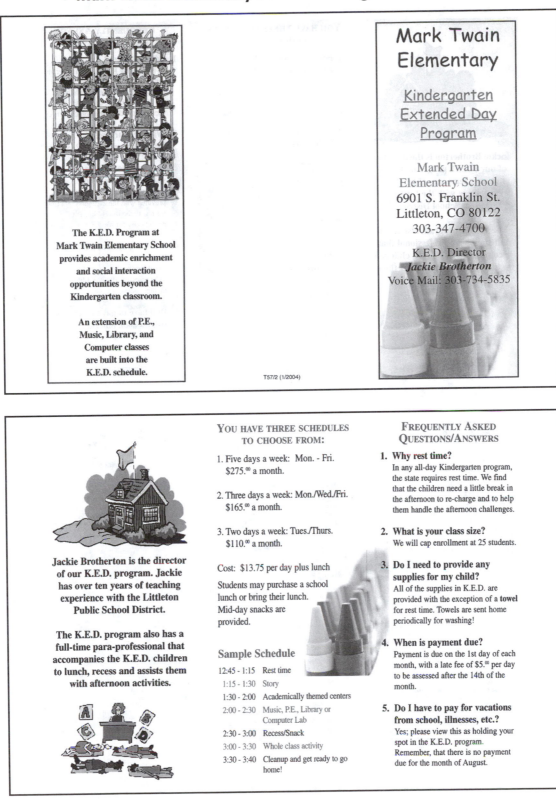

Mark Twain Elementary

Kindergarten Extended Day Program

Mark Twain
Elementary School
6901 S. Franklin St.
Littleton, CO 80122
303-347-4700

K.E.D. Director
Jackie Brotherton
Voice Mail: 303-734-5835

The K.E.D. Program at Mark Twain Elementary School provides academic enrichment and social interaction opportunities beyond the Kindergarten classroom.

An extension of P.E., Music, Library, and Computer classes are built into the K.E.D. schedule.

T57/2 (1/2004)

Jackie Brotherton is the director of our K.E.D. program. Jackie has over ten years of teaching experience with the Littleton Public School District.

The K.E.D. program also has a full-time para-professional that accompanies the K.E.D. children to lunch, recess and assists them with afternoon activities.

YOU HAVE THREE SCHEDULES TO CHOOSE FROM:

1. Five days a week: Mon. - Fri. $275.⁰⁰ a month.

2. Three days a week: Mon./Wed./Fri. $165.⁰⁰ a month.

3. Two days a week: Tues./Thurs. $110.⁰⁰ a month.

Cost: $13.75 per day plus lunch

Students may purchase a school lunch or bring their lunch. Mid-day snacks are provided.

Sample Schedule

12:45 - 1:15	Rest time
1:15 - 1:30	Story
1:30 - 2:00	Academically themed centers
2:00 - 2:30	Music, P.E., Library or Computer Lab
2:30 - 3:00	Recess/Snack
3:00 - 3:30	Whole class activity
3:30 - 3:40	Cleanup and get ready to go home!

FREQUENTLY ASKED QUESTIONS/ANSWERS

1. **Why rest time?**
   In any all-day Kindergarten program, the state requires rest time. We find that the children need a little break in the afternoon to re-charge and to help them handle the afternoon challenges.

2. **What is your class size?**
   We will cap enrollment at 25 students.

3. **Do I need to provide any supplies for my child?**
   All of the supplies in K.E.D. are provided with the exception of a **towel** for rest time. Towels are sent home periodically for washing!

4. **When is payment due?**
   Payment is due on the 1st day of each month, with a late fee of $5.⁰⁰ per day to be assessed after the 14th of the month.

5. **Do I have to pay for vacations from school, illnesses, etc.?**
   Yes; please view this as holding your spot in the K.E.D. program. Remember, that there is no payment due for the month of August.

Fernbrook Elementary School Kindergarten Brochure

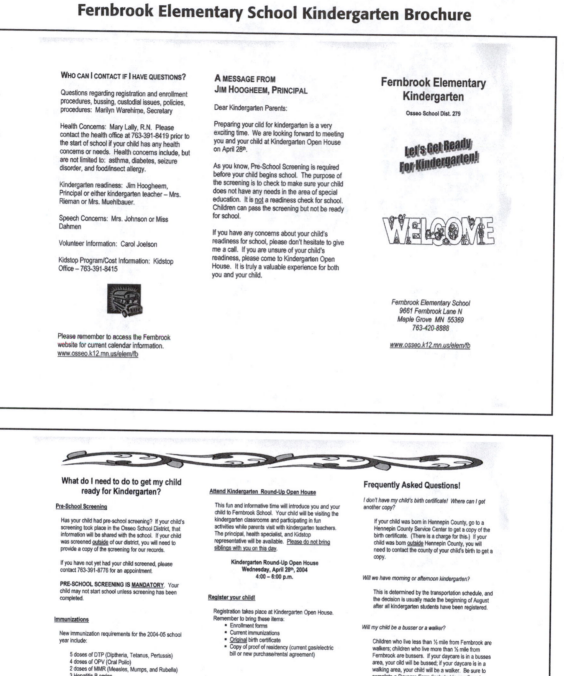

WHO CAN I CONTACT IF I HAVE QUESTIONS?

Questions regarding registration and enrollment procedures, bussing, custodial issues, policies, procedures: Marilyn Warehime, Secretary

Health Concerns: Mary Lally, R.N. Please contact the health office at 763-391-8419 prior to the start of school if your child has any health concerns or needs. Health concerns include, but are not limited to: asthma, diabetes, seizure disorder, and food/insect allergy.

Kindergarten readiness: Jim Hoogheem, Principal or either kindergarten teacher – Mrs. Rieman or Mrs. Muehlbauer.

Speech Concerns: Mrs. Johnson or Miss Dahmen

Volunteer Information: Carol Joelson

Kidstop Program/Cost Information: Kidstop Office – 763-391-8415

Please remember to access the Fernbrook website for current calendar information.
www.osseo.k12.mn.us/elem/fb

A MESSAGE FROM JIM HOOGHEEM, PRINCIPAL

Dear Kindergarten Parents:

Preparing your cild for kindergarten is a very exciting time. We are looking forward to meeting you and your child at Kindergarten Open House on April 28th.

As you know, Pre-School Screening is required before your child begins school. The purpose of the screening is to check to make sure your child does not have any needs in the area of special education. It is not a readiness check for school. Children can pass the screening but not be ready for school.

If you have any concerns about your child's readiness for school, please don't hesitate to give me a call. If you are unsure of your child's readiness, please come to Kindergarten Open House. It is truly a valuable experience for both you and your child.

Fernbrook Elementary Kindergarten

Osseo School Dist. 279

Let's Get Ready For Kindergarten!

WELCOME

Fernbrook Elementary School
9661 Fernbrook Lane N
Maple Grove MN 55369
763-420-8888

www.osseo.k12.mn.us/elem/fb

What do I need to do to get my child ready for Kindergarten?

Pre-School Screening

Has your child had pre-school screening? If your child's screening took place in the Osseo School District, that information will be shared with the school. If your child was screened outside of our district, you will need to provide a copy of the screening for our records.

If you have not yet had your child screened, please contact 763-391-8776 for an appointment.

PRE-SCHOOL SCREENING IS MANDATORY. Your child may not start school unless screening has been completed.

Immunizations

New immunization requirements for the 2004-05 school year include:

     5 doses of DTP (Diptheria, Tetanus, Pertussis)
     4 doses of OPV (Oral Polio)
     2 doses of MMR (Measles, Mumps, and Rubella)
     3 Hepatitis B series
     1 dose Varicella (Chicken Pox) new this year!

We urge parents to make appointments for immunizations as soon as possible. Physicals are not required but it is suggested that kindergarten students have physicals before starting school.

IMMUNIZAITONS ARE MANDATORY. Your child will be excluded from school if these are not provided prior to the beginning of the school year. Parents may file a medical exemption signed by a health care provider or a conscientious objection signed by a parent/guardian and notarized to be excluded from the immunization requirements.

Attend Kindergarten Round-Up Open House

This fun and informative time will introduce you and your child to Fernbrook School. Your child will be visiting the kindergarten classrooms and participating in fun activities while parents visit with kindergarten teachers. The principal, health specialist, and Kidstop representative will be available. Please do not bring siblings with you on this day.

**Kindergarten Round-Up Open House
Wednesday, April 28th, 2004
4:00 – 6:00 p.m.**

Register your child!

Registration takes place at Kindergarten Open House. Remember to bring these items:
- Enrollment forms
- Current immunizations
- Original birth certificate
- Copy of proof of residency (current gas/electric bill or new purchase/rental agreement)

Pay for school supplies!

Kindergarten Supply Kits may be purchased for $20, payable to the kindergarten teachers at the Fall Open House. Each student will then have a complete kit with all necessary supplies.

Frequently Asked Questions!

I don't have my child's birth certificate! Where can I get another copy?

If your child was born in Hennepin County, go to a Hennepin County Service Center to get a copy of the birth certificate. (There is a charge for this.) If your child was born outside Hennepin County, you will need to contact the county of your child's birth to get a copy.

Will we have morning or afternoon kindergarten?

This is determined by the transportation schedule, and the decision is usually made the beginning of August after all kindergarten students have been registered.

Will my child be a busser or a walker?

Children who live less than ½ mile from Fernbrook are walkers; children who live more than ½ mile from Fernbrook are bussers. If your daycare is in a busses area, your cild will be bussed; if your daycare is in a walking area, your child will be a walker. Be sure to complete a Daycare Form (included in enrollment packet) and turn in with enrollment materials; this information is vital.

I'm interested in the Kidstop Program. How do I register?

Kidstop is a before and after school child care program. Representatives from the program will be available during Kindergarten Open House to help with registeration.

Clark Elementary School Brochure

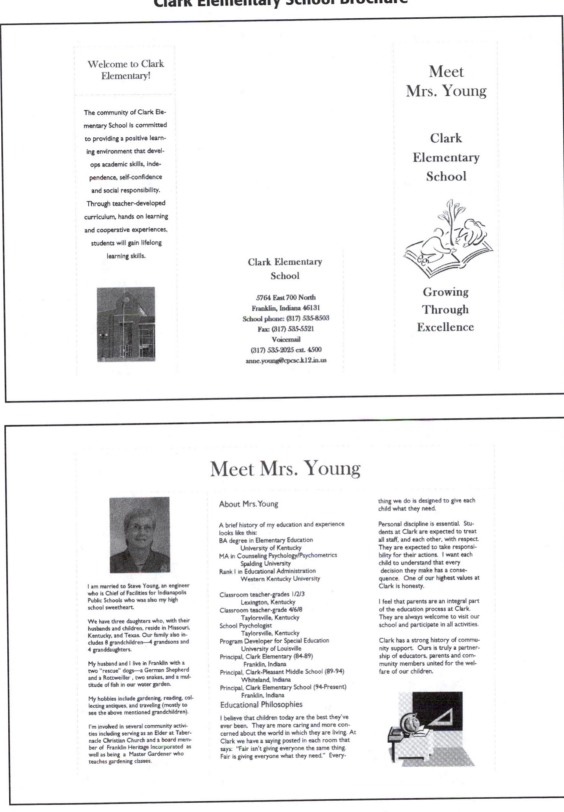

Welcome to Clark Elementary!

The community of Clark Elementary School is committed to providing a positive learning environment that develops academic skills, independence, self-confidence and social responsibility. Through teacher-developed curriculum, hands on learning and cooperative experiences, students will gain lifelong learning skills.

Clark Elementary School

5764 East 700 North
Franklin, Indiana 46131
School phone: (317) 535-8503
Fax: (317) 535-5521
Voicemail
(317) 535-2025 ext. 4500
anne.young@cpcsc.k12.in.us

Meet
Mrs. Young

Clark Elementary School

Growing Through Excellence

Meet Mrs. Young

I am married to Steve Young, an engineer who is Chief of Facilities for Indianapolis Public Schools who was also my high school sweetheart.

We have three daughters who, with their husbands and children, reside in Missouri, Kentucky, and Texas. Our family also includes 8 grandchildren—4 grandsons and 4 granddaughters.

My husband and I live in Franklin with a two "rescue" dogs—a German Shepherd and a Rottweiler , two snakes, and a multitude of fish in our water garden.

My hobbies include gardening, reading, collecting antiques, and traveling (mostly to see the above mentioned grandchildren).

I'm involved in several community activities including serving as an Elder at Tabernacle Christian Church and a board member of Franklin Heritage Incorporated as well as being a Master Gardener who teaches gardening classes.

About Mrs. Young

A brief history of my education and experience looks like this:
BA degree in Elementary Education
    University of Kentucky
MA in Counseling Psychology/Psychometrics
    Spalding University
Rank I in Educational Administration
    Western Kentucky University

Classroom teacher-grades 1/2/3
    Lexington, Kentucky
Classroom teacher-grade 4/6/8
    Taylorsville, Kentucky
School Psychologist
    Taylorsville, Kentucky
Program Developer for Special Education
    University of Louisville
Principal, Clark Elementary (84-89)
    Franklin, Indiana
Principal, Clark-Pleasant Middle School (89-94)
    Whiteland, Indiana
Principal, Clark Elementary School (94-Present)
    Franklin, Indiana

Educational Philosophies

I believe that children today are the best they've ever been. They are more caring and more concerned about the world in which they are living. At Clark we have a saying posted in each room that says: "Fair isn't giving everyone the same thing. Fair is giving everyone what they need." Every-

thing we do is designed to give each child what they need.

Personal discipline is essential. Students at Clark are expected to treat all staff, and each other, with respect. They are expected to take responsibility for their actions. I want each child to understand that every decision they make has a consequence. One of our highest values at Clark is honesty.

I feel that parents are an integral part of the education process at Clark. They are always welcome to visit our school and participate in all activities.

Clark has a strong history of community support. Ours is truly a partnership of educators, parents and community members united for the welfare of our children.

Map of the School

At DeLaura Middle School in Satellite Beach, Florida, principal Robert Spinner coupled the need to have a map of the school displayed prominently inside the entrance of the school's office area with a student project in the Computer Assisted Design (CAD) class. A student new to the school indicated that she needed to complete a project for the class. She mentioned how much easier it would have been for her to learn the school's floor plan if there was a map to follow. She created the map, to scale, and her teacher helped make the frame and plexiglas cover for it.

Welcoming Students—Orientations

Taking away the anxiety many students feel when they know they will be going to a new school can be minimized if they have an opportunity to visit the school before the actual first day. Many middle schools have a visitation day set up for students from their feeder schools. Some school principals plan the visitation day to include a tour of the school and a planned presentation with comments from students who attended the same elementary school and have made a smooth transition to the middle school. Question-and-answer opportunities have proven to be a welcome part of the Hoover Middle School plan. Planned visits to Melbourne High School in Melbourne, Florida, are held on special visitation days and times for new students a few weeks before each school year begins. Guidance counselors and student council representatives take the students and their parents on tours and discuss with them the details of their schedules.

When Dr. Lynn Long was a first-grade teacher at a school I worked at in South Carolina, she sent a personal note to students who would be in her first-grade class each year. The note contained an invitation to come to her home to visit and have afternoon tea and cookies. These small group get-togethers (usually no more than four to five students at a time per visit) allowed the students opportunities to see Dr. Long as a person in addition to being their teacher. Parents were invited to stay for the one-hour sessions. Needless to say, all parents wanted their children to be assigned to Dr. Long's classroom each year. One veteran teacher at Southdown Elementary School in Houma, Louisiana, takes time to call every student's parents after the first days of school. After she introduces herself and invites the parents to contact her at any time, she makes sure to say something nice about each student.

Years ago, when my teacher colleagues and I were required to call all of the parents of our students with something positive to say about the children, I had a special experience. It seems that my call to one mother caught her by surprise because I made only positive comments about her son. She had received calls from teachers in the past, but they always were about bad things her son had done. Anne Young, principal at Clark Elementary School, and Kelly Forey, the school's counselor, have developed a program called New Kids on the Block to help orient new students to the school. On the first day of school, every child goes to the gym for the orientation program. Room by room, each teacher is called to the center of the gym, and the names of the students assigned to the teacher are read. Each new student receives a small booklet with a page for each staff member (e.g., the secretary, school nurse, custodian, librarian, and head cook). Each student locates the 13 people with the help of a buddy and receives stickers to put on the appropriate pages. When the sticker book is complete, the principal gives the student a coupon for a free book from the book fair and two tickets to invite a special guest to school for a complimentary lunch. Principal Patricia Green of Cedar Heights Junior High School in Port Orchard, Washington, starts sending copies of the school's monthly newsletter to parents of incoming students in March. They are invited to an informative night visit to the school in May. Dr. Les Potter, principal at Silver Sands Middle School in Port Orange, Florida, greets new sixth graders at the WEB event—"Welcome EveryBody!"

Years ago, I prepared a letter to parents of children who were enrolling in kindergarten. The letter gave an overview of what to expect during the year plus a promise that additional information would be shared as the start of the school year approached. Principal Dr. Lolli Haws of Avery Elementary School in Webster Groves, Missouri, sends a personal letter to each child of the school. I prepared a letter of welcome, which was given to the parents when they registered their child at our school. The letter was updated regularly to include current information. Principal Dr. Doug Fiore of South Aurora Elementary School in Montpelier, Vermont, rides each school bus once during the first month of school. His school serves a large attendance area, and by riding the buses, he gets to see where the students live.

School Displays in Businesses

When I was the principal of an elementary school in South Carolina, we celebrated May as "Arts in the Schools Month." We had student musical performances as well as a display of student art work. One of the local pediatric dentists in the area always walked through the art display. He would select various student art pieces and ask us to have the parents contact him because he wanted to display the art work in his dental office. When he received permission, he framed the pictures, displayed them with the students' names attached, and after a year gave the professional-looking items to the student artists to have at their homes. A side benefit to him was that some of the students became his patients!

The Wachovia Banks have displayed student art work as well. The monthly displays feature artwork from an elementary school one month, a middle school another month, and a high school for another month. This cycle is repeated throughout the school year. Other schools have had student artists, under the direction of their teachers, paint store windows with seasonal scenes and messages.

Assisted Living/Senior Homes

These facilities will welcome visits and materials from school children. Choral groups from Longleaf and Suntree Elementary Schools in Melbourne, Florida, make regular visits to share their talents with the residents. As part of their presentation, the choral teachers make certain the students sing songs from the past—ones to which the residents can tap their toes. Students at Cypress Park Elementary School in Orlando, Florida, participate in the Taft Community Center Christmas Party. The annual Saturday event showcases performances by students in the primary grades, followed by students in grades 3 to 5. Some schools have involved students in the creation of place mats to be donated to the senior homes. Oftentimes this is done for seasonal purposes, but some principals have found that there are other times of the year when these items are also welcome.

Evening Principal Office Hours

When Bob Ziegler was an elementary school principal, he began a process of having evening office hours. He announced the day, date, and times in the previous month's newsletter to parents so that they would be aware of the opportunities to informally discuss school-related events or issues. Light refreshments were made available by the PTA, and Bob indicated he always had a small group of parents participate in the two-hour sessions each month.

Years ago I followed the lead of the principal I succeeded, Edith Underwood, by having Fireside Chats. She began the tradition and when I was appointed to succeed her, I was faced with the question, "Do you plan to continue the Fireside Chats?" My reply, of course, was yes! On cold Ohio winter evenings we even built a fire in the fireplace. I also had a faithful group of parents and community folks join me in various discussions each month. From suggestions that were received at these gatherings, we developed other evening learning opportunities such as guidance counselor presentations on parenting skills and discussions by the media specialist about new good books for children of all ages.

Community Projects

Students should be encouraged to be involved with projects that will enhance the community or help individuals. A middle school student who had a serious ailment and spent time in the Ronald McDonald House began a campaign to collect soda can ring pulls. What started as an individual project quickly spread by word of mouth to be a schoolwide activity (helped by an article in the principal's newsletters), a local newspaper article, and a television story. In a short time, 1.5 million ring pulls were gathered and donated. The physical education teacher at Mark Hopkins Elementary School in Centennial, Colorado, organized a 13.5-mile student walk sponsored by "Friends Make a Difference" from the school to a local hospital to help parents who had lost one child in an automobile accident pay the medical bills of another one of their children who was hurt in the accident. Support for the event was shared in the principals' newsletters from their schools in the district. The event found lots of sponsored walkers and much additional support from the community.

Real Estate Sales Meetings

In most areas of the United States, realtors meet on a regular, if not weekly, basis to discuss newly listed homes and strategies to sell other homes. These gatherings of agents are perfect opportunities for principals to share information about their schools. Following a carefully prepared presentation, packets of information can be shared with the sales force. Some items to include are copies of the trifold brochure about the school, recent principal newsletters, information about before- and after-school activities, qualifications of the teachers, accomplishments of the teachers, and successes of the students and other members of the school's "family." Some principals, the author included, followed up with the visit to the realtors' meeting with an invitation to have a meeting at the school. Following their regular meeting agenda, they were given tours of the school led by members of the student council. The meeting can conclude with a brief presentation by the principal and distribution of additional packets of materials to have for prospective home buyers. From my own experience, I found that several of the agents did revisit the school with new buyers. In addition, I always left several copies of every principal newsletter at the real estate agency. One real estate agency even included our school's name as the school the children would attend if a particular home was purchased.

Gold Passes for Seniors

In many communities, there is an increasing number of citizens who do not have children to send to the local schools. To get them informed and interested in your school, offer them the opportunity to receive a Golden Pass to attend school events free. Several high school principals have found these passes are great goodwill gestures for those citizens whose homes are near or adjacent to the school's campus. Other principals indicated they were able to the get seniors citizens to become involved with school activities as volunteers or mentors of students.

Grandparents' Day

An activity that has become an annual event at many elementary schools is Grandparents' Day. The process can be done in several ways, depending on the location and size of the schools and the interest shown by everyone. The positive aspects of having a student's real or surrogate grandparents visit the school are worth the effort. Door prizes and student-prepared gifts help to make the day memorable. Parent organizations usually are willing to provide refreshments.

Volunteers/Mentors

School principals and teachers have relied on the donations of time and talents from volunteers. Many of the volunteers are the parents of students, although in more recent years, many are also members of the community. Some school systems and states require the volunteers to pass strict screening techniques to ensure that child molesters or pedophiles are not among them. Mentors provide different means of support to students by giving time to support students who are having personal problems. In some instances, the mentors are business women or men who come to the school to eat lunch with the students. Most schools recognize the volunteers and mentors for the hours of service with performances by students and refreshments provided by the parent–teacher organizations. Volunteers at Mark Twain Elementary School are known as VIPs They are treated to a VIP's Tea each April. The highlight of every tea is the student musical program.

Alumni Recognition—Wall of Fame

When Martin Kane was the principal at Rocky River, Ohio, High School, he established an Alumni Wall of Fame. The inductees are high school alumni who have distinguished themselves in their professional careers. Some of the inductees include news reporters, a professional comedy writer, several doctors, clergy, community leaders, and athletes. The photos and plaques honoring each member of the Wall of Fame are prominently displayed in one of the main corridors of the school. This tradition has been maintained by other principals who have served at the school.

A school's foundation or other major funding group can provide the money to sponsor such a program. An organizing committee should be established to set the criteria for induction to the wall of fame. The selection committee should comprise community leaders and school staff. All honorees should be well respected and attribute a portion of their success to the time they spent at the high school. The induction should be a special event, such as a community luncheon or dinner. If possible, have opportunities for current students to meet with each year's inductees.

Showcases of Accomplishments

Most high schools have showcases in which the athletic trophies from the school's sports teams are displayed. In more recent years the academic achievements have begun to appear, too. Middle schools have also put their students' achievements and awards on display. Some elementary school principals are displaying, in a prominent place at school, photos of student council officers, safety patrol members, and other students who have distinguished themselves. These photos are changed each school year.

Birthday/Anniversary/History of the School

Is your school celebrating a birthday or anniversary in an upcoming year? To help commemorate the occasion, invite the members of the school's family to write short pieces about their memories of the school when they first came. For those new to the school, have them write projections about what they anticipate in future years. If made in poster format, these memories and projections can be displayed in prominent places for others to enjoy. Many schools have developed brochures that highlight the history of the school. These are distributed to new families and placed in prominent locations in the community, such as libraries, hospitals, doctors' offices, and real estate offices.

Videos/CDs/DVDs of "A Year at" Your School

One way to preserve the elements of a year at a school can be accomplished with videos, CDs, and DVDs, One process would be to make a DVD for every grade level and classroom, as well as for the school in general. Duplicate copies can be made and sold to help raise money for a school. In return, parents and students will have lifelong memories of a year at the school. For $40, students at Lee's Summit High School in Missouri receive a hardcover yearbook and a 45-minute companion CD with video and sound highlights of the past year. The CD includes footage from sporting events, prom highlights, and even teacher tours of their homes. The same strategy regarding the CDs can be used for elementary and middle schools by class or grade level or for the whole school. Once the master CD is created, it only takes a nominal amount of time and cost to make additional copies. This could be a source of support money for schools.

School Mascot

Do you capitalize on your school's mascot? By displaying the mascot in prominent places at the school, such as the cafeteria, gymnasium, or office area, you will be adding support to the spirit of the school. Schools where I have been the principal have the eagle, frog, and leprechaun prominently painted on the wall of the gymnasium and two school cafeterias. The design was transferred by projecting the image from an overhead projector, using the image from T-shirts, and other spirit items. Each mascot was painted in the school's colors on a wall in a prominent place. Not only did the image serve as an inspiration for the students and staff, but parents, volunteers, and visitors immediately knew what the school's mascot was. When a new school is built, selecting a mascot can be an important decision for years to come. Involving other people in that decision is a very wise move for a principal to consider. In some cases, contests were held for names and supporting reasons to be considered by a committee and voted on by students, teachers, and parents.

School Motto/Slogan

A school motto or slogan can serve as a reminder to parents and others receiving communication from a school what the main focus is at the school. For instance, Mark Twain Elementary School in Colorado is known as The Peak Performance School, and its mission statement is "I know where I'm going and how to get there." The motto "Growing Through Excellence" serves as a ready reminder of Clark Elementary School in Indiana. Students at Cypress Park Elementary School in Florida are reminded, "We've Got the Power!" Dr. Les Potter and his faculty at Silver Sands Middle School in Florida share their goal, "Linking Learning to Life." The cooperative focus at Hunter's Creek Middle School in Orlando, Florida, is apparent in the school's slogan, "Together We Reach Beyond Today." Jacqueline Norcel and her faculty at Frenchtown Elementary School in Trumbull, Connecticut, have a different motto for each year. Recently, "Together We Reach New Heights" served as the guiding focus for a school year. Dr. Jim Jordan, principal of Chapin High School in South Carolina, reminds his students the school was "Built on Pride and Tradition," and that it is their duty and responsibility to maintain them. Meanwhile, Dr. Scott Holinger, principal at Christa McAuliffe Elementary School, urges everyone to remember they are STARS (Stellar Teachers And Respectful Students).

Atlantic High School in Port Orange, Florida, has the shark as its mascot. But the school's culture is taken from the word *sharks*: S–search for knowledge; H–honesty; A–acknowledge and accept human worth and dignity; R–responsibility; and K–kindness and tolerance. The administration, teachers, and staff at Indian Trails K–8 School in Palm Coast, Florida, are reminded that they are there "to educate children while emphasizing responsibility, respect, and rapport." Here are some additional mottos and slogans:

- Where Exploration Is the Key to Our Future
- Where Educational Excellence is "A" Reality (used at a Florida school with an "A" rating)
- A Safe and Caring Place to Learn
- United We Learn
- Where Our Roots Go Deep and Our Children Blossom
- Our Children Are Our Future
- One Community with One Goal—Student Success

- Building a Brighter Future—One Child at a Time
- Strive for Success
- There Is No End to What a Child Can Achieve
- Be Not Conformed…Be Transformed! (used at a magnet middle school)
- Renew Your Mind Through Music
- A Shining Pathway to Success
- Enter to Learn, Depart to Serve

Other Yearly Events

Although there are myriad opportunities to get students, teachers, parents, and others involved in a school, look for some ways that your school can have one or more that other schools don't have. Consider the following (or variations of them):

- Celebration of the Arts
- Family Evenings
- Field Day
- Holiday Boutique
- Holidays Around the World
- Talent Show
- Egg Drop

The Egg Drop is the kickoff activity to the June Fair weekend at Daniels Farm Elementary School in Trumbull, Connecticut. Principal Gail S. Karwoski reported that each homeroom, with the assistance of parent helpers, designs and creates packaging for a raw egg. This package, with its egg held safely inside, is then dropped from the top of a fire truck bucket. The winning homeroom receives recognition and special treats from the cafeteria.

Letters to the Editor

An effective method to communicate with audiences not related to a specific school is through letters to the editor of the community's newspaper. One principal submitted a letter to the editor to add information about a relevant school-related issue, overweight students. Gary Shiffrin, principal of Merritt Island High School in Florida, argued that the banning of any food or drink that does not have nutritional value—which includes carbonated beverages—would not solve the problem. His main method of getting leaner students would be through more opportunities for wholesome activities. Other principals have written letters of thanks to their schools' community for the support they received during the academic year.

Hotlines

A convenient way for parents and students to get information about home-work assignments or other school events is through the use of telephone hotlines. Several varieties are available to schools—each has its own unique qualities to make its mark. Points to remember, as the school principal: you will need to have a "voice box" for people to call, and the information must be kept current, changed daily in most cases. When I introduced the concept to the faculty at one school where I served as principal, there was some natural apprehension. The teachers and I received inservice in the use of the system, and we went "live" to work out the bugs for a period of time before we told the students and parents about the new opportunities they had available. After we were convinced the process had value, we informed everyone via the principal's newsletter and with an article in a local newspaper. At the end of two weeks I received an accounting of whose extension had the most hits. To my surprise, it was mine! Seems the teachers were checking my daily message to see if it had changed each day. (As the school administrator, I had the power to check where each call to a mailbox came from; the majority of mine were from the teachers.)

Web Sites/E-mail

Advancements in technology continue to change the way we are able to communicate with each other. In some school districts, each school has a link to its Web page on the school district's Web page. Many other schools provide links to individual teachers, grade levels, departments, and the school's administrators. To help the external publics linked to a school, the electronic possibilities are limitless and restricted only by the imagination of the school's technology personnel. At many schools, students have been trained to help teachers create and maintain the Web sites and/or pages. Like anything else related to effective communication, the information must be kept current.

Summary

An effective school–community relations plan is based on several sound principles. According to the NSPRA definition, school public relations is a planned, systematic, two-way process of communicating between a school and its internal and external publics. It appropriately uses both interpersonal communication and mass media. The uncommon ideas presented in this chapter are common ideas as they are used at the identified schools. More in-depth presentations about other ways to communicate will be presented in later chapters.

Case Problem

Review the uncommon ideas presented in this chapter and select at least five that should become part of the common practice at your school. Brainstorm ideas for implementing them before you involve others in the process. Brainstorm with others, finalize plans, and then implement the strategies at your school.

> **The progress of a school as an institution of democracy requires the support of the public it serves.**
>
> *– Unknown*

2

The Need for a School–Community Relations Plan

Why Have a School–Community Relations Plan?

- More choices, other than the public school, are available for parents to consider.
- More households do not have children of school age than at any other time in our history.
- More families from other countries are sending their children to the public schools.
- The multicultural makeup of the students attending the public schools will require extra interest and support from school administrators and all members of the school's "family."
- Opportunities are provided for principals to emphasize schools as places where children and young adults come together for learning.
- The major concepts of a school–community relations plan serve as a road map to follow.
- The organizations and groups that exist in all communities have opportunities to impact the local students.
- Realizing the needs and interests of the publics comprising a school and its community is essential.
- Sending and receiving information should be a major goal of every school.

Often the leaders in school administration view school public relations as deciding what they want to communicate and then communicating it. Or they decide how they want their school to look and then they make it look that way. They generally perceive public relations as a collection of techniques, ideas, or approaches without considering the broader framework of a school–community relations plan.

Edward Bernays, the father of modern-day public relations, defined public relations as *social accountability*. He applied this concept, for example, to the private sector in this way. If a store were built in a commercial and residential neighborhood, Bernays would say that a store manager has a social obligation to that neighborhood. For instance, if a safety hazard had been created because of the store's parking lot, Bernays would feel that the manager should seek the assistance of city officials to make sure there were lights or crosswalks (Yeager, 1985).

The Public Relations Function: Accountability

Bernays did not see public relations as just customer service or quality of merchandise or techniques of advertising. He really saw public relations as accountability to one's public.

Social accountability applied to public education means being answerable or accountable to all the members of the public that we serve at our school, including teachers, students, neighborhood, parents, nonparents, and senior citizens. Today is the age of accountability, and that accountability is built into the jobs of educational administrators.

Very often, members of the nonschool public groups and the numbers of people in each of these groups are growing each year and do not know how their schools are doing; they reflect on the information they have gathered from the news media or from personal observations. They continue to read and hear about the high dropout rate, the incidents of vandalism and violence, the need to set goals and standards, and the need to reform education. This is why an organized effort to accurately disseminate information about a school is necessary.

School–Community Relations

Before addressing the *how* of school–community relations, the *what* and *why* first must be discussed. Many principals confuse school–community relations with public relations, which has led to many ill-conceived programs to increase community support for public schools. Public relations is a process used by schools and other organizations to influence public opinion in an attempt to gain support for the organization. This is typically a one-way process involving news releases, reports, newsletters, and other methods of distributing favorable information to the public.

Through the years, educators and other professionals have worked to define more clearly what an effective school public relations plan would resemble. A review of the literature on the topic yields little of significance but for the work of one researcher. Professor James Grunig of the University of Maryland developed four models of public relations practice along with a situational theory to identify various *publics.* The reason his work is significant is that the field of public relations is a relatively young field of study. As a field of study, it came into its own in the late twentieth century. So, Grunig's work has traced the development of public relations from its publicity stages to its current two-way, symmetric structure —a structure that is more conducive to developing and maintaining relationships. Schools and other organizations that adopt this model use balanced, two-way communication to establish mutual understanding (Grunig & Hunt, 1984).

Coupled with Grunig's model of two-way communication is his notion of situational interactions. Much like the theories of situational leaders school administrators study, Grunig's situational theory supposes that communication behaviors of individuals will vary in line with their perceptions of situations of the organization in which they find themselves. In other words, the extent to which individuals recognize problems and possible constraints, along with their involvement with these problems, will determine their responses (Grunig & Hunt, 1984).

Many years ago, as I was preparing to become a school principal, I elected to take a course, School–Community Relations, that helped to shape my interactions with the people I worked with inside the school—the internal publics—and everyone else outside the school—the external publics. So, since my first encounter with the subject of public relations, I was taught that a broader, more inclusive term would be *school–community relations.*

Cutlip (1994) indicated there are two striking differences between the practice of school public relations and school–community relations. First, school–community relations has a direct link to students. Its purpose is to directly improve and enhance learning opportunities for students, thereby improving their achievement. The aim of school public relations is to provide information so that citizens can become knowledgeable about schools and support their school system.

The second difference discovered by Cutlip is that school–community relations activities are not controversial as compared to school public relations. Who could, or would, argue or find fault with a school's efforts to work with parents, volunteers, or community members to establish partnerships?

Thus, school–community relations goes beyond simply telling the good side of a school's story. Rather, it involves the community in a process of two-way communication with the school and emphasizes not increasing the community's understanding of the school but instead increasing understanding between the school and its community. The school–community relations process involves working closely with teachers, parents, other school personnel, students, nonparents, businesspeople, and other members of the community. This is done to get input, feedback, and assistance in establishing and maintaining that which is responsible to every internal and external spectrum of the community. Although the aim of public relations programs is to create favorable impressions of the local public school and community support for that school, the goal of the school–community relations plan is to find ways to involve the community in the educational process in ways that help students to learn.

Establishing and maintaining an effective school–community relations plan is one of the seven main responsibility areas of the principalship.

Responsibilities of School Administrators

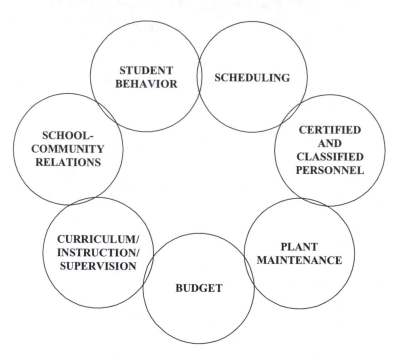

Educators' influence in improving education rests on their ability to guide public opinion and to be guided by it in meeting society's needs. Failure to establish this cooperative partnership frequently results in defeats of needed bond issues. It is also the source of much of the criticism of teaching methods and curricula content.

The Public School in the Modern Community

Because the public school is an integral part of every community, it has a unique function to perform. A school's community comprises the immediate area and population within the individual school's boundaries. It is this local community that sends its children to the school and it is the residents of the community with whom an administrator likely will have the greatest contact. These same residents are also the ones with whom school personnel need to communicate because their opinions about the school are likely to be the most influential when the educational organizations are discussed.

Although communities have some common characteristics, there are factors that make communities differ one from the other. Six factors that make communities differ from each other are the following:

1. Tradition and cultural background
2. Sets of values the community holds
3. Economic bases
4. Geographic features
5. Social structure
6. Political structure

It would be difficult to find two communities in which all six factors are identical. The spread of multicultural issues has had an impact on how communities deal with the complexity of the issues. The concept of a modern community offered here is that of a constantly emerging social entity of which the school is a key institution. Therefore, five characteristics of a modern community are the following:

1. A community is changing.
2. A community is diverse.
3. A community is structured.
4. A community is organized.
5. A community makes decisions.

As more and more communities experience large influences of foreign-born families, the schools must rise to still another challenge. School personnel should never take for granted that just because a person seems fluent in English that he or she really understands everything that is said. If a sizable nonnative population resides in a school district, guidance and help must be provided to the school staff to alert them of the dos and don'ts of dealing with people of diverse cultures. Many school principals have begun sending out school information, newsletters, and/or invitations in multiple languages, or having persons call who can speak the specific language. These actions send the message that the school is trying to help bridge the culture gap.

Getting to Know the Local Community

The American experience strongly suggests that an effective way to promote a cause, or to bring about some desirable social change, is to interest and involve people. The school administrator must provide the leadership to get the school's staff to develop specific professional responsibilities. Some of those responsibilities include acquiring knowledge of the community the school serves. Some ways that can be accomplished are the following:

- Take a bus tour of the community.
- Map the community area.
- Plan, conduct, and evaluate organized field trips.
- Invite key community personnel to share information with students at school.
- Cooperate and join community groups and organizations.
- Understand other current community public relations plans.
- Campaign with civic groups to improve community facilities.
- Become acquainted with minority groups and leaders.
- Be involved plotting the community's probable future development.

My career as a school principal found me at several schools. Fortunately for me, when I made the move to an elementary school with a very diverse student population, one of my new principal colleagues took me for a ride around the community that my school served. He also made certain that many of the above strategies were met during that first year. I found the bus tour to be such an eye opener that I took the teachers and support staff on a similar tour during one of the school district's mandatory staff development days.

Other Educational Settings

School leaders, now more than ever before, are faced with the challenges of maintaining the support of parents who send their children to a given school. The age of accountability in education has arrived! In the last decade, parents, politicians, and the community at large have increasingly demanded accountability from their schools. To keep up in the new education marketplace, public schools must sell themselves aggressively. The burden of proof rests largely with the school administrator to provide the leadership in getting all members of a school community involved.

This "selling of a school" must, of course, be based on fact and the outcomes of the children who attend the school for, as many schools and districts around the country have found, parents and other taxpayers are becoming increasingly dismayed with schools that do not meet the learning needs of the students. They have become vocal in sharing their dissatisfaction with school boards, state and national policymakers, and politicians. Those school leaders impacted by disgruntled parents and others have found that if the school didn't meet expectations, the parents told other parents, school leaders, politicians, and anyone else who would listen, with the result that some educators were either reassigned or removed from leadership positions. In addition, many parents removed their children from public schools and enrolled them in other schools.

But that renewed interest and push for accountability should not be viewed as only negative. As the number of school choices has increased, the pressure has been put on public schools to sell themselves harder. Since 1991, when Minnesota passed the first charter legislation, many other states have followed suit. According to the National Center for Educational Statistics data, there were 1,010 public charter schools operating in the United States during the 2000 school year, with 266,721 students enrolled in those schools (Snyder, 2003).

As school administrators know, nearly every dollar that goes to a charter school is subtracted from the public school's budget. School administrators can learn from the charter school movement. First, they must learn how to respond to the needs of the school community. This will be addressed more thoroughly in Chapter 3. Second, rather than ignore the needs of students of a one-size-fits-all model, administrators must work to create and maintain an institution that acknowledges and supports the often diverse student populations. Third, administrators should focus on a base of established standards and assessments, as well as the consequences when these are not realized.

A second movement away from both public and private schools is homeschooling. In recent years, growing numbers of parents have forsaken public and private schools to teach their children at home. Although homeschooling is not a recent phenomenon, it has been an option for many years. Until about the 1970s, homeschooling was mostly limited to students living in remote areas and those who had chronic illness or disability. The latest government numbers, from 1999, put the total of homeschooled students at 850,000, but Brian Ray, president of the National Home Education Research Institute, contends that between one and two million children, representing 2%–4% of all U.S. schoolchildren, are taught at home. Ray indicated that the federal figure is low because some homeschooled students do not report themselves (Ray, 2003).

So what benefits can school administrators obtain from homeschooling? Perhaps by examining homeschooling as a source of data, administrators can learn how to improve parent involvement, individualize instruction to meet learners' needs, and use computer technology to enhance learning.

Good public school administrators will rise to the market challenges of school choice—such as charter schools and homeschooling—by improving. They will view these options not as the end of public education, but rather as their renaissance. And their counterparts, the citizens of the community, will be reaching for and filling the civic imperative of building better communities.

An effective school–community relations plan should be systematic, comprehensive, and ongoing. School–community relations should never be a haphazard process or left to chance. To do so confines the school to a *reactionary* approach, where the style of communication must be adapted to fit the situation (which is usually negative), as opposed to a *proactive* approach, where the style of communication can be adapted to the audience in a positive manner. As a result, an effective school–community relations plan involves a written plan to deliberately communicate with and involve all segments of the community. Some specific components of an effective school–community relations systematic plan are that it

- specifies the goals and objectives of the school–community relations plan;
- identifies the *publics* with whom the school must communicate and how the communication will be carried out;
- specifies when and how the communication should take place; and
- identifies the person(s) responsible for carrying out each activity.

A school–community relations plan is a study in communication. Reduced to its essentials, communication in this context is concerned with *who* says *what*, to whom, through which *channels*, and with what *effects*.

Because it is impossible to not communicate, an effective plan should be ongoing. As Renihan and Renihan (1989) note, every institution has an image—whether it is intentional or not. The image, in the eyes of the public, of an organization, such as a school, may not be built on facts but rather on perceptions. Those perceptions of individuals, when influenced by media reports, can have an impact on the success or failure of a school. In some cases, perceptions can be altered by the stories from the media with the resulting confusion a change from positive perceptions to more negative ones.

One way to deal with the perceptions others may have of your school would be to look at the school through the *eyes of a total stranger*. The way to accomplish that would be to walk the school campus and really look at it with a critical eye. For instance, are the school grounds maintained? Are there broken windows or graffiti present? Is the message on the school's marquee current? These are just a few areas where the publics who pass by a school regularly can form their perceptions about a school. They might be thinking that if the school building, grounds, and message are not tidy and current, then what goes on inside the school might be equally unappealing.

Effective public relations and positive public perceptions are essential keys to the successful operation of a school. The perceptions of a school's outward appearance are almost as important as what goes on in the school's classrooms.

> **Communication is the key to understanding...and understanding could be the key to success for a school's programs. That is why an effective school–community relations plan is essential.**
>
> *– Anonymous*

An effective school–community relations plan, then, is a planned, systematic, two-way process of communication between the school and its community to build morale, goodwill, cooperation, and support. The plan must include the following:

- Communicating with the internal publics
- Communicating with the external publics
- Involving parents
- Involving nonparents, businesses, and community members
- Dealing with rumors, public attacks, and criticism
- Dealing with crisis situations

Building an effective school–community relations plan is the responsibility of every person associated with the school, but it is the *school principal* who must be in the leadership role at the school.

Principals Set the Tone for Accountability

The Metropolitan Life Survey on the American Teacher 2003: An Examination of School Leadership revealed a striking disconnect between school principals and the school community. MetLife interviewed 1,017 public school (K–12) teachers, 800 public school (K–12) principals, 1,107 parents, and a representative sample of students in grades three to 12. The only thing they (parents, teachers, students, and principals) fully agreed on was what they considered to be the principal's most important roles: motivating teachers and students to achieve and keeping the school safe. Some of the findings of the MetLife survey are the following:

- Principals believe their relationships with teachers are open, friendly, supportive, and respectful. Teachers are not as positive.
- About half of the surveyed parents do not feel welcome or connected to their children's school. Principals are satisfied with their relationships with parents.

Several suggestions from respondents focused on making the school have a sense of community:

- Teachers suggested that principals listen more, give more credit for hard work, and keep the school clean and orderly.
- Parents suggested the principals be more visible and friendly, get out of the office more often, and communicate better.

The MetLife survey is at www.metlife.com (search for "teacher"). The questions could be repeated in the school newsletter or sent by e-mail. Listening to your community is good for your school and promotes great school–community relations.

The principal is the key person to develop understanding of, and the need to have, an effective school–community relations plan in the minds of colleagues. The principal is constantly imitated and observed by others, which may be called the *echo effect*. This means that the person in charge is echoed or mimicked by all the other employees in the organization. This manifestation may not be a conscious echoing. The attitudes and priorities of the person in charge bounce off the other people in the setting and could be repeated many times, perhaps at no one's conscious awareness level.

Principals must show leadership as the school–community relations plan is developed. Good school–community relations practices can positively affect public perception and expand the influence and support of school leaders and their schools. To accomplish this, school principals need to use a variety of tools and strategies, including strategy planning and message development, low-cost materials about the school, media relations, partnerships, and coalitions. Having an effective school–community relations plan enhances the image of the school and everyone associated with it.

The principal sets the tone for the school building and its appearance. It is essential for the principal to determine the type and frequency of communications to staff, students, parents, nonparents, and other citizens of the community. The principal also sets the tone for the manner in which the school staff, students, parents, and other people are treated and determines the manner in which telephone calls are handled and school visitors are greeted when they are on the school's campus.

There is no question that changes will continue to take place in schools as a result of the many initiatives and pressures to reform education. Most states have enacted legislation that requires teachers, parents, and other community members to have a greater say in the decision-making process at an individual school. School improvement councils or committees, comprising elected teachers, elected parents, community members, business partners, and students, are helping school principals make decisions that have an impact at the school.

When changes need to be made, the principal who is known, accepted, respected by, and is in touch with the community will achieve the changes more easily with community support than the principal who is not known and has not gained the support and confidence of the community.

The principals who practice *managing by walking around* (MBWA) (Peters & Waterman, 2004) are using more effective leadership strategies than their counterparts who remain in their offices most of the day doing paperwork. Principals in effective schools are out and about because they recognize the value of maintaining personal contact with the many publics working in the school.

The visible principal knows on a firsthand basis what is going on daily in the school and seems to be everywhere: classrooms, hallways, the cafeteria, bus loading areas at strategic times, school plays, athletic events, and other special programs or events. The visible principal considers instruction to be one of the most important goals of the schools.

Teachers continue to report that they appreciate the feedback received from their school administrators. They especially look forward to and welcome frequent classroom visits by the administrators. Their comments must be heeded by school leaders because the teachers are key personnel in sending out information about a school. Because drop-in classroom visits are a familiar occurrence, teachers and students seldom vary their routines to acknowledge the principal's presence. Smith and Andrews (1989) characterize visible principals as administrators who are positive, cheerful, and encouraging. These principals make themselves accessible to teachers, staff, students, and parents. They also move frequently through the campus while they interact with teachers, staff, and students.

So, it is better to be known as a *classroom* principal rather than an *office* principal. Those teachers who at first don't agree with this perception will eventually become accustomed to your daily visits. Your 5 × 5 plan—five classroom visits of five minutes each—will yield positive results.

Marshall (1996) indicated the principal must focus on observations on active teaching and arrange visits at the elementary school level when such subjects as reading and math are being taught. He supports the notion of keeping drop-in visits to five minutes. Marshall also suggests making a master list, visiting all teachers on a cycle basis, and jotting down a brief description of each visit, including the date, subject observed, and a few descriptive words. This information was a staple of my daily trips around the school campuses where I worked. My notes were recorded on 3 × 5 index cards. These note cards served as a resource to write follow-up comments to teachers, staff members, and students.

My message to each principal about school–community relations is to leave no stones unturned in attempting to implement the community relations techniques featured in this book. What a principal does will be believable to the publics if *you* believe it makes a difference. The backbone of your entire school–community relations plan is the attitude you have. In the years I served as a public school administrator, I developed an understanding of what effective school–community relations are. School–community relations

- are a function of management;
- operate in the public interest;
- have social significance;
- include two-way communication;
- place a high value on active listening;
- place the accent on human values; and
- involve meaningful citizen participation and cooperation.

When we see the practice effective school–community relations as social accountability, then it is no longer just an extra, it is an essential. It is part of the philosophy of why we are in education. It is at the heart of what is done when teachers teach. It is no longer just a means to an end, but rather it is a fundamental, integral part of what is done, what money is spent on, and what amount of time is given to accomplish specific goals.

When we look at effective school community relations as accountability, we create a sense of integrity and honesty that generates, in turn, much goodwill on the part of other people. Also, when the public relations of a school are seen as a part of our social accountability, we broaden the base of ownership for the plan. Now it becomes not just another expectation, or a one-shot inservice that teachers and staff are required to participate in at the beginning of the school year. If everyone has to account for what they are doing as educators, then it makes sense for all employees to see an effective school–community relations plan as social accountability.

An effective school–community relations plan is based on solid action. Ann Barkelew, former National School Public Relations Association (NSPRA) president, said that 90% of school public relations can be traced to what is done in a school, 7% is how effectively the school listens to its publics, and 3% is what is said through publications. An effective school–community relations plan promotes quality education by establishing and maintaining a program of internal and external communications that is both ongoing and comprehensive.

Jerome C. Kovalcik, former NSPRA president, offers the following checkpoints for evaluating a school–community relations plan (Cutlip, Center, & Broom, 2000):

- Is the program child-focused? Is the child the primary client?
- Is reporting accurate and truthful?
- Is the program based on what goes on in the schools—and not on window dressing?
- Are weaknesses as well as strengths reported?
- Is it a multimedia program?
- Is it sensitive to various publics?
- Is there inservice public relations training for all staff members?

Finally, it might be worthwhile to restate this in another way.

Public relations is the planned effort to influence opinion through good character and responsible performance, based upon mutually satisfactory two-way communication.

– Anonymous

A Closing Thought

In this chapter, the need for a school–community relations plan was presented. School leaders must provide the proactive initiative to prepare their school to meet the needs of the school. Understanding the community structure, the formal and informal groups that function in the community, can be an asset to the success of the school. As a school administrator (current or "wannabe"), you have to focus on three important issues. First, do you understand the significance of your proactive involvement in developing and maintaining positive community perceptions, interest in, and support of your school as well as other schools in the district? Second, will you spend time and energy reflecting on efforts? (Remember, you expect teachers to reflect on their teaching.) Third, what will you do on a regular basis to keep all segments of your school community informed? As Stephen Covey (1989) has suggested, "We should seek first to understand, then to be understood."

Summary

The need to have a plan for establishing effective relations with a school's community was discussed in this chapter. Social accountability should be an integral part of the reason a school should communicate with the various publics of its community. Although the definition of an effective school–community relations plan may vary from community to community, more and more school administrators are recognizing that effective programs require twin efforts: to raise the level of public information through information programs and to enlist community support by drawing citizens into meaningful participation in school affairs.

Case Problem

The newly hired school district superintendent has been charged with reviewing and updating the district's school–community relations plan. Because he/she has recently hired you to be the principal of one of the district's schools that was criticized for not having effective relations with its community, the superintendent wants you to be involved with this project. The superintendent has asked you to develop a statement about why a school–community relations plan is needed. Develop what you would consider to be an effective statement.

References and Suggested Readings

Covey, S. (1989). *The 7 habits of highly effective people: Restoring the character ethic.* New York: Simon and Schuster.

Cutlip, S. M. (1994). *The unseen power: Public relations, a history.* Hillsdale, NJ: Erlbaum.

Cutlip, S. M., Center, A. H., & Broom, G. M. (2000). *Effective public relations* (8th ed.). Upper Saddle River, NJ: Prentice Hall.

Grunig, J. E., & Hunt, T. (1984). *Managing public relations.* New York: Holt, Rinehart and Winston.

Marshall, K. (1996). How I confronted HSPS (hyperactive superficial principal syndrome) and began to deal with the heart of the matter. *Phi Delta Kappan, 77*(5), 436–445.

Peters, T. J., & Waterman, R. H. (2004). *In search of excellence: Lessons from America's best-run companies.* New York: HarperBusiness Essentials.

Ray, B. (2003). More families opting for home schooling. http://www.cnn.com.

Renihan, F. I., & Renihan, P. J. (1989, March). *Institutional image: The concept and implications for administrative action.* NASSP Bulletin, 73(515), 81–90.

Smith, W. F., & Andrews, R. L. (1989). *Instructional leadership: How principals make a difference.* Alexandria, VA: Association for Supervision and Curriculum Development.

Snyder, T. D. (2003). *Digest of education statistics, 2002.* Washington, DC: National Center for Education Statistics.

Yeager, R. J. (1985). Introducing Edward L. Bernays, the "father of public relations." *Momentum, 12,* 28–29.

3

Communicating With the School's Internal Publics

Why Communicate With the Internal Publics?

♦ The various groups of people who collectively make up the internal publics can "make or break you."

♦ What goes on in a school each day is the base from which an effective school–community relations plan is built and maintained.

♦ The messages the internal publics' members carry from the school are generally believed to a higher degree than the messages that come from an administrator.

♦ The large army of public relations agents—the students—in every school is a key conduit to sharing the proper story about a school.

Effective school–community relations plans must include ways and means of communicating with the *internal* publics—the employees and students. As more school systems and schools are switching to shared leadership or shared decision making, it is imperative that all members of a school's *family*—teachers, paraprofessionals, secretaries, cafeteria workers, custodians, and bus drivers—be informed about the school's operations.

Employees who are informed and involved in decision making often can be counted on to make constructive suggestions or share valuable ideas if they are listened to or their written comments read. The fact that someone has informed them and listened to them serves as motivation to become more socially accountable. The positive feelings that develop from a sense of belonging or being recognized for contributing also can enhance involvement, accountability, and productivity.

> **The most important reason an effective internal communications plan is needed can be found in the fact that an effective external communication plan cannot exist without it.**

Family Meetings

Whenever possible, all staff members should be involved in planning the meetings of the school's personnel. *Family meetings*, rather than just faculty meetings, are great examples of involving the total staff in activities such as planning open houses or other events in which the cooks, custodians, and other staff members can set up displays and be available to talk with parents. I remember the time I asked the cafeteria manager/dietician if she would be present and participate in the annual open house activity. She was delighted to have been asked and was an active participant for the remaining years I was at the school.

Family meetings should be limited to situations or events that affect the entire teaching and nonteaching staff. Some of those times might be open houses, a potential crisis situation, changes in school boundaries, or changes in personnel. It's entirely possible that a school principal wouldn't have more than two or three family meetings a year. One of these meetings may represent a major step in improving communication and understanding, as well as the *climate*, within the school.

Some school administrators make it a habit to energize their school's internal publics by having monthly talk sessions. By meeting with smaller groups of school personnel, you will be providing opportunities for people to be willing to share their thoughts more openly.

Some principals stop by the cafeteria to chat with the workers while they are eating their lunches—usually before they serve the students their lunches. Midmorning is usually a good time to meet with custodians, office personnel, and classroom paraprofessionals. At the least, principals should *meet quarterly* with office staff, teacher assistants, cafeteria staff, and custodians.

The principal should meet with *various personnel weekly* to discuss issues relevant to their job description. Personnel to be included in these separate meetings are the elementary resource teacher, speech teacher, ESE/ESOL (exceptional student education/English for speakers of other languages) consultative teacher, head custodian, guidance counselor, and cafeteria manager. The secretary and principal should meet on a daily basis, if possible, to review the current day's happenings and focus on the events of the next day or two.

Because members of a school's *family* interact with people in the community, each of them must be informed about important details concerning a school's operation. Various studies have confirmed that community members base a great deal of their attitudes on the information they obtain from employees of the schools or students who attend the school.

By *managing by walking around* (MBWA) or *dip sticking*, a term borrowed from the automotive world, a principal will have many opportunities to recognize praiseworthy performance of all school employees. There is no better way for a principal to show a school's family members that he or she is aware of their performance on the job, the contributions they make to children, and whatever hardships they have to endure than by observing them while they are working.

Each member of a school's internal family—teachers, office personnel, paraprofessionals, cafeteria workers, nurses, custodians, crossing guards, and bus drivers—make contributions to the image people have of a particular school. Thus, it is imperative that each of them be included as a contributing player in the school–community relations plan, because each of them is important to the plan.

Nothing improves a person's hearing more than sincere praise.

Support Staff Personnel

Several years ago, the National School Public Relations Association (NSPRA) conducted a survey of who in the school district has the most credibility in the community. The most believable person a school has is the custodian. When school custodians speak highly about their school, the teachers, staff members, students, or the principal, people who are not on a school's staff believe them. Remember, the custodians not only work for the school district but they also live and vote in the school district. Because they are considered highly reliable sources of information about the schools, it is up to the principals to keep the total school family informed and ready to share ideas and suggestions to make a school's program more effective.

The second most believable person is the school bus driver, followed by cooks, secretaries, teachers, and the school principal. No one from the central administrative office or the school board made the list. So, then, school-based employees are perceived to be the voice of the school. These individuals have an important role to play in a school's communication plan.

Getting Input from Support Personnel

Look for ways to include classified staff members in school meetings and activities. If work requirements do not make this difficult, plan at least one session a month to exchange ideas and explore concerns with the secretarial, paraprofessional, custodial, and food service workers. Some principals invite the head custodian, cafeteria manager, and office secretary to give updates at the school's faculty meetings. This is a good opportunity for teachers to share comments with these key people, too. I always referred to my faculty meetings as *family* meetings.

> **A school's own staff is key to good school–community relations.**

Ken Williams, a New Hampshire elementary school principal, believes that everyone in his school is an educator, degree or not. Williams recognizes his entire staff, especially during American Education Week. An Ohio elementary principal agrees that the support staff are vital to the school's team. They participate in the school's annual Reading Night. When I was an elementary principal, we ended each school day with a 20-minute silent reading time. Everyone—and I mean *everyone*—stopped what they were doing, grabbed a book, and read for the 20-minute time period. The secretary would read but answered any phone calls that came to the school during the time period. The custodial staff members had their books to read in classrooms, too. They realized the importance of reading and of being role models for students, too.

Getting to Know the Support Personnel

Introducing kindergartners and other students new to a school can be a learning experience. Connecticut elementary principal Karen Smith has the students go on a "school hunt" to locate where secretaries, custodians, cafeteria workers, the media specialist, and others work and to find out what they do. Earlier you read about the New Kids on the Block activity that Indiana elementary principal Anne Young and guidance counselor Kelly Forey have developed. Some principals invite support personnel to be at the school to be introduced to the parents who attend an open house or back-to-school-night activity. In many cases, parents and others attending these activities make positive comments to these school personnel.

> **A healthy, growing organization has used a variety of suggestions in becoming effective.**

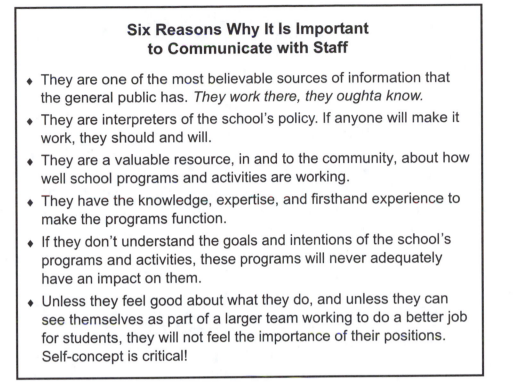

So what do school employees want? Actually, the answer to that question is quite simple, and the principal has the ability to answer it and to make it happen.

> **What employees want most is appreciation for a job well done.**

Having a well-informed and happy support staff as members of a school's family is good for children, and it's good for school–community relations.

There are several ways the support staff can be recognized and rewarded for a job well done. A special note, card, "sunshine note," or even a "bouquet of flowers" can be written and given to the support person and teachers, too. (See an example of a sunshine note and bouquet of flowers at the end of the chapter.) Colorado principal Lori Kinney of Mark Twain Elementary School presents each support staff person with a pin that has a glue bottle (support staff on it) and "The glue that holds it all together" printed on the glue coming out of the bottle.

Improving Communication Techniques

Good Listening

As mentioned earlier, high visibility is one certain way to get to know everyone who works at a school. Dr. Harold Border, assistant principal at Hunters Creek Middle School in Florida, walks the campus each morning with the school's head custodian. During their travels around the school, they discuss their families, hobbies, and ways they will spend vacation times. Florida principal Joe Loffek and his assistant principal eat lunch at different times and spend a few minutes chatting with staff members. Be willing to listen, and practice active listening. People have the need to be heard.

Business Cards

In many school districts, the educational foundation provides all employees with their own business cards. Some principals have solicited donations from businesses, and even the printer, to provide a limited number of business cards for every member of a school's family. One creative, and some might say brave, teacher bought a sheet of small magnets with adhesive on them. She attached a magnet to the back of her business cards for parents to take when they visited at open house.

Being Available and Visible

If you profess to have an open-door policy, then you need to be available and accessible to teachers and others when they come to your office area. Some principals increase their availability to everyone by being in areas where lots of students, teachers, and others are. The hallways (when students are moving between classes), open courtyards, and before- and after-school student arrival and dismissal times are just a few of the places and times. One place I always found to be a fun place to be to give information is the lunchroom when the students are eating.

Getting to Know the Teachers

Frequent trips around the school (MBWA) can provide opportunities for informal meetings with individual teachers or groups of teachers to discuss issues related to their teaching or matters outside of the school. Getting to know teachers on a personal level can add to your understanding of each of them and what they do outside of the school. Some principals schedule times to attend grade level or subject matter planning and preparation times. Whatever the purpose or motive, the point is the principal was out where the action was.

Meeting the Professional Needs of Family Members

Most school districts provide opportunities for professional staff members to give their opinions and identify needs through surveys. The most-often expressed professional needs become the focus of staff development for the following school term. The Brevard County Schools in Florida use the same approach with support personnel, too. Their inservice needs are identified, and appropriate activities are planned and made available to them. A South Carolina high school principal provides lunch coverage for teachers to have an extended lunch away from the school's campus. He and the other school administrators provide the "oversight" so the teachers can be rewarded for their efforts. He does the same for the office personnel and classroom professionals. Dr. Beth Sharpe, principal at English Estates Elementary School in Florida, uses a variety of techniques to address the needs of her teachers. She gives them a "Give Me a Break" certificate for 30 minutes of free time. Everyone at the school receives "A Treat from Ghirardelli Square" certificate and some chocolates to go with it. (See the examples on p. 59.)

Meeting the Personal Needs of Family Members

Most schools have a voluntary "sunshine fund" to provide small gifts or flowers for birthdays, weddings, births, funerals, and accomplishments such as achieving National Board Certification. "Curves" classes at the school have been replacing the aerobics classes offered in years past. Some school principals have used the services of physical therapy students to give everyone at the school a 10- to 15-minute massage. In some cases this event takes place at the midpoint of each semester and again during Teacher Appreciation Week. The costs are nominal, but the rewards are phenomenal!

Recognition of Family Members

The most influential way this can be accomplished is through personal contact with everyone each day. A welcoming greeting early in the morning as people enter can help to set the tone for the day. The late Laurel Pennock, a friend to many principals, once said, "Start each day with a smile on your face, keep smiling until 10 a.m., and the rest of the day will take care of itself." Try it—it works!

Here are some other ways to give recognition to deserving school people:

- ♦ Recognize the person in the principal's newsletter, as Dr. Patricia Ramsey, a Florida principal, did when she wrote, "Congratulations to Mrs. Joyce Powell, our media clerk, who will represent our school as one of the five finalists for Employee of the Year. Mrs. Powell works very hard to make sure that the children are exposed to books and reading. When you see her, make sure you thank her for all she does for our school."

- ♦ Write personal notes of thanks or recognition. (See the sunshine notes and bouquet of flowers samples included in this chapter.) A handwritten note often means more than one generated by a computer program. "Sharpie" permanent markers are wonderful! Colorado principal Lori Kinney sends her thoughtful messages on "Peach of a Person" note cards. Shorter notes are penned on 3 × 5 cards printed with these messages: "I love what you are doing for our kids," "You are making a difference," "You're Terrific," and "Superb Teaching."

February Picker-Upper

The months of January, February, and March can be long months because of the cold, rainy weather in some parts of the country and can be a problem because they follow the winter holiday break when no days off are usually scheduled. Instead of having a faculty meeting, have an ice cream social. Make it an unexpected, last-minute thing where everyone who wants to participate can have dessert before the main course—something some people advocate. Provide a variety of ice cream flavors and toppings and beverages. A social event!

Family Meeting Giveaways

Most restaurants in a school's community will provide gift certificates to be used in drawings for everyone at a school to try to win. Grocery stores, movie theaters, and other venues have been known to support schools with giveaways, too.

Golden Garbage Can Award

This special award is given out every two weeks to the classrooms that are the neatest and require the minimum of cleaning time and effort from the custodial staff. A new, regular size garbage can should be spray-painted gold before the custodial staff members review the top contenders and then makes their selection(s). Depending on the size of the school, more than one can should be available and presented.

Recognize Special Occasions

Birthdays, weddings, births, and adoptions of family members' children are all events that need to be acknowledged and celebrated. Some schools have a birthday party for everyone born in a particular month. Summer birthdays have their own special days during a school month. For new babies, have a T-shirt-stenciling company add the school's name and mascot on the smallest children's

T-shirt available. Add the words "Future Student at" along with the school's name and mascot. This same shirt can be given to parents of a student in the school when a new baby is welcomed into the family. The faculty member's new child will be wearing the spirit T-shirt the next time the family visits the school.

Beginning and Ending Year Gatherings

Bringing a school's family together at the start and end of a school term can be critical opportunities to develop relationships among the members. Involve the staff in planning and carrying out the event.

Standardized Testing First Aid Kit

Elementary principal Lorrie Butler at Cheney Elementary School in Florida provides support to her teachers and students as they prepare the students to take the Florida Comprehensive Achievement Tests (FCAT). The following items are placed in a Ziploc bag for each student taking the tests, along with a note that says the following:

FCAT Bag Items

1 pencil—to help you record the knowledge you have learned

4 stickers—to help you stick to the task at hand

1 eraser—to use when you check over your work

1 highlighter—to highlight all of your success

3 Hershey's hugs—for all the hard work you put into the test

Rx: For best results combine with

   1 night of restful sleep

   1 nutritious breakfast

   1 positive attitude

Possible side effects: Improved test taking skills and awesome FCAT scores

---

Internal Publications

Some schools have begun to use electronic newsletters in place of the printed kind to convey important information. Although this approach may work for the school's personnel who have access to computers, some people will not be kept up to date. Paper newsletters can still serve the purpose of sharing information in a timely manner. Those publications should have identifiable characteristics, a masthead, dates of coverage, important events, news of a specific or general nature, and thoughts for the week, and they should be printed on colorful paper.

Some principals have them three-hole-punched, too. Everyone on a school's staff should get a copy of the newsletter. *Faculty/staff handbooks* provide a valuable service to everyone at a school. Included in the handbook of most schools is information about district policies and procedures, school-level procedures, the school's mission statement, and myriad other topics. The publication needs to be updated on a regular basis—at least once a year.

New Staff Orientation Procedures

Florida Odyssey Middle School principal Christopher Bernier and his administrative team have developed *A Practical User's Guide* for all new teachers. Each new teacher receives the guide at a daylong inservice called "Meet and Greet Welcome: Getting to Know You—It's About Excellence." Ms. Kim Marlow, grade-level administrator, put the information packet together and leads the daylong inservice. Other new members of the school's family receive the same type of welcome to the school.

Communication Helpers

To preserve the importance of instructional time, pagers or walkie talkies should be made available to the administration, head custodian, secretary, and others as needed. In addition to avoiding the interruption of the teaching and learning process, they make immediate communication possible.

School Crisis Plans

Most schools have developed and update crisis plans more regularly since September 11, 2001. Teachers are required to review and be responsible for knowing all aspects of the crisis plans for their school. The information presented should be reviewed and updated as needed—but at least once a year. The crisis plan should be a topic of discussion at the start of every school year. Most school districts require that the crisis plan be available for use in the classroom or work area. Two school districts that have prepared exceptional crisis plans are the Clark-Pleasant Community School Corporation in Indiana and the Trumbull, Connecticut, Public Schools. (A more comprehensive discussion of the crisis plans is in Chapter 9.)

Substitute Teachers

In past years, substitute teachers were viewed as baby-sitters for a day; they were expected to keep students occupied and out of trouble, and little learning took place. Those lost days are not part of the expectation these days. Most school systems now require teachers to have an updated *substitute folder* that is given to the sub on arriving at the school or classroom. The folder should contain items that will help the sub's day go smoothly while promoting active learning by the students. A typical sub folder should contain the following:

- A diagram or map of the school
- Daily schedules
- Lesson plans
- Forms for attendance and lunch counts
- Up-to-date class rosters
- Seating charts or plans
- Lists of class rules, procedures, and discipline policies and procedures
- Special notes about students with special needs or who receive special services
- Emergency procedures
- Names and locations of teachers who might be a resource to answer questions or assist
- Form(s) for the sub to complete regarding what was taught and to add notes about how the day went

Substitutes are required to have complete background evaluations prior to being hired. In addition, many school districts require the substitutes to complete a number of inservice hours prior to being assigned to work in classrooms. This is true in the Brevard County, Florida, School District and Lexington County 5 School District in South Carolina. School districts are beginning to require substitutes to complete evaluation forms about the experiences they had at the schools. This is true at North Canton High School in Ohio, and if the sub expresses concerns about the day's experiences, these concerns will be discussed with the principal the next time the sub works at the school. Teachers at that school also complete a sheet about the substitute's performance. Students are a great source of information about how things *really* went when the teacher was absent. Substitutes should be invited to participate in family meetings and other activities while assigned to the school. Some schools take photos of the substitutes to be reused and posted in the teacher's lounge when the person is working in the school.

Other Ways to Recognize School Personnel

- Purchase inexpensive gifts that relate to individual special interests, for instance, a small bird house for someone who loves birding, a picture frame for someone with a new child, fishing tackle for the fisher person on staff, or a book of crossword puzzles for the puzzle fan.
- Write a personal note of thanks or appreciation to family members. Keep a copy to possibly be used when the year's evaluations are written.

- Have a *jeans day* when everyone can wear jeans to school on specific days.
- Give donated gift certificates to personnel who have perfect attendance for one month. The certificates might be for a CD, DVD, a movie, or a dinner.
- Give each family member a freshly cut flower on the first day of spring.
- Include a joke or two as a part of the weekly principal newsletters to school personnel.
- Purchase a coffee mug for each member of your school's family—and personalize with each person's name on it.
- Keep the faculty lounge clean, updated, and attractive with fresh paint, new pictures, curtains, and new or reconditionedfurniture.
- Place school supplies in teachers' mailboxes at the semester break.
- Provide dinner between the end of the school day and an evening meeting (PTA or open house).
- Take photos throughout the year and compile them in a video at the end-of-the-year luncheon.
- Encourage parents to write notes or letters of appreciation to teachers or other personnel.
- Have a message of thanks posted on a local bank's or business's marquee.
- Purchase books, with book plates with the teachers' names included in them, for the media center.

Be Enthusiastic

A school leader sets the tone for the school. The impact each principal has on the climate and culture of a school has been documented and written about extensively. One surefire way to make that positive impact is through an enthusiastic approach to daily activities. *Enthusiasm is contagious!*

Communicating With Students

Students are the most influential messengers of a school's internal publics. Much of the information and attitudes held by the general public are carried from the students to the community by the students and then through the community grapevine. All too often, the students are *not recognized as the key communication link* they are with their parents and the community in which they live. Although the school's head custodian has been identified as the number one source of believable information about a school, the students are also viewed as reliable sources of information about a school. Parents certainly base their opinions about the school in general on what their children tell them about their own school. People who don't have children in school base their opinions on what friends or neighbors who have children in school tell them. If that is true, it follows that one of the best ways to improve the image of a school is to consider the *perceptions* the students in a school have about the school. The core of the school–community relations plan should be the regular school experiences of the students.

According to the data presented in the National Center for Education Statistics *Projections of Education Statistics to 2013*, the projected enrollment of students in American elementary and secondary public schools will increase from 48 million in 2004 to almost 50 million in 2013. More than 14 million students are projected to be attending private elementary and secondary schools. Therefore, if the image of the school is to be improved, one sure way it can be done is through the eyes of students—either young or old. First impressions do count! Little things mean a lot! From the welcome new students receive on the first day in the school to the last day they are there, they should be treated with care and respect.

Students at any school can be the catalyst and conduit to get the good news out to listening ears. Following are ways that school principals can enlist the students in the school–community relations plan.

First Impressions—Lasting Impressions

Principals at schools of all levels have developed successful techniques to welcome students to their schools. David Butler, an elementary principal in Volusia County, Florida, makes a personal telephone call to every incoming kindergarten student during the summer before the school year begins. After talking first with parents and inviting them to visit the school, he talks directly with each student. When the parents and the child visit the school, Mr. Butler sees them. Ron Nathan, elementary principal in Seminole County, Florida, developed a program, Bridging the Gap, to help some students facilitate the transition from home to school. Mr. Nathan and the guidance counselor meet with students who have started to have difficulties with other students or their teacher. Lots of positive reinforcement is part of the individual group sessions.

Students and parents are often uncertain about what school supplies the children will need in the new school year. Many school systems in the Central Florida area require elementary teachers to include the following grade level's supply lists with the student's final report card. Some large retail stores, like Target and Wal-Mart, display copies of the grade level supply lists for the schools in their immediate area. Ron Pagano, principal at Atlantic High School in Volusia County, Florida, has followed the lead of the principal he succeeded by making personal contacts with each of the incoming freshmen to the school. He does this through the postcards he sends to the students. His handwritten messages are short, but they convey a thought of interest and caring from the principal. Mr. Pagano also makes random telephone calls to students during summer vacation to discuss the upcoming year. As a result of suggestions offered by some students, some changes in procedures were made.

Donna Kelley, a fourth-grade teacher in Westminster, Colorado, reported to *Education World* writer Gary Hopkins that she gives her students opportunities to use her classroom telephone to make *brag calls* home when they have exceeded expectations. Kelly returns student papers with "brag call" added to the grade and other comments. She reported that the benefits and rewards of brag calls are numerous: lots of smiles, reinforcement of quality work, positive affirmation for parent and child, plus additional support from home for her teaching efforts.

Principals can accomplish the same thing by carrying a cell phone on MBWA trips around the school. When students are seen doing something noteworthy, the student can place the call home on the principal's phone. When I served as an elementary principal, cordless phones were just coming into popularity. My colleagues and I were given them so that our area superintendent could call and reach us at any time and not be told, "He's visiting classrooms." We got around that by turning off the phones except when we wanted to make calls—the majority of calls from my phone were made by children calling home.

Postcards

The administration, faculty, staff members, and all members of Silver Sands Middle School in Port Orange, Florida, use postcards to share "Good News" with parents and others. Dr. Les Potter, the school's principal, reports the cost of the special postcards and postage is minimal when the benefits are evaluated.

Spend Time Where the Students Are

The MBWA strategy used to promote visibility in a school is also a strategy to get to know students. *High visibility* and *enthusiasm*, when coupled, can be a useful strategy to employ. Parents and their children expect to see the school's principal at all school activities when students are involved. High school principals have the difficult task of making personal appearances at student activities that occur at the same time and at different locations. Martin Kane made his presence known at swim meets, wrestling matches, and basketball games. He stayed for a

Good News! Postcard

short time at each event, conversed with parents in attendance, and then excused himself to travel to another site. Amazingly, the parents understood his plight and were accepting of his need to move on to another event. He was seen; he spoke with parents, students, and others; and he was updated about the details and final results of each event by the coaches' phone calls to his home. Eat lunch with students, and talk with them while they are in the cafeteria. Middle and high school principals in Brevard County, Florida, are expected to be on duty for part of each day's lunch period. Part of the time they are also expected to spend time in the common areas or courtyards where students go after they have finished lunch. MBWA works there as well, and the presence of the principal helps to get students to their classes when the lunch period ends.

Details…Details…Details

Trying to remember details that could be used for various purposes can be a lofty expectation when the size of some large schools is considered. Some principals handle the expectation by carrying a *portable handheld tape recorder* to hold significant details until the principal returns to the office for follow-up. PDAs and cell phones are other devices on which details can be stored for later use. Often principals prefer to use *3 × 5 index cards* to record important details. The cards are an inexpensive way to keep information for later reference. So, however you keep track of important details is a matter of choice—the important item to remember is that the details and accuracy of what is said and done should impress people who are on the receiving end.

Getting to Know All Students

Some students will go out of their way to do things that will help you to get to know them. But, most principals have large numbers of students who didn't do things that made them stand out. Learning the names of students, all of them if possible, is a first-rate way to let them know you care about them. Some principals take the groups of students' photos home and begin to "place a face with a name." The sharing of lunch times is another effective way to get to know the names of students. Involving students in school-related activities, like morning announcements and safety patrols, and as school supply store salespersons, are a few ways to get them involved, visible, and ready for recognition by significant persons—one being the school principal. Some elementary principals, and I was one of them, invite students to come to their offices to "show off" or to spend a short period of time away from the classroom. I enjoyed the experience of listening to children read a few pages of early reading books. I shared the excitement they had when they realized they could read is something they might have forgotten but I haven't. Silent reading periods, mentioned elsewhere in the book, were and are special times to get to know students, especially if you are with them during those times. On some days I took my books (selected by the media specialist for me to read so I could recommend them to the children) to classrooms. On other days I invited students to join me in my office to read with me for the 20-minute period. My invitation is shown on page 52. For each session I invited two or three students from various grade levels; for instance, children in first, third, and fifth grade would be invited. On other days second, fourth, and sixth graders were invited. Suitably sized chairs were available for the students' use, and, of course, I sat in my large, black leather chair for the periods. One day I had an experience of a lifetime because one small first grader, the last one I greeted at my door, arrived with an armload of easy readers to enjoy. Instead of heading for "his" first-grade-size chair, he headed for my large, black leather chair. As I closed the office door to welcome the students and get them started on their reading, I noted what he had done. The remaining students were all watching to see what I would do, and I made my choice without hesitating—I sat for 20 minutes on a first-grade-level chair! What do you think the dinnertime discussion might have been at the homes of the children who witnessed this?

There May Be "Silver" on the Playground

Another effective way to get to know the students at an elementary school is to be present on the playground when they are there. Years ago, I learned about a great way to involve students in removing trash from the school's play area. The late Laurel Pennock, a longtime Minnesota elementary principal, revealed how he would walk around the playground before the students came out for their recess sessions. As he walked around, he would pick up pieces of paper trash and put a few nickels, dimes, and an occasional quarter in each. After placing the "loaded" trash back on the ground, he would return to the building to finish his MBWA. When recess time arrived, he would return to the playground to interact with the teachers and students. As he walked and talked with the children, he would "find" one of the special pieces of trash. Naturally, when the children saw the money he found, they spread out to find more. Some of the students were rewarded, some were not, but the main objective was accomplished—the playground was cleaned of litter.

I used the technique and found that it works. It is not necessary to add money to the trash all the time. Also use the approach when different grade levels are on the playground. I carried two large plastic trash bags—one for the girls and one for the boys. Sometimes I rewarded the group that picked up the largest amount of trash with an extra cookie at lunchtime. They did not know they were working to be rewarded.

Students to Read with the Principal

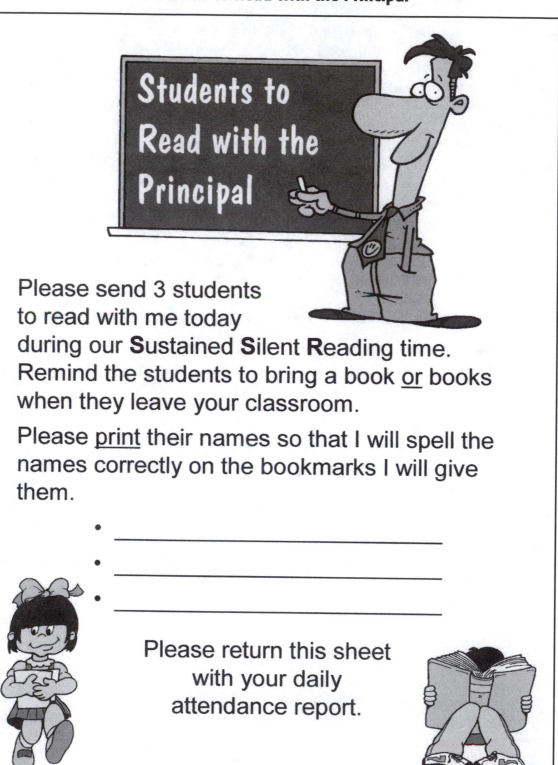

Students to
Read with the
Principal

Please send 3 students
to read with me today
during our **S**ustained **S**ilent **R**eading time.
Remind the students to bring a book <u>or</u> books
when they leave your classroom.

Please <u>print</u> their names so that I will spell the
names correctly on the bookmarks I will give
them.

- _____
- _____
- _____

Please return this sheet
with your daily
attendance report.

Positive/Negative Consequences

Each year Judi Madsen, the principal at Westview Elementary School in Northglenn, Colorado, involves her school family in determining the theme for the school year. "Flying Toward the Future" was the theme in a recent year. Students at the school had the opportunity to earn a Kid Caught card when they did something positive that deserved special recognition. Students who earned a Kid Caught were eligible for the weekly drawing to select a prize from the office treasure chest. One student's name per trimester was drawn from all previous winners for a gift certificate at a local retailer such as Borders.

Flying Toward the Future Card

Student Recognition

There are limitless ways students can be recognized and rewarded. Various awards and certificates can be purchased for different special occasions. Some principals have incorporated suggestions from family members in designing award certificates that have special meaning at a particular school. Some sample communication items, "The Good News Is…," "Blue Ribbon," "You're Thumbody Special Because," "Hooray for…," "Excellent Science Project," and "Missing Tooth Award" are displayed on pages 62–64. "Student of the Month" and other such certificates should be used to make the event special for the students who receive them. Have a self-inking rubber stamp made that might have a simple message such as "Principal's Stamp of Approval," "Your Friend," and the school's mascot and your signature on it. As you MBWA, carry the stamp with you, and if the students' papers are displayed in classrooms and no one is in the classroom, select a few papers on which to affix your stamp. One such stamp is shown on page 60.

> **If a child "turns out" well, it is because, consciously or unconsciously, he/she has been given a response— warmth, attention, affection—to positive behavior.**
>
> *— Jacob Azerrad, PhD*

Birthdays

A child's birthday is a special day to honor the student. These days are usually exciting times for them. At Mark Twain Elementary School in Colorado, birthdays are recognized with treats for the kindergarten classes only. The school principal requests that birthday invitations for private parties not be distributed at school, unless every child in the class receives one. The same expectations are included in the parent handbooks at Clark Elementary School in Indiana and Daniels Farm Elementary School in Connecticut. Some school principals announce each child's birthday during the daily announcements. Students may be given a birthday card and school pencil. When I was an elementary principal, I did this. The school pencil was special because it was coated with gold paint. I added some other magic to these pencils by saying if the pencil was used for tests or other projects, the student might do better on all of these assignments. Amazingly, some of the students reported that they did do better.

Be Enthusiastic and Positive

Just as enthusiasm is contagious with teachers, it is equally so with students. Your smiles, nods, and winks are great nonverbal ways to communicate with students. *Dare to be different!* Find reasons to do common things uncommonly well! Capitalize on the many opportunities to develop support from all members of your school's internal family and the students who attend the school.

The impact that school personnel have on students is often never considered or measured. The eighth-grade students at Monarch K–8 School in Louisville, Colorado, took it upon themselves to let the significant people in their lives at the school know how much they appreciated them. They also recognized their families and friends in their "8th Grade Continuation Ceremony." Eighth-grade students Lindsay Pawlas and Kaila Terwilliger worked with assistant principal Marsha Orr to put the ceremony together. This was the first time students were in charge of putting the program together. Those who attended it reported that it was the best, and it set a standard for others to come in the future. The outline of the program and actual comments read by the two students are presented on pages 56–57.

Summary

We need to listen to our publics, especially the students, the way Peters and Waterman (2004) talk about being "close to the customer." The best companies learn from the public they serve. In the case of America's schools, these customers would be the students.

Case Problem

At a recent meeting of school principals, the superintendent expressed concerns about the morale of the teachers and an overall negative attitude students have about the schools. He expects every principal to develop a plan to improve the morale of the teachers at each school while also working to improve the students' attitude toward their school. Develop your plan to include five strategies that you would incorporate at your *present* school. Also, include five strategies that you would use to improve the students' attitudes toward their school.

Reference and Suggested Reading

Peters, T. J., & Waterman, R. H. (2004). *In search of excellence: Lessons from America's best-run companies.* New York: Harper Business Essentials.

Monarch K–8 8th Grade Continuation Program

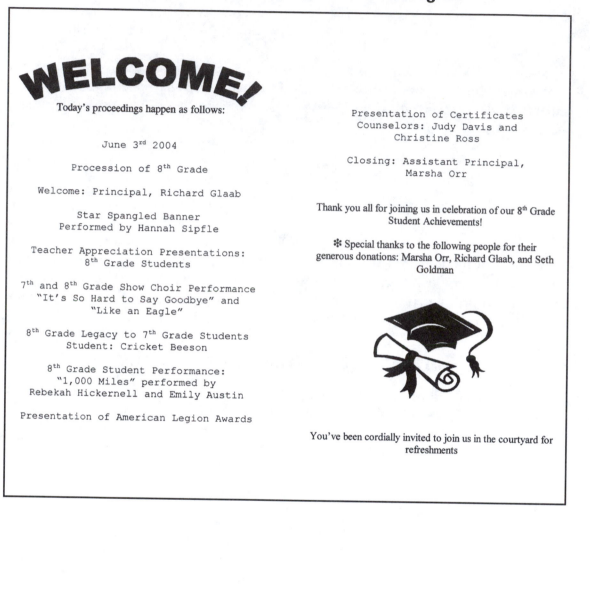

WELCOME!

Today's proceedings happen as follows:

June 3rd 2004

Procession of 8th Grade

Welcome: Principal, Richard Glaab

Star Spangled Banner
Performed by Hannah Sipfle

Teacher Appreciation Presentations:
8th Grade Students

7th and 8th Grade Show Choir Performance
"It's So Hard to Say Goodbye" and
"Like an Eagle"

8th Grade Legacy to 7th Grade Students
Student: Cricket Beeson

8th Grade Student Performance:
"1,000 Miles" performed by
Rebekah Hickernell and Emily Austin

Presentation of American Legion Awards

Presentation of Certificates
Counselors: Judy Davis and
Christine Ross

Closing: Assistant Principal,
Marsha Orr

Thank you all for joining us in celebration of our 8th Grade Student Achievements!

❊ Special thanks to the following people for their generous donations: Marsha Orr, Richard Glaab, and Seth Goldman

You've been cordially invited to join us in the courtyard for refreshments

To Our Families, Teachers, and Friends

To Our Families:
"Other things may change us but we start and end with family." - Anthony Brand
Throughout all the smiles and tears in our middle school years, you've been here for us. You've helped us learn from our mistakes. You gave us love and support when we needed guidance. You never failed to fulfill your duty as parents. When everyone else seemed to walk out of our lives, leaving us alone, you stayed by our side. And for this we thank you!

To Our Teachers:
"A child's life is like a piece of paper on which every person leaves a note." - Chinese Proverb
Throughout our middle school years at Monarch, each teacher has had an opportunity to sign our book of life, and each one has with love. Those memories will be with us forever. They have given us a gift worth saving, and we will forever keep them in our hearts.

6th grade teachers: *"I wish they would only take me as I am."* - Vincent Van Gogh
As we entered our middle school lives everyone at one time or another felt like this. We all wanted to fit in and be the "cool" one. The teachers are the ones who truly saw us as we were and accepted us for who we wanted to be. Without them we would have never realized that it's okay to be anyone you want to be. Thank you!

7th grade teachers: *"Maturity begins to grow when you can sense your concern for others outweighing your concern for yourself."* - John MacNaughtan
At the beginning of 7th grade we were confident, independent, and sure that the world revolved around us. Our teachers helped us realize that our friendships were more important than ourselves. By the end of the year we cared for those around us. We learned that we need love from others to get through the hardest times in our lives. Our teachers taught us this by giving us the love we needed. Thank you!

8th grade teachers: *"There is always one moment in childhood when the door opens and lets the future in."* - Deepak Chopra
8th grade was hard. The teachers pushed us to give our all in everything we presented. We experienced life from a new point of view. We had new worries. We struggled to find someone who we could trust to always be there when times got hard. Our teachers are the ones who held our hands and lead us to that open door, our future, in this case high school. We are now waiting to step through. Thank you!

To Our Friends:
"A friend is one who knows you as you are, understands where you've been, accepts who you've become and gently invites you to grow."
Through thick and thin our friends have been here for us right through to the very end. We shared secrets and jokes and made a million memories. We Love You! Thank you!

Lindsay Pawlas, Kaila Terwilliger & the 8th Grade Student Body.

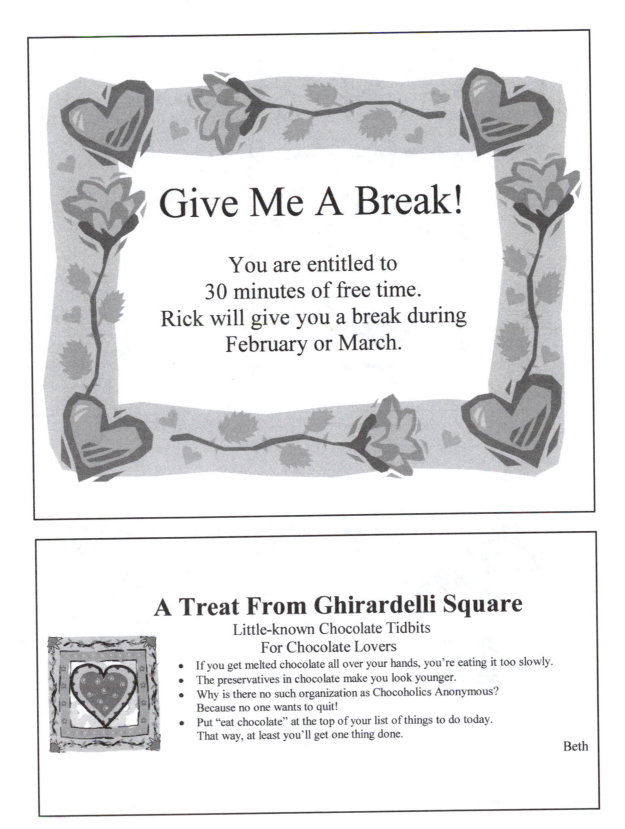

Give Me A Break!

You are entitled to
30 minutes of free time.
Rick will give you a break during
February or March.

A Treat From Ghirardelli Square

Little-known Chocolate Tidbits
For Chocolate Lovers

- If you get melted chocolate all over your hands, you're eating it too slowly.
- The preservatives in chocolate make you look younger.
- Why is there no such organization as Chocoholics Anonymous?
  Because no one wants to quit!
- Put "eat chocolate" at the top of your list of things to do today.
  That way, at least you'll get one thing done.

Beth

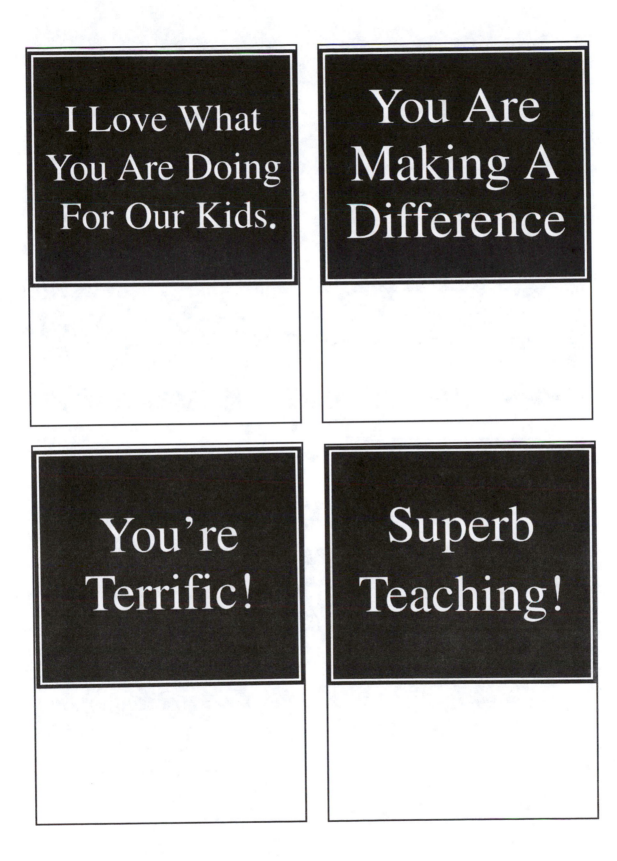

I Love What You Are Doing For Our Kids.

You Are Making A Difference

You're Terrific!

Superb Teaching!

The good news is...

LEXINGTON 4 PUBLIC SCHOOLS

"Where Excellence is the Rule"

———————————————— work deserves a BLUE RIBBON.

——————————

Date

——————————

Signature

EXCELLENT

TO _____

1981–1982
MILL CREEK SCIENCE FAIR

for your OUTSTANDING work in science.

★ _____ ★ _____ ★

MISSING TOOTH AWARD

Today _____

is special for _____

because _____ lost a tooth!

CONGRATULATIONS!!

© GP82

SIGNATURE

4

Communicating With the School's External Publics

Why Study About Communicating With the School's External Publics?

- ◆ The external publics will base their opinions about a school on the messages they receive from the members of the internal publics.
- ◆ Parental involvement with their children's education is an indicator of an effective school.
- ◆ Key communicators help to keep other members of the external publics informed while also sharing their questions, comments, and concerns with the leadership of the school.
- ◆ More citizens do not have school-age children, so strategies need to be used to keep them informed.

> **Good public relations is not always telling a particular public that which it wants to hear.**
>
> **– David Martinson**

In the previous chapter we learned that efforts to build good school–community relations outside of school, in the community at large, have as their foundation the things that are done in school. When staff members have a good feeling about their school, they tell the community. Therefore, all of the strategies for building staff morale have a direct effect on school and community relations.

Efforts to involve parents in school activities in effect advertise to the community what is going on in the school. Parents who are made to feel they are welcome in a school become supporters of the school and relay that message to the community.

At the core of a school's community relations plan is a strong educational program. This makes educating children the mission of the school and allows the principal to advertise honestly to the community about the good things going on in the school. The message of the effective school learning program, once communicated to and acknowledged by the students' parents, will spread throughout the community. The plan must be developed and publicized to promote parent and community involvement.

Parents entrust schools with two of their most valued assets: their children and their money. They are deeply concerned about the care each receives from the school system. When students feel good about school, and learning, they tell their parents and grandparents, their neighbors, their religious-school teachers, their dance teachers, their karate teachers, their coaches, and their scout leaders. All of the strategies for making students feel successful have a direct effect on the school and the impact it has on the community.

In addition to the parents of the students who attend the schools, other external publics include

External Publics		
◆ Taxpayer groups	◆ Preschool parents	◆ Industry
◆ Alumni groups	◆ Ethnic organizations	◆ Substitute teachers
◆ Service clubs	◆ Churches	◆ Single adults
◆ Legislators	◆ Businesses	◆ Media
◆ Teachers' union	◆ Athletic boosters	◆ Retirees

Waler (1998) offered 12 guidelines to school leaders as they work to involve parents and other members of the school community in the workings of the school. His suggestions stress the need for school leaders to reach out and touch parents and other citizens in personally meaningful ways.

What Do the External Publics Want to Know?

These people want to know how the students in the school district are doing. Years of administrative experience and contact with various publics have led to the following questions people want to ask principals. Some specific areas in which they are interested are the following:

- How do the students' performances on standardized test scores compare to those of neighboring school districts? Also, how do their performances compare to the national averages?
- What is each school's and the school district's dropout rate?
- What percentage of the students who graduate from high school go on to college?
- Are graduates who are not going to college prepared to enter the workforce?

They are also interested in the adults who interact with the students. Some of their interests include the following:

- How much training and what degrees do the teachers have?
- How is their teaching evaluated? How often is this done?
- What support is given to the teachers?
- How much teacher turnover is there? What are the ages of the teachers?
- What qualifications do substitute teachers need? Are enough qualified substitutes available?

The academic program is of interest to the school's external publics. They want to know:

- How are features/components of the learning program determined?
- Is there a regular plan to review, revise, and evaluate the curricula?
- Are computers available for the students? How much time/how many periods can a student spend each day/week on one?
- What percentage of the students are in special education? How are their needs served?

Some other areas of interest to members of various external publics include the following:

- What is discipline like inside the schools?
- How safe are the schools?
- What is done with people who are involved with drugs?
- How are visitors welcomed at the school?
- How many students are bused?
- How much time do students spend on the bus?
- Do parents have options in selecting what schools their children can attend?
- Are any of the schools on year-round schedules?

- What are magnet schools? What learning programs are offered in any magnet schools in the district?
- Is there any type of child care available, either before or after school?
- Are before- or after-school activities available for students?
- If a person has questions about the schools, who should be contacted?
- When, where, and how often does the school board meet?

Not all members of the external publics will want to know the answers to each of these questions, but enough of them do. Helping those people who do have questions is a necessary expectation for the school to meet. To do this effectively, support from other members of external publics must be obtained.

Communicating With Parents

People's opinions about a school system in general, and their local community school in particular, are based primarily on information received from students. Parents are strongly influenced by their children's comments. Other community members base their opinions of a school and school system on their personal encounter with parents of the students or the students themselves. If students comment favorably and with enthusiasm about their school, the school staff and principal are likely to benefit from the support and confidence of the school's external publics.

Ned Hubbell (1981) spent a lifetime and a career in education—with a focus on school–community relations. He wrote about a special telephone call he and his wife received from their son's homeroom teacher. The call was one of many made by every teacher and was made during the dinner hour. It was a special personal invitation to attend the school's open house. Hubbell recalled that he could tell that the teacher was following an outline giving information about the evening, but he felt compelled to reply that they would attend. How could he turn his back on a teacher who had said to him, "You know, your son Gary just starts my day. He's really great to have around. I'd love to meet his folks" (p. 66). The mass telephone call campaign resulted in the largest turnout of parents to ever attend the school's open house. Hubbell concluded, "Come to think of it, if my wife and I want guests to come to our house, we don't send them a dittoed invitation, or put a notice in the newspaper. We call them up and invite them" (p. 66).

In addition to communicating with parents of students who attend the school, the other parents must also be considered. They include parents of preschool children, single parents, married couples with no children, married couples whose children are beyond public school age (empty nesters), and young marrieds who have no children yet.

Efforts must be made to ensure that all parents feel like part of the school's community. One of the most effective ways to do this is through regular contacts with parents. The telephone is an effective way to accomplish this mission. By making at least 10 telephone calls a week to parents, a principal can get valuable information about how they perceive the school. Many principals who have effective community relations plans make these calls either at breakfast time or during the dinner hour, because most parents are available then. The focus of the call can be to ask how the parents and their neighbors are reacting to a new instructional program, a revised procedure, a potential problem, or the school year in general. Ask the question and be prepared to listen. Promise to get back with information you don't have at hand. Then do it! Again, the credibility of the organization is at stake. These calls, because of the times they are made, should be brief and concise in nature.

The school's communication plan will be strengthened if every member of the teaching staff, including the principal, is expected to make a specific number of telephone calls each week to the parents of students. Their telephone calls can be made to share positive comments about the work habits and specific achievements of students. They can also enable parents to share concerns and questions. If follow-up responses are needed, they must be made. These telephone calls should be made in addition to the positive written communications that are sent home regularly.

Some principals expect their teachers to make two-minute phone calls to each of their students' parents during the first two weeks of school. These short calls can serve as an introduction of the teacher to the parents. The positive aspects of the experiences the teacher has had with each student should also be included. The first invitation to the annual school open house can be made during this call. Also, parents who have just moved into a community appreciate a welcoming call from their child's teacher or principal. This small investment in time can yield large dividends in the future.

Another effective way to communicate with parents is by writing notes. Happy grams, sunshine notes, or other personalized school stationery or note cards should be used. (See samples in Chapter 3.) Letters of congratulations, with brief handwritten messages, are effective in recognizing not only the achievements of students but also their parents and citizens in the community. One sample includes pictures of the school's mascot as well (see p. 71). This was printed on quality paper, with the sun and mascot colored in by student volunteers. The envelope used to send positive messages home can be upbeat and convey a message, too. One was used by the author at several schools (see p. 70). Volunteer students added colors to the pictures of children before the envelopes were used.

Notes can be sent home with students; this usually works effectively with younger students. For older students, notes can be mailed home. The notes can show awareness of these qualities:

◆ Improved behavior

◆ Improved grades

◆ Improved or perfect attendance

◆ A student's or a parent's kindness to another

◆ Sharing of a talent

◆ The loss or illness of a loved one

Education is simply not something which is provided either by teachers in schools or by parents and family members in the home. It must be a continuing cultivation of the child's experiences in which both schools and families jointly take part.

**– Fraser School Newsletter
(Edmonton, Alberta, Canada)**

"Hi!" Envelope

Mill Creek Elementary School
925 Universal Drive
Columbia, South Carolina 29209

Congratulations Note

Some principals are using communication methods based on recent developments in technology use. Carroll and Carroll's book, *EdMarketing: How Smart Schools Get and Keep Community Support* (2000), contains valuable information and suggestions for school principlas who use these and other techniques.

The electronic age has opened up new opportunities for ways to communicate with parents. Principals at all levels are finding that e-mail is a great way to communicate to parents. Dr. Gary Dunkleberger of North Carroll High School in Hempstead, Maryland, reported to *Education World* that his new-found strategy is great for many reasons. He uses the technique for emergencies, to shut off rumors by making sure certain parents get accurate information, and to simply communicate good news. Dr. Dunkleberger collects the e-mail addresses at the beginning of the school year. He sets up a list serve or e-mail group and adds to it as new addresses are made available to him. Each summer he purges the old list and rebuilds it anew the following year. Every time he sends a newsletter out, he requests parents to send their e-mail addresses to him. This information source could also become a part of the items parents complete when they register their children at a school. Another high school assistant principal, Marilyn Brewster at Parkview Arts/Science Magnet High School in Arkansas, reported to *Education World* that she uses e-mail to notify parents if a student is late for school or received a referral for a minor discipline problem.

Involving working parents in school activities is often difficult to do. Some school principals have invited them to visit the school for breakfast on their way to work. These before-school sessions are great opportunities for the school to highlight the learning program through short presentations made by key staff members or a short tour of the school with a stop in their child's classroom. The children who have participated in these events—"Muffins for Moms" and "Donuts for Dads"—reported that they enjoyed the extra times with their parents.

Many principals of secondary schools use personalized letters to students to recognize academic and/or athletic accomplishments. Letters from Dr. Fred Anderson, retired principal of Custer County District High School in Miles City, Montana, are included as examples of how he recognized students at his high school (pp. 73–75). Principal Anderson also paid attention to recognizing the accomplishments and efforts of people who worked at his school. Imagine the positive reactions of the employee who received the letter. Remember that sincere, honest praise is appreciated and usually results in continued efforts by the people who receive them.

(Text continues on page 76.)

Science Bowl Congratulations Letter

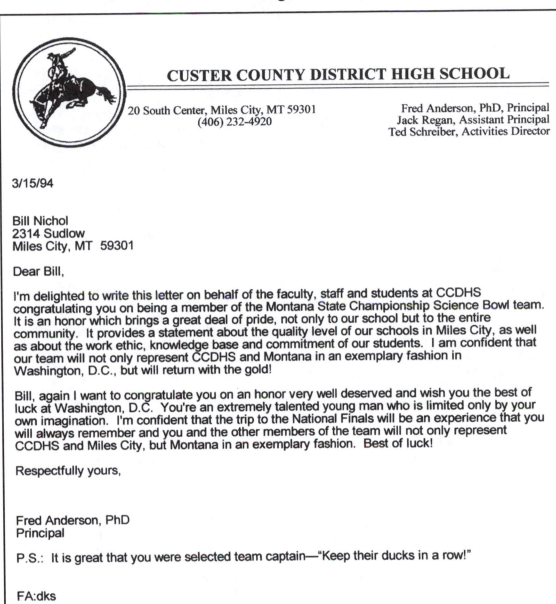

CUSTER COUNTY DISTRICT HIGH SCHOOL

20 South Center, Miles City, MT 59301
(406) 232-4920

Fred Anderson, PhD, Principal
Jack Regan, Assistant Principal
Ted Schreiber, Activities Director

3/15/94

Bill Nichol
2314 Sudlow
Miles City, MT 59301

Dear Bill,

I'm delighted to write this letter on behalf of the faculty, staff and students at CCDHS congratulating you on being a member of the Montana State Championship Science Bowl team. It is an honor which brings a great deal of pride, not only to our school but to the entire community. It provides a statement about the quality level of our schools in Miles City, as well as about the work ethic, knowledge base and commitment of our students. I am confident that our team will not only represent CCDHS and Montana in an exemplary fashion in Washington, D.C., but will return with the gold!

Bill, again I want to congratulate you on an honor very well deserved and wish you the best of luck at Washington, D.C. You're an extremely talented young man who is limited only by your own imagination. I'm confident that the trip to the National Finals will be an experience that you will always remember and you and the other members of the team will not only represent CCDHS and Miles City, but Montana in an exemplary fashion. Best of luck!

Respectfully yours,

Fred Anderson, PhD
Principal

P.S.: It is great that you were selected team captain—"Keep their ducks in a row!"

FA:dks

Sportsmanship Award Congratulations Letter

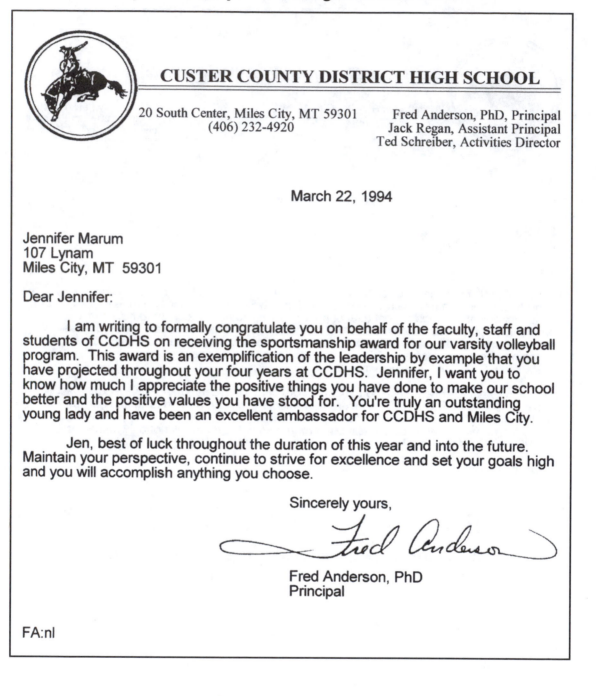

CUSTER COUNTY DISTRICT HIGH SCHOOL

20 South Center, Miles City, MT 59301   Fred Anderson, PhD, Principal
(406) 232-4920   Jack Regan, Assistant Principal
                                            Ted Schreiber, Activities Director

March 22, 1994

Jennifer Marum
107 Lynam
Miles City, MT 59301

Dear Jennifer:

I am writing to formally congratulate you on behalf of the faculty, staff and students of CCDHS on receiving the sportsmanship award for our varsity volleyball program. This award is an exemplification of the leadership by example that you have projected throughout your four years at CCDHS. Jennifer, I want you to know how much I appreciate the positive things you have done to make our school better and the positive values you have stood for. You're truly an outstanding young lady and have been an excellent ambassador for CCDHS and Miles City.

Jen, best of luck throughout the duration of this year and into the future. Maintain your perspective, continue to strive for excellence and set your goals high and you will accomplish anything you choose.

Sincerely yours,

Fred Anderson, PhD
Principal

FA:nl

Letter of Appreciation

CUSTER COUNTY DISTRICT HIGH SCHOOL

20 South Center, Miles City, MT 59301
(406) 232-4920

Fred Anderson, PhD, Principal
Jack Regan, Assistant Principal
Ted Schreiber, Activities Director

November 12, 1993

Mr. Wayne Hert
Box 1514
Miles City, MT 59301

Dear Wayne:

It is a pleasure to write this note of congratulations to you for a job very well done. Wayne, the pride you take in our school and in the job you do is very evident. Your area is clearly outstanding in terms of cleanliness and attention to detail. Beyond that, I also want to let you know that I deeply appreciate the pride you take in the entire school and your willingness to work beyond the call of duty to make CCDHS a better place for all of us.

Again, thank you for a job very well done!

Respectfully,

Fred Anderson
Principal

FA:nl

Key Communicators

The system of key communicators is generally formalized at the superintendent's office. And although it is important to suggest people to that office who will have an impact on the school district, the concept should be formalized at the individual school, too. The reasons for doing so are identical: School leaders need people who can, and will, share vital information with other community members while also sharing information from the community with school leaders. So although the numbers of key communicators will vary by the size of the school district, the same will also be true for an individual school.

Some of these people in the external publics are known as *key communicators*. In addition to being the power people behind the scenes, the opinion leaders, and the people who influence the directions and actions of the various community organizations, they may be the people who work in places that everyone frequents on a regular basis. Some of those people include barbers, beauticians, grocery store managers and cashiers, bank tellers, leaders of cultural groups, clergy, and real estate agents. Each comes in contact with large numbers of people. The messages they share with others about what is happening in a particular part of the community—a school, for instance—can have a significant impact on the organization. In some cases, key communicators for a specific school may also be key communicators for the school district. Their role, then, may be considered *very* important.

Key communicators are sincere people who are concerned about the school, and they want to be involved. Very often they have contacts with many people inside and outside of the school community. Generally, they are respected by others, and their messages are heard. Because of their contacts, they can get the word out quickly to large numbers of people. The messages from the key communicators are often viewed with more credibility than those of school district employees because they don't have a vested interest in the issues.

A network of key communicators can be a positive influence on an entire school's community-relations plan. If rumors are circulating in a community, there is a strong likelihood that some key communicators have heard the rumors because of their relationship with others in the community. Their opinions are valued, and their thoughts are sought to verify a situation or to clarify or amplify a position. Rumors can grow and get out of hand, and rumors are usually inaccurate; an established system of key communicators helps to control rumors and spread correct information instead. The key communicators play an important role in helping school leaders keep their fingers on the pulse of a community.

Whom Do You Select to Be Key Communicators?

Anyone who has contact with a large number of people in the community could be considered a key communicator. Included in that group, in addition to those mentioned earlier, may be local business people, parents, PTA officers, members of the clergy, school crossing guards, bus drivers, key students, and staff members. Also, be sure to include as many of the external public groups as possible—senior citizens, preschool parents, nonparents, single adults, and parents of nonpublic-school students. Don't eliminate the *negative* members of the community from consideration. Sometimes, by giving them advance information, their questions will be answered, and unfounded attacks and rumors will be defused.

Staff members can be asked to identify people they consider to be key communicators. Use your own knowledge of people to identify key communicators. By reading the local newspapers you will be able to identify people whose names are mentioned frequently through their involvement with various organizations. Your discussions with parents, staff members, and others should also be useful in identifying some key people. Remember, some of these people may be the silent, behind-the-scenes people, sometimes referred to as the power brokers. You may find them working with political, social, charitable, or ethnic groups. You might also find them in the school's parent–teacher–student organization or in the business community. Once the word is out that you want to talk with them, others will help you with your search. A person who is identified as such by several people should be considered a strong candidate for the role of key communicator. In asking other people to identify these important people, encourage them to volunteer themselves if they feel it is appropriate.

The number of key communicators to select will vary depending on the size of the school. It is best to start with a number the principal can feel comfortable with—fewer is probably better than more. The program can grow as needed. Members of the group can change as people who lose interest are removed and others with interest are added.

Follow up a letter of invitation from the principal with a personal call to encourage the key communicators to attend a brief meeting. The personal telephone call from the school leader will increase greatly the number of people who accept the invitation. At the meeting, their role can be explained and any questions answered. By keeping the meeting attendance to 8 to 10, the key communicators and the principal can communicate more informally, which can lead to more personal exchanges of information. The main purposes of their role should be shared. These are featured in the following list.

The Role of the Key Communicator

- ◆ Be informed via information that is given to them.
- ◆ Share information if they are asked to do so.
- ◆ Share any questions or concerns they hear about the school or school system.

Two-way communication is essential. It is imperative that regular communication be maintained with key communicators. Once the key communicators have been identified, a mailing list that includes all relevant information about contacting each person, including e-mail addresses whenever possible, could allow for a quick, inexpensive method to contact the key communicators on a regular basis. However, care must be exerted to remember the key communicators who cannot be reached that way. By sharing your e-mail address with each member, you can expect their messages and information to reach you promptly. This can be done through a monthly letter with important school highlights mentioned. Other school leaders who have established successful key communicator programs have sent copies of their school newsletters, press releases, abstracts of school and district school board meetings, information and fact sheets about the school and district, as well as good news related to the school's adult personnel and students. The information sent to them can help them in their role as a source of information about your school. Telephone calls can also serve as a survey for seeking information from them or as follow-ups to e-mail messages you receive. Remember, the continued personal touch yields better results. Occasional meetings of the key communicators can be useful in meeting new staff members or school board members. These meetings can be used as a forum to answer questions, to show off a new learning program, to sample cafeteria food or to witness new procedures in the kitchen, or to tour a renovated or new school facility.

Because the key communicators are important links with the community, it is crucial to answer all comments, messages, questions, letters, and telephone calls with a personal phone call or letter. It is important to have an answer or response, and if a response or answer to a question isn't known, a call should be made anyway. At the same time, the appropriate person, if not at the school, should be asked to make a formal response, too. Last, follow up with the key communicators to be sure a response was made, to ensure that the key communicator feels equipped with accurate information about a specific question or concern. At stake here is the credibility of the organization—the school—because the key communicator needs to have accurate information to be a credible supporter of the school.

It is important to get feedback from the key communicators at least once a year. An annual system check and evaluation, done at an annual meeting, should yield information about how key communicators feel the partnership is working for them, whether they want to continue their work, and if they have the names of other people who might be good candidates as key communicators.

If representatives from the various external publics have been included, their opinions and temperament should be a good example of how the school's support network feels about the school. Having an open, honest effort to communicate, in a two-way manner, should contribute to the overall success of the school and ultimately the school district. Those school leaders who listen attentively to the concerns of constituents take action when and where appropriate, are willing to share information, and are successful in their roles. Their strategy can work for every school in the nation. Key communicators are resources that can support the dedicated efforts of all school employees. And like any other valuable resource, they need to be nurtured and appreciated.

Getting Parents Actively Involved at School

Parents who are actively involved in the school's learning program often become strong advocates of the school. Some parents are reluctant to volunteer to help at school but will respond favorably if they are invited to help. Some options for a principal to offer parents to get them involved in the school's program include doing the following:

- Helping a teacher
- Judging a competition
- Assisting in the media center
- Decorating a bulletin board
- Assisting in the office
- Serving as a mentor for a new family
- Assisting in classrooms
- Sharing information about a skill
- Sharing information learned from recent travels
- Helping with student/staff recognitions
- Serving on a committee

Target specific persons for tasks and issues in which they are most likely to have interest and competence. Not everybody needs to be invited to do everything in the same way. Don't be afraid to let people know that you've asked them to help in a particular way because of the unique talents and experience they would bring to the task. They will appreciate your recognition of their abilities and probably will be flattered by an offer to make a difference in the school.

Casual encounters with parents and others can be opportunities to invite them to become involved in important school issues. I made significant contacts while attending and working athletic events and managing by walking around (MBWA) during open house sessions and at other community events. You will connect with people who would not respond to less personal invitations.

Teachers need to be trained to seek, welcome, and use parent and community involvement effectively. Most teachers will agree that these forms of involvement can benefit their programs; few of them will be confident to accept the help without additional training and experience. This is a job for principals to share, model, and recognize ways in which teachers can effectively collaborate with those beyond the classroom.

Dr. Ann Kohler, the technology coordinator at Lyman High School in Seminole County, Florida, invited a neighbor who was retired, but who at one time had students in the school system, to visit the school to see how computers were being used to enhance the students' learning in the academic subjects. Dr. Kohler said, "After Mrs. Albertson saw how we were enriching the students' understandings, she was hooked. I can count on her to be at the school, serving as a volunteer 'dividend,' at least three days a week." This story reflects the power that can be felt from a personal invitation to a nonparent to observe the positive impact a school's instructional program has on students.

Because both parents in some families work each day, it is often difficult for them to communicate with the school. Those with a home computer have found the task easier because their e-mail messages can be sent, received, and responded to more rapidly than ever before. To accommodate the needs of these and other parents, some principals maintain evening office hours once or twice a month. The hours are announced in the principal's newsletters and on the school's outdoor sign board. Parents are encouraged to call the school or come in. Bob Ziegler, retired principal at New Hope, Minnesota, Elementary School, kept evening office hours for a number of years. He reported that the time was well spent and informative. Parents who worked all day and who would have had to take vacation time to meet with him appreciated his willingness to stay later in his office.

Catherine Roach, principal at Cypress Park Elementary School in Orlando, Florida, schedules Coffee Talks in the principal's conference room three times a year. The announcement she sends home is written in English and Spanish and is shown on the facing page.

As I moved about the country serving in various elementary schools, I made it known that I would travel to the homes of parents who would host a short daytime or evening meeting with me. It turned out that these meetings were well received and usually were done by grade levels. The agendas were open—that is, parents could come with questions, concerns, and suggestions for me to consider. At the same time I was always asked to share my vision for the school. Because these sessions were held in the fall, I couldn't be very specific about changes I

Coffee Talks

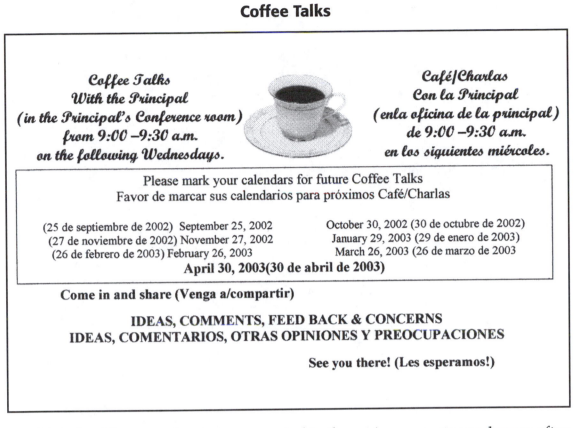

Coffee Talks
With the Principal
(in the Principal's Conference room)
from 9:00 –9:30 a.m.
on the following Wednesdays.

Café/Charlas
Con la Principal
(en la oficina de la principal)
de 9:00 –9:30 a.m.
en los siguientes miércoles.

Please mark your calendars for future Coffee Talks
Favor de marcar sus calendarios para próximos Café/Charlas

(25 de septiembre de 2002) September 25, 2002
(27 de noviembre de 2002) November 27, 2002
(26 de febrero de 2003) February 26, 2003

October 30, 2002 (30 de octubre de 2002)
January 29, 2003 (29 de enero de 2003)
March 26, 2003 (26 de marzo de 2003

April 30, 2003(30 de abril de 2003)

Come in and share (Venga a/compartir)

IDEAS, COMMENTS, FEED BACK & CONCERNS
IDEAS, COMENTARIOS, OTRAS OPINIONES Y PREOCUPACIONES

See you there! (Les esperamos!)

would make. These sessions were repeated in the spring semester and were often held in different homes and in the evenings.

According to the National School Public Relations Association (NSPRA) (1981), effective parent involvement programs seem to have common factors. The five factors are *climate, relevance, convenience, publicity,* and *commitment* (see p. 82).

Communicating With New Parents and Parents With Preschoolers

Parents who are new to the school should be made to feel welcome and needed. After the initial telephone call and welcome letter have been made, the next scheduled activity should be an information-sharing meeting. If the family has arrived before the school year begins, the parents can be invited to attend an orientation meeting with their child. At the session they can be introduced to the faculty members and key staff members. (See sample letters sent to kindergarten students and their parents, and parents of ninth-grade students whose children will be attending a high school for the first time, pp. 83–84.)

(Text continues on page 85.)

Climate, Relevance, Convenience...

Climate

A warm, caring atmosphere is apparent. The school said to the parents, "Welcome! We're glad you're here."

Relevance

Programs for parents were based on what they cared about, had an interest in, and enhanced their parenting skills.

Convenience

Successful programs make it easier for parents to participate by dealing with the factors that keep them home: providing transportation and child care.

Publicity

People need to know what has been planned. Fliers, posters, and newsletters help to spread the news, but the most effective method is the personal invitation.

Commitment

A successful parent involvement program is time consuming. Although it demands time and commitment, the payoff is worth the effort.

Welcome Letter, Beach Elementary

Rocky River City School District

BEACH ELEMENTARY SCHOOL
1101 Morewood Parkway • Rocky River, Ohio 44116 • (216) 333-6000

GEORGE E. PAWLAS, PRINCIPAL

Welcome

27 August 1976

Dear

A hearty welcome to you and your family from all of us at Beach School. I am sure you will have a very interesting year with us with many opportunities for new and exciting experiences.

Many people have been hard at work cleaning, repairing, decorating and planning so that everything will be in good order when you come to Beach on Wednesday, September 8.

Entering a new school is an exciting experience. In time, you will make many new friends. I anticipate you will become a good citizen of Beach and will do what you can to make everyone proud of Beach.

Classes begin at 8:45 a.m. on Wednesday, September 8. The morning session ends at 11:30 a.m. After lunch, school begins again at 1:00 p.m. and is dismissed at 3:45 p.m.

On Wednesday, you will receive a list of supplies which you will use during the year. You will have an opportunity to purchase the supplies on Thursday or Friday.

Your teacher,   , is expecting you in room

If you would like to visit Beach before school begins, do not hesitate to visit. Someone is in the office until 4:00 p.m. every day.

Cordially,

Mr. Pawlas, Your Principal

GEP:ms

Orientation Letter, Custer County

CUSTER COUNTY DISTRICT HIGH SCHOOL

20 South Center, Miles City, MT 59301   Fred Anderson, PhD, Principal
(406) 232-4920   Jack Regan, Assistant Principal
Fax: (406) 232-4923   Ted Schreiber, Activities Director

August 6, 1994

Dear Parent/Guardian:

The school year is about to begin and your child is about to embark on his/her high school career. These next four years will be very important in the formation of their futures.

To help insure a positive start, we at CCDHS would like to invite you and your incoming freshman to an orientation picnic on Monday, August 22, 1994, at 6:30 p.m. The picnic will be held in front of the high school on Center Street.

We will be explaining the curriculum, graduation requirements, school policies, and activity opportunities, and will present the freshmen with their final class schedules and locker numbers. Parental involvement is very important in a student's educational success. This is your school and we want to establish open lines of communication so we can work as a team to make your child's stay at CCDHS both enjoyable and profitable. A tour of the building will be provided at the end of the picnic.

We look forward to seeing you the evening of August 22nd!

Sincerely,

Fred Anderson

Fred Anderson, Principal

Jack Regan

Jack Regan, Assistant Principal

FA:nl

It is important for these new parents to receive written information about the school and school district. The Orange County Public Schools in the Orlando, Florida, area distribute to all parents a comprehensive publication, "Parent's Guide to Orange County Public Schools." Included in the publication is a Quick Reference Guide that contains information on registration procedures, curriculum, special programs, transportation, parent/community involvement, and frequently called numbers. The 24-page publication is a handy reference for all parents. Some other districts have put relevant information, written in English and Spanish—including a handbook for students and parents, past copies of the principal's newsletters, information about special programs (outdoor education, gifted program) provided by the school, opportunities to volunteer to join parent support groups, and community information and activities—in a pocket folder. In addition, a "Who's Who at School" brochure, which gives brief educational background information about teachers and administrators, will give important details about them.

Many states require each school and school district to prepare and distribute annual performance reports. The Clark-Pleasant Community School Corporation in Indiana publishes such a report. Their report contains a message from the Superintendent of Schools, the School Corporation (District) Performance Summary, and reports from each of the seven schools. The January 2004 report was included as an insert in the *Daily Journal* newspaper.

School Tours and Visits

Tours of the school can be arranged with students or key personnel acting as the guides. If the parents receive a map of the school, they will be able to orient themselves as they are guided around the school. It is important to post a map of the school near the school office. Also, copies of the map should be available in the school's office to be distributed to visitors. Remember how Bob Spinner of DeLaura Middle School in Florida enlisted the services of a student in the creation of a map of the school, to scale, that was framed and displayed near the entrance of the school's office area.

For parents in one Indiana town, finding out about their children's school activities is as easy as picking up the telephone. The homework hotline at Fegley Middle School in Valparaiso, Indiana, provides parents the homework assignments given and a brief update on what each class is studying. The hotline also allows parents to check lunch menus, get a complete schedule of after-school sports and activities, or report a sick child. Parents just have to enter a special code assigned to each teacher. Assistant principal Chris Evans says it's almost like having a parent–teacher conference very day, without meeting face-to-face.

As part of her school's comprehensive parent/student handbook, principal Lori Kinney of Mark Twain Elementary School in Colorado has included a complete listing of how her school personnel will communicate with parents.

Communication (From *Twain Newsletter*)

To facilitate school-to-home communication, a wide variety of tools are used. The *Twain Newsletter*, our school newsletter, is published monthly and sent home with the youngest child or only child in the family. The newsletter also can be accessed from our Web site. Our address is http://twain.littletonpublicschools.com.

The *Twain Bulletin Board* is located in the main hallway and is updated weekly. Be sure to check our Web site for up-to-date information also.

Each teacher at Twain has *voice mail*. Parents will receive voice mail telephone numbers for the staff at the beginning of the year. Because teachers are not available during class time to take calls, please leave a voice message so the teacher can get back with you. The staff is committed to keeping parents informed about their children and uses traditional forms of communication as well as technology-based methods. Also, we would very much appreciate making communication a two-way process. Please call the school (303-347-4700) or the voice mail for your child's teacher if you are concerned about your child, if you want to share good news and celebrations, or if you want to exchange information. The *Mark Twain Marquee* in front of the building lists major school events.

The district Web site is another excellent source of updated schedule information on all LPS schools. The Web site address is: www.littletonpublicschools.com.

Ms. Kinney's complete listing of ways in which the school personnel let parents know what is happening at the school should enhance understanding at the school. She also welcomes unsolicited communication from the parents. She and her colleagues understand the value of two-way communication. One additional technique Ms. Kinney uses to help parents communicate with the school is through the refrigerator magnet each family receives. All relevant information about the school is included on the magnet.

Mark Twain Magnet

Printed information sheets about your school and relevant events should be available for the new parents to take home. As part of a course assignment for a school–community relations course I teach, one graduate student, Junella Handley, prepared an informative trifold brochure (see p. 88) about her school, Cypress Park Elementary. The school principal recognized the need to have such a communicative device and was so pleased with the final product that she had multiple copies made to give to new parents, real estate personnel, and others.

Other Strategies

Another effective component of an orientation session for new parents is a color DVD or videotape presentation. Either of these techniques is an effective way to show teachers and support staff members in action. Be sure to include examples of all parts of the typical school day, including special services provided to students, lunch, media center operations, and arrival and departure procedures. The events can be narrated by students and members of the professional staff. Some schools allow the parents to take the videotape home to share with other members of the family who were unable to attend the orientation. The DVD and/or the videotape can become a part of an annual school open house event. Many schools have them playing continuously in the media center during the event. Either can become a part of a presentation that might be made to various out-of-school organizations.

The parent–teacher association or organization (PTA/PTO) president should also receive information about new parents. Their involvement can be initiated through a telephone call to the home to invite the parents to come to a special orientation meeting to learn how to become active in the school and to receive questions about the school. To keep parents informed of upcoming PTA/PTO events and activities, Indiana elementary principal Anne Young, like many other principals, includes "PTO News" as part of her weekly "Clark's Wednesday Express" newsletter to parents. In one of those publications, she included a reminder about a spaghetti dinner that was soon to occur. Dr. Fran Duvall, principal at Altamonte Elementary School in Florida, includes valuable information about her school's PTA in the pocket folder, which is also her school's student handbook.

Two follow-up activities for the new parents include inviting the parents to have lunch on a specific day with their children during the first several weeks of school. If possible, the principal should also try to have lunch with them. This can be done by grade levels and on different days of the week. In addition to sharing lunch with each new parent and student, another effective method is a telephone call to the parent about a month after arrival to inquire how the student is doing. This can also provide the parent with an opportunity to ask questions or share concerns.

Cypress Park Elementary Brochure

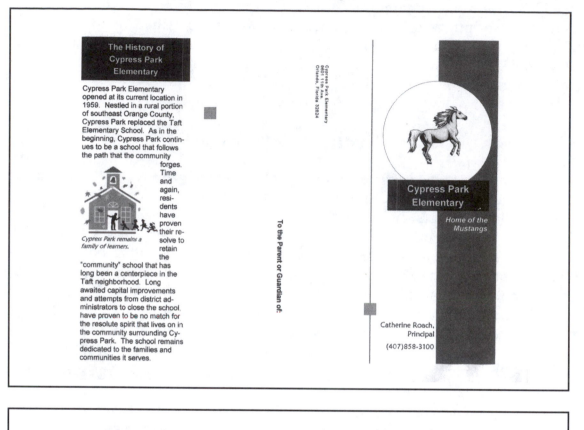

The History of Cypress Park Elementary

Cypress Park Elementary opened at its current location in 1959. Nestled in a rural portion of southeast Orange County, Cypress Park replaced the Taft Elementary School. As in the beginning, Cypress Park continues to be a school that follows the path that the community forges. Time and again, residents have proven their resolve to retain the "community" school that has long been a centerpiece in the Taft neighborhood. Long awaited capital improvements and attempts from district administrators to close the school, have proven to be no match for the resolute spirit that lives on in the community surrounding Cypress Park. The school remains dedicated to the families and communities it serves.

Cypress Park remains a family of learners.

Cypress Park Elementary
9601 11th Ave.
Orlando, Florida 32824

To the Parent or Guardian of:

Cypress Park Elementary
Home of the Mustangs

Catherine Roach,
Principal
(407)858-3100

All About Cypress Park Elementary

Our Vision

Cypress Park Elementary School's vision is to engage all members of the learning community in a school-wide effort to provide the skills, knowledge, and opportunity necessary for students to perform successfully on the state standards and in everyday life.

Our Plan

We maintain high standards and expectations for our students and school. To achieve our goals, our staff adapt programs to meet individual needs and provide a positive learning environment that promotes critical thinking. We strive to continue improving, sharing the responsibility of developing life long learners. Cypress Park's School Improvement Plan emphasizes a community-wide effort to meet the needs of every child- in school and at home.

Cypress Park is dedicated to meeting students' needs.

Our Staff

Cypress Park Elementary employs 54 faculty members, including classroom teachers, support teachers, paraprofessionals, office staff, custodians, lunchroom staff, and administrators. Thirty percent of our staff have earned a degree beyond a bachelor's degree. One hundred percent of our teachers and staff received satisfactory annual evaluations through the district's assessment system.

Our Students

Cypress Park student enrollment ranges from between 340 to 360 proud Mustangs each year. Our diverse population includes approximately 40% Hispanic students, 10% African American students, 43% Caucasian students, 6% Asian students, and less than 1% students in an "other" category.

Our Community

The rich history within our community has allowed Cypress Park to maintain close relations with parents, community members and local businesses. Our school offers parents resources for helping their children at home. Our Accelerated Reader program features adult books for parents to continue their reading improvement as well. Our ADDITIONS volunteer program and Partners in Education program provide opportunities for volunteers and businesses to share resources for maximum student learning opportunities.

Our Campus

Originally built in 1958, our school's main building now serves as our office, media center, resource classrooms, and cafetorium. More recent construction on campus has revitalized our look with a new 16 classroom building.

Contact Information:

Catherine Roach, Principal
Cypress Park Elementary
9601 11th Ave.
Orlando, Florida 32824

Phone: (407) 858-3100
Fax: (407) 858-2222
http://www.cypresspark.ocps.net

Some school districts set aside days during the school year when parents and other members of the community are invited to visit the schools to see learning in action. These opportunities are in addition to the National Education Week activities. Copies of the school newsletters, information brochures, and sign-up sheets to volunteer or mentor should be available to give to the visitors.

Communicating With People Without School-Age Children

As the world outside the school is surveyed, the segment of the community that is farther away from direct contact with schools must not be overlooked. Who are the people in this group?

- Senior citizens
- Adults whose children are grown (empty nesters)
- Married adults without children
- Newly married couples who have no children as yet
- Single adults ages 18 years and older

What do these people want to know? Earlier in this chapter, a comprehensive list of needs was shown, but basically they fall into these categories:

- What is being taught?
- What teaching methods are used?
- How effectively are the students learning?
- How do the students' test results compare with other schools and districts in the state and nation?
- How are decisions made by the administration and school board?

The answers to these questions can be shared in the school newsletters, which can be sent or taken to churches, civic organizations, service clubs, the media, and legislators. In some cases copies can be carried to barber and beauty shops, doctors' offices, and real estate offices on a regular basis. Some other ways to inform and involve these large groups of people are listed on page 90.

The percentage of senior citizens in the total population continues to grow each year. Because in many cases it has been years since these people have had children in schools, or even visited a school, it is important for school principals and their staffs to find ways to get these citizens interested in the schools and to get them involved in the programs in the schools.

Sharing good news about a school in the community is another challenge a principal must accept. Dr. Pat Ramsey, principal at Orla Vista Elementary School in Orlando, Florida, distributes bumper stickers (p. 92) to parents of students at her school who have received very good grades and have achieved the honor roll.

Other Ways to Inform and Involve
People Without School-Age Children

- ◆ Hold special observances: Grandpersons Day, Career Exploration Day, Graduates Day, School Community Open House, Community Leaders Day, and Retired School Employees Day.
- ◆ Use radio public service announcements for taped messages from parents, graduates, teachers, students, and neighbors about school accomplishments.
- ◆ Use public access time on cable television to share the talents of performing groups of students, share information about a new educational program, or mark a special observance of community or national importance.
- ◆ Invite the senior citizens and community leaders to lunch, plays, concerts, sports events, and assemblies, and to see for themselves children who are busy learning.
- ◆ Arrange for students to visit community organizations, clubs, and senior centers.
- ◆ Communicate with the neighbors who reside near the school. The most effective way is through a personal visit to the homes. These are great opportunities to get to know these people, to share information about the school with them, and to invite them to visit the school.
- ◆ Share information about graduates' accomplishments or the school staff's community service and honors.
- ◆ Use a newspaper's local interest section to announce events and activities that are open and available to the public.
- ◆ Make school facilities such as auditoriums, gymnasiums, and classrooms available to community organizations for meetings. This will bring people to the school and expand interest and awareness.
- ◆ Develop a graduates' "Hall of Fame" to highlight people who have been students in the school and have gone on to make worthy contributions or have become celebrities.

Principal Joe Loffek of Port Malabar Elementary School in Florida distributes bumper stickers (p. 92) that reveal that a student has received a Principal Award for some special efforts at the school. Principal Patty Martin of Gardendale Elementary Magnet School (GEMS) makes certain all her students' parents are given a bumper sticker that indicates that their child attends the school, a nice way to let other parents know about the fact the school is a magnet school that houses four distinct schools. Those are the School of Arts and Cultures, the School of Microsociety, the School of Math and Science, and the School of Performing Arts. Principal Ken Winn of Hoover Middle School and his faculty convey a different message to their community through the school's bumper sticker (p. 92). They recognize that students of that age group do not like to have their achievements announced and recognized, so their school's message is more generic in nature. The wrestling coach and team of Melbourne High School have the support of principal Jim Wilcoxon in the distribution of their bumper sticker to people in the Florida attendance area. Middle school principal Dr. Les Potter of Silver Sands Middle School in Ormond Beach, Florida, distributes bumper stickers (p. 92) to his teaching staff to let others know they are proud to be members of the school's faculty.

Some schools successfully use their sign boards to communicate messages to parents and citizens who pass by the school. Sample messages from Golfview Elementary School (p. 93) and Kennedy Middle School (p. 93) reflect different messages to the community. Principal Ken Winn of Hoover Middle School is proud of the fact that his school achieved the state's A rating for the achievement of the students and the hard work of the school's family.

Several school districts around the country have issued *gold cards* to senior citizens that enable them to attend band concerts, sporting events, and dress rehearsals of plays, in addition to other school events. Local agencies that interact with the seniors can help in identifying the seniors as well as distributing the gold cards to them. A more personal touch, of course, would be achieved if the principal attended a meeting of the groups, shared a few comments about the school, and then issued the gold cards to those interested in receiving them.

The letters to the editor section in local newspapers is another effective technique to use to get a message to a large number of citizens. Retired principal Connie St. John used the column to share her thanks for the support her school community gave while renovations were being made (p. 94).

Sometimes the letters to the editor section can also be used by parents to recognize the efforts of school personnel. As an example, a parent, Laura Wilcox, showed her appreciation for the conscientious job the principal of her child's school, Mary Cassidy, did to ensure that children left school on the correct buses (p. 94). Another person, Tim Kozusko, who attended a school more than 40 years ago but who was currently actively involved with students, wrote to let others know of the school's successes on the Florida Comprehensive Assessment Test (FCAT) (p. 95).

(Text continues on page 95.)

Bumper Stickers

Sign Boards

Community Aids Its School

By Constance R. St. John, Principal, Retired
Spessard Holland Elementary School, Satellite Beach

With our year of renovation, our Satellite Beach community has supported us in an excellent manner. Patrick Air Force Base has extended help to us as needed.

We appreciate the "family atmosphere" given to us by volunteers, merchants and the police department. Thank you for understanding our problems this year and being there when we needed you. Your support makes us a better school.

Principal Gets Kids On Right Bus

By Laura Wilcox
Melbourne

As a parent of a bus-riding student at Riviera Elementary School, I want to thank Principal Mary Cassidy for ensuring that my son got on the right bus.

With 11 buses, 1,050 students and the confusion of the first week of school, children could very easily have boarded the wrong bus.

Instead of condemning Cassidy for writing bus numbers on the hands of their children, parents should be thanking her for caring enough to get their children home. And also sparing them the trauma of missing their bus altogether or riding the wrong bus.

Her biggest concern is for the safety and well-being of the students. She has demonstrated this by arranging to have new sidewalks poured in front of the school. She also secured a crossing guard for dismissal time.

Let's appreciate and support the caring principal whom we are fortunate enough to have.

Scores Show Freedom 7 Gets Education Right

After looking through the recently announced scores for area schools on the Florida Comprehensive Assessment Test, I couldn't help but notice the amazing performance by students at Freedom 7 School of International Studies in Cocoa Beach.

I attended this school in the 1960s and led field trips into the Thousand Islands with the fifth-grade students this year, so I had more than a passing interest in how the school did.

The average scores in all grades, in all subjects, rate the highest in Brevard County. The average scores in each grade are within the top 5 places in the entire state. In fifth-grade science, Freedom 7 students had the highest average score in the state.

This seems to demonstrate what happens when great educators, administrators and support staff are met with bright students whose parents take an active role in raising their own children.

Congratulations are in order for all involved with this superior performance. It should be a source of great pride for Freedom 7 and the community.

Tim Kozusko,
Cocoa Beach

The 26th Annual Phi Delta Kappa/Gallup Poll of the Public's Attitudes Toward the Public Schools, which was released to the public in September 1994, contained the responses of the 1,326 adults who were surveyed. One of the topics the pollsters sought the public's perceptions on was "Citizen Contact with the Schools." The results of answers received are presented on pages 96–97 (Elam, Rose, & Gallup, 1994). These questions have not been asked again but they should be—they are important!

(Text continues on page 98.)

Citizen Contact with the Schools

Recent emphasis on the importance of parental knowledge about and involvement in the life of the public schools may be paying off. Over the last decade the frequency of many forms of public contact with the schools has doubled or nearly so. Areas showing the greatest gains are attendance at school board meetings, attendance at meetings dealing with school problems, and attendance at plays, concerts, and athletic events. Even adults with no children in school now claim to participate in the life of the schools to a certain degree.

The question: **Since last September, which of the following, if any, have you done yourself?**

	National Totals, %	No Children in School, %	Public School Parents, %	Nonpublic School Parents, %
Attended a school play or concert in any local public school	54	43	79	51
Attended a local public school athletic event	53	46	70	59
Met with any teachers or administrators in the local public schools about your child	31	6*	87	48
Attended any meeting dealing with the local public school situation	28	18	51	34
Attended a PTA meeting	21	7	49	50
Attended a meeting to discuss any of the school reforms being proposed	20	13	35	34
Attended a school board meeting	16	10	27	38
Been a member of any public school-related committee	15	8	31	18

*Parents of a child approaching school age might consult school personnel about enrolling him or her.

	National Totals		
	1994 %	1991 %	1983 %
Attended a school play or concert in any local public school	54	30	24
Attended a local public school athletic event	53	30	25
Met with any teachers or administrators in the local public schools about your child	31	27	21
Attended any meeting dealing with the local public school situation	28	16*	10
Attended a PTA meeting	21	14	14
Attended a school board meeting	16	7	8

	Public School Parents		
	1994 %	1991 %	1983 %
Attended a school play or concert in any local public school	79	56	42
Attended a local public school athletic event	70	49	42
Met with any teachers or administrators in the local public schools about your child	87	77	62
Attended any meeting dealing with the local public school situation	51	36*	18
Attended a PTA meeting	49	38	36
Attended a school board meeting	27	16	16

*In 1991 this category was worded: "Attended any meeting dealing with the local public schools."

Source: *Phi Delta Kappan*, September 1994, Vol. 76, No. 1

An extensive study conducted by Phi Delta Kappa (PDK) in 1988 explored the topic of public confidence in schools. Responses from a sample of 240 public and private schools and 65 school districts that seemed to have high levels of public confidence were reported by PDK. The five most frequently reported characteristics of schools with high public confidence follow (Wayson et al., 1988).

Most Frequently Reported Characteristics of Schools With High Public Confidence

♦ Respondents described students' characteristics far more frequently than any other elements of their school.

♦ Schools with high public confidence were characterized by a lively, yet orderly, environment and a caring and cooperative climate.

♦ Teachers in these schools were described as well-prepared, competent, and caring about their students.

♦ School personnel in these schools saw the communities as supportive and deserving of high levels of service.

♦ These schools reported that their curriculum is diverse and their instruction is varied to meet many different interests and abilities.

How to Improve School–Community Relations With Minority Communities

The classrooms of America are becoming a microcosm of the world. More and more students of different cultures, and who speak different languages, are attending schools in the United States. In fact, almost one in three students in U.S. public schools belongs to a minority group. The Orange County, Florida, Public Schools, like many other school districts around the country, have found that the various minority student populations, when combined, produce a *majority* student population. Because 199 different languages are spoken in the schools, an English for speakers of other languages (ESOL) program is available in every elementary, middle, and high school. Students receive instruction in English from an ESOL teacher every day, and they are placed in regular classrooms for their academic courses. Bilingual instruction is also available for other students. Instruction is available in Spanish, Vietnamese, and Haitian Creole. Students attending one of the 23 elementary or 13 middle school bilingual centers study science, math, and social studies in their home language while working on reading and writing in English every day. The job of effectively communicating with and involving these people in their children's schools has appeared on the principal's responsibility sheet. Dr. Barbara C. Cruz, professor at the College of Education at the University of South Florida , has developed a 10-point tip sheet for secondary principals to use (Cruz, 1993). Her suggestions, which have been adapted, are included here.

10 Steps to Fostering School–Community Relations with Minority Communities

- ◆ Provide inservice opportunities for teachers and other administrators to learn more about the cultures represented in the school.
- ◆ Communicate with the home in the home language.
- ◆ Help students become more proficient in standard English.
- ◆ Involve faculty and staff members in interpreting the home language for others.
- ◆ Whenever possible, meet with the parents in their homes.
- ◆ Recognize that households do not necessarily consist of traditional nuclear families, and the primary contact at home might not be a parent.
- ◆ Use every opportunity to communicate signs of progress, exceptional effort, good behavior, and attendance to the parents.
- ◆ Ensure that students are not penalized for having limited financial resources.
- ◆ Become more knowledgeable about and sensitive to the many cultures reflected in the school.
- ◆ Do not automatically assume you know how a particular student will think or behave based on the student's ethnic background.

Although this is a short list of suggestions, it should be used for awareness purposes and to stimulate discussions within a school. The power of many people thinking about, and discussing, how to meet the needs of students from other cultures is important. Additional, specific suggestions for counselors to use when they work with students of other cultures can be found in a book, *Counseling the Culturally Different: Theory and Practice,* by Sue and Sue (2003). The ideas presented in the book can be used by other members of a school's staff, too.

It is important to respect the cultural sensitivities and life experiences of the people you would like to become involved with the school. Some parents and community members are uneasy about interacting with teachers and administrators because of language and educational barriers. However, others may be reluctant to get involved because of a firsthand poor school experience. School personnel, especially principals and teachers, need to address these obstacles with compassion and in a forthright manner.

Other Sources Report
School Effectiveness

In many parts of the United States, local newspapers report the effectiveness of the schools in their service area. In the past, these assessments were based solely on the test scores of the students. Now, however, a growing number of newspapers are investing heavily in time and resources on special reports on education that go far beyond the mere reporting of test scores. Some newspapers' reports often surpass the documents produced by districts and states in their level of detail, sophistication, and accessibility; and most are available on the World Wide Web.

This new way of reporting information creates new challenges and opportunities for educators. On one hand, the potential for a more in-depth, complete picture of education could result. On the other hand, the possibility of misleading or incomplete information could result. In any case, the news media's interest in more comprehensive reporting of this information stems from the public's hunger for information about schools. In our mobile society, many people shop for school districts before they actually shop for a home.

Schoolmatch.com, an Ohio-based business, conducts audits of school districts across the United States. The comprehensive reports that are prepared are presented to school boards, community organizations, and citizens. The results are available to people who might be interested in moving to specific locations. Real estate agents report that they make wide use of the information generated by the audits.

The second source of information about every school in the United States is GreatSchools.net, which uses test data and other statistics developed and reported by every state's department of education. In addition, each school's principal can request a special code to enter the school's site to add additional information to enhance the school's profile. Parents can also submit comments about their impressions about a school.

This additional source of information about schools should send a message to principals that their school is in competition with every other school in the country. Our mobile society has made it necessary for school personnel to keep the data about their school current and impressive. Sharing these Web sites with real estate agents who sell homes in a school's attendance area can provide them with additional sources of support for purchasing a home in a particular area.

A Closing Thought

Various research studies have revealed that a large percentage of adults do not have children attending schools. Their lack of active involvement in the functioning of a school has been attributed to some of the problems facing the schools.

School leaders must make concerted efforts to reach these publics while also focusing attention and efforts on the parents of the students in the schools.

Summary

Schools that make *extraordinary* efforts to foster parental involvement should benefit from strong community support. There must be frequent communications with parents and the broader community. Students who might otherwise fall between the cracks must be helped. Students should be involved in many, and varied, extracurricular activities. Perhaps the most compelling reason might be found in the participatory management techniques used. Conscious efforts should be made to enlist the participation of nonparents in the activities of the school.

Case Problem

The school board has requested that the superintendent conduct a demographic survey of the school district. This was done as a follow-up to a county government report that revealed changes were occurring rapidly in the overall population of the county. William Wannamaker, a newly appointed school principal who was hired after a national search, listened attentively as the superintendent outlined the school board's request. What items should he anticipate that would be included in his school's survey? Outline the steps you think he should follow. Whom do you think he should include in his efforts? Develop a demographic study of your school.

P^5 = *Prior Planning Prevents Poor Performance*

Learning is the shared responsibility of the school, the student, the home, and the community.

References and Suggested Readings

Carroll, S. R., & Carroll, D. (2000). *EdMarketing: How smart schools get and keep community support.* Bloomington, IN: National Education Service.

Cruz, B. C. (1993, October). *Tips for principals—How to improve home–school relations in minority communities.* Reston, VA: NASSP.

Elam, S., Rose, L., & Gallup, A. (1994). The 26th annual Phi Delta Kappa/Gallup poll of the public's attitudes toward the public schools. *Phi Delta Kappan, 76*(1), 41–56.

Hubbell, N. A. (1981). Why we went to parents night. *Educational Leadership, 39*(1), 66.

National School Public Relations Association. (1981). *Involvement is key to support or commitment. Principal's survival kit.* Arlington, VA: NSPRA.

Parent's guide to Orange County public schools 2004–2005 (2004). Retrieved February 9, 2004, from http://www.ocps.k12.fl.us

Sue, D. W., & Sue, D. (2003). *Counseling the culturally different: Theory and Practice* (4th ed.). New York: John Wiley and Sons.

Waler, J. A. (1998, February). *Tips for principals—How to promote parent and community involvement in school issues and activities.* Reston, VA: NASSP.

Wayson, W., Achilles, C., Pinnell, G. S., Lintz, M. N., Carol., L., & Cunningham, L. (1988). *Handbook for developing public confidence in schools.* Bloomington, IN: Phi Delta Kappa Educational Foundation.

5

Written Communications

Why Are Effective Written Communications Important?
◆ The written word is as important as the spoken word—and it lasts longer…forever.
◆ School personnel, parents, students, and community members have a need and a right to know.
◆ A surefire way to gain support or to share concerns would be through the written messages sent from a school.
◆ Clearly written and easily understood communications between the school and the community will enhance collaboration with families and community members.

The public's view of its schools is based on many factors: the quality of the teaching, the achievement of the students, the physical condition of the school, and the communication received from the school. The principal plays a key role in controlling both the quantity and quality of the communications distributed within and sent from the school.

Many of the same principles for effective speaking apply to effective writing. There are, however, differences between oral and written communications. These differences should be considered as the choice is made about which form to use. Two differences are immediate feedback, which can be present with oral communications but is often not obtained in written communications, and permanency, which exists with written communications, but not in oral communications.

In addition, the writer must consider those people who will receive the written message. Those members of a school's internal publics (the "family" of the school) should receive messages written in a different manner and tone than those who are part of the external publics.

To be an effective writer, the principal must recognize and acknowledge these constraints while selecting the communication method best suited for the task at hand. The next consideration should be deciding the purpose the written communication will meet. What is to be accomplished? Two additional considerations for all written documents are the target audience to be reached and what they should know or do as a result of the message they receive.

Dr. Dianna Lindsay, principal at Ridgefield High School in Ridgefield, Connecticut, in cooperation with her administrative team, developed six major goals for a school year. Goal 1, "To Increase and Enhance School-Wide Communications and Conversations about Learning," had nine related objectives. Objective I states, "Review all communications documents for clarity of understanding by internal and external publics to model the standards indicative of our expectations for learners." Dr. Lindsay and her team identified the measures of success of this objective by doing the following:

- Reviewing all mailed items produced for students and parents, such as
  - high school profile
  - handbooks
  - program of study
  - college planning guide
  - all forms, programs, and brochures;
- Establishing an official font, font size, use of logo, and general formal layout for electronic and print materials at Ridgefield High School (RHS);
- Communicating the print standards to all employees at RHS; and
- Using the same standards for
  - the administrative office
  - the athletics office
  - the guidance office
  - the PTSA (Parent–Teacher–Student Association) office
  - the student activities office
  - the student government office
  - the health office.

The changes and standardization procedures were to be in place at the start of a new school term. By establishing the goal and related nine objectives, this principal and her subordinates have set the marks regarding the value of communications with the internal and external publics of the school.

Note the to-the-point tone of her message to the members of the internal publics at Ridgefield High School. The academic calendar page is only one of nine pages distributed to the school's family members. In addition to the school vacations/staff development pages, Dr. Lindsay included pages on testing dates; faculty meetings—purpose, expectations, dates, time, and location; leadership team meetings; staff council meetings; department meetings; administrative team meetings; and other meetings—PTSA, Athletic Council, Board of Education, and Central Office Administrative Council.

Principal Lori Kinney of Mark Twain Elementary School in Colorado communicates with the school's internal publics through her "Lori-Grams" (p. 106) Notice how she uses important sayings to set the tone for each of the two "Lori-Grams" she shared with us. The August 18 message set the tone for the start of a new school year, and the April 26 communiqué has a future focus to it.

Lenore Stoia developed two types of stationery (p. 107) to use at the school she hopes to lead one day. Although she is a teacher at Cheney Elementary School in Orlando, Florida, she saw the relevance to the idea of developing a meaningful school letterhead to use for sending messages from the school. The other letterhead is one she developed and will use to send messages to the members of the school's internal family.

The next consideration of effective written communications is the selection of what is to be shared. Care must be taken to use words that convey a message of what is intended to be said and, more important, have meaning for the reader. Words selected in the written message, then, must correct misunderstandings, educate where there is a lack of knowledge, and clear up confusion. A cardinal premise is that you cannot tell anyone something he or she cannot understand (Cutlip, Center, & Broom, 2000). To make other people understand something you have to understand it first. Educators have been criticized because they tend to infuse both written and oral communications with jargon (educationese), which parents and others often cannot understand. This failure to communicate properly leads to misunderstanding and, even worse, lack of trust. Besides the jargon educators may want to use, care must be taken to avoid using slang, dialects, and exaggerations in written communication.

Good educator-to-parent communication can go a long way in improving student achievement. Dr. William L. Bainbridge, CEO of SchoolMatch, cited the work of the late Ron Edmonds, which found that clear and concise communications are a standard of effective schools (Bainbridge, 2002).

(Text continues on page 108.)

April 26, 2004 Lori-Gram

LORI-GRAM
April 26, 2004

Dance like no one is watching; sing like no one is listening;
love like you've never been hurt; and live like it's
heaven on earth.   Mark Twain

Twain Day...was terrific! Thanks to all of you who made it so. I thoroughly enjoyed going from class to class with the digital camera. While I thought a half-day of celebrating was plenty, some feedback I've received indicates that shorter sessions didn't allow for projects that take a bit longer. Also, some folks want to do this every year. E-mail me or see me with your feedback. Leslie Farley will be distributing a survey within the next week or so asking for staff input.

Future planning...I received a memo from Bonnie Miller, Asst. of Learning Services, stating that the morning of Friday, August 13th is being reserved for all district level meetings, i.e. ICs, assessment facilitators, special ed staff, curriculum councils, etc. Staff should return to their buildings by 1:00p.m., that day.

Scheduling Committee. Thank you to Liz, Julie C., Tammy, Susan, and Julie K-I for joining this committee. Our specials schedule really only needs tweaking. The one goal we said we would try to achieve(don't yet know if we can)is to get all teachers at least one planning time a day. We shall see. We will also be working on the before/after school duty schedule. If you have input for the committee see any committee member.

D.C. trip...I leave this Friday afternoon for what appears to be my final meeting of the Principal Preparation Task Force with NASSP. I have been on the task force for 3 years. I hope that the work of our group continues to make a difference in the lives of novice building principals. I'll be back at school on Wed., May 5th. Cheryl Houser, principal at Ames, is in charge in my absence.

Tutors...Attached is a copy of the district-wide list of tutors. Keep it for reference purposes in the event a parent asks about available tutors.

Calendar...
Mon., April 26th...non-student day...9-11:30a.m...Gwen's inservice...atrium...the afternoon is to be used for class placement work...no other staff development work planned for that day.
Mon...April 26th...noon -1:00p.m...lunch link...grades 4-5 + resource...atrium
Tues...April 27th...8:00-9:00a.m...chess club...media center
Tues...April 27th...8-9a.m...scheduling committee...Lori's office
Tues...April 27th...9:30-11:00a.m...5th graders visit Powell
Tues...April 27th...9:30-10:45a.m. and 12:50-1:55p.m...kindergartens visits HHS
Tues...April 27th...9:15-1:30..3rd grade field trip
Wed...April 27th...3:45-5:00p.m...scrapbooking club...art rm.
Wed...April 28th...9:30-1:15...4th grade field trip
Wed...April 28th...3:45-5:00p.m...theatre club...gym/cafeteria
Wed...April 28th...6:30-8:30p.m...TAC mtg...atrium
Thurs...April 29th...7-7:30p.m...5th grade music program
May 2nd-8th...Teacher Appreciation Week
May 2nd -13th...2nd grade District Writing Assessment window
Tues...May 4th...Mom & Me lunch...Zyzda...courtyard
Tues...May 4th...3:45-5:00p.m...Etiquette Class...atrium
Wed...May 5th...newsletter deadline(LAST NEWSLETTER OF 03-04 SCHOOL YEAR)
Wed...May 5th...Joint PTO Scholarship presentations...ESC board rm.
Thurs...May 6th...8-9a.m...Staff meeting...atrium
Thurs...May 6th...Teacher Appreciation Luncheon
Thurs...May 6th...PTO mtg...media center(by-laws decisions)
Fri...May 7th...8-9a.m...classified staff mtg...atrium

August 18, 2003 Lori-Gram

LORI-GRAM
August 18, 2003

"Quality is never an accident; it is always the result of high intention, sincere effort, intelligent direction, and skillful execution; it represents the wise choice of many alternatives."   William A. Foster

Let me begin my first Lori-Gram Of 2003, by telling you how very proud I am of you. The time, energy, enthusiasm, and preparation, you bring to a new school year is amazing! Thank you also for exhibiting patience and understanding as we worked our way through planning time discussions and the new Xerox machine procedures for this year. Together Each Achieves More = TEAM!

- There is no "formal" staff meeting this Wednesday. However, the 8:00-9:00a.m. timeframe that day would be an appropriate time to pass on the portfolios from grade level to grade level. Here's the schedule we'll follow in the atrium:

8:00-8:30a.m.	8:30-9:00a.m.
Kdg. Passes folders/info to 1st	1st meets with 2nd
2nd meets with 3rd	3rd meets with 4th
4th meets with 5th	

- This first week of school will bring us much information regarding the new student pick-up and drop-off system. Would those of you who do not have assigned duties this week, please assist students and parents outside both before and after school? If primary folks would sprinkle yourselves out front all along the driveway, intermediate folks can assist kiddos from school to bus stop, and specials folks can keep an eye on the parking lot. I know this is "extra" but you are truly needed. Your eyes and ears will guide us in how to provide ultimate safety for kids, i.e. formulating new routines, need for new and/or additional signage, etc. Thanks.

- **Reminder**...take your walkie-talkies with you when you are outside for recess times, duty times, etc.

- **Calendar dates to remember...**
  - Aug. 19th , first full-day with students.
  - Aug. 21st, first day of kindergarten..."Kleenex times" for parents held in atrium at 9:05a.m. and again at 1:00p.m.
  - Aug. 27th, staff mtg., atrium, 8:00-9:00a.m.
  - Aug. 27th, Vision/Hearing bus here for kindergarten
  - Aug. 30th--Sept. 1st...Labor Day weekend
  - Sept. 3rd , grade level mtgs., 8:00-9:00a.m.
  - Sept. 4th, Curriculum Night, 6:30-7:30(K-2), 7:30-8:30(3-5)

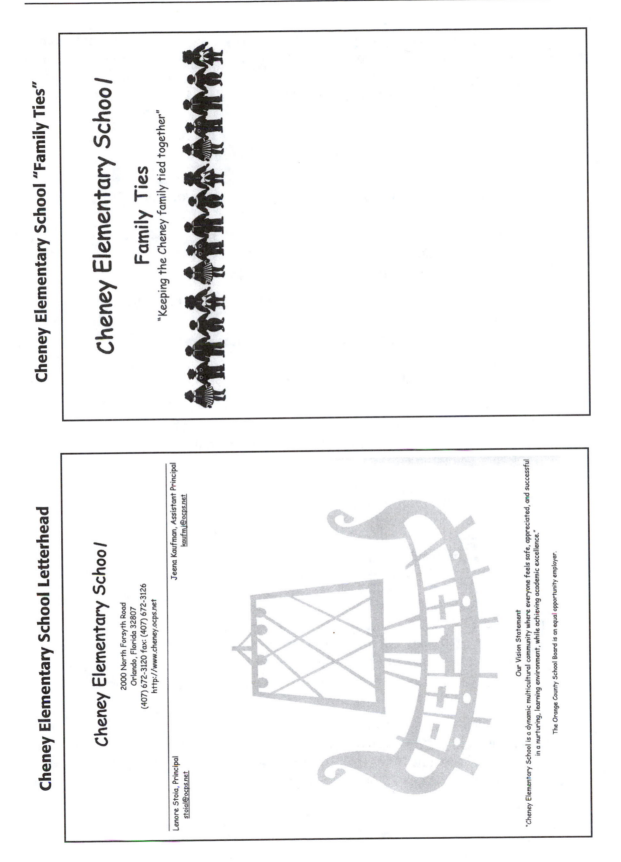

Cheney Elementary School "Family Ties"

Cheney Elementary School

Family Ties

"Keeping the Cheney family tied together"

Cheney Elementary School Letterhead

Cheney Elementary School

2000 North Forsyth Road
Orlando, Florida 32807
(407) 672-3120 fax: (407) 672-3126
http://www.cheney.ocps.net

Lenore Stoia, Principal
stoial@ocps.net

Jeena Kaufman, Assistant Principal
kaufmj@ocps.net

Our Vision Statement

"Cheney Elementary School is a dynamic multicultural community where everyone feels safe, appreciated, and successful in a nurturing, learning environment, while achieving academic excellence."

The Orange County School Board is an equal opportunity employer.

Some people will view writing as hard work, and it is, but it need not be painful. Yerkes and Morgan (1991) indicate that effective writers realize it takes only three special ingredients to write well. They say good writers strive to be organized, clear, and friendly. Some additional guidelines for clear and effective writing follow.

Write-Ability Makes for Readability

- ◆ Control the length of the words used. Remember, you don't get paid by the syllable.
- ◆ Write as you talk. If your tongue gets tangled as you read your message aloud to yourself…simplify.
- ◆ Use active verbs to keep the reader's interest.
- ◆ Organize your thoughts before you put them on paper. Make a list of points you want to make and work from it.
- ◆ Vary the length of the sentences used; shorter is better.
- ◆ If your message is lengthy, pull out the "meat" of it to use as a headline to be followed by the details.
- ◆ Maintain plenty of white space around the outside margins.
- ◆ No matter how the message is reproduced (typewriter or word processor), make sure the final copy is well proofed and clean of extraneous materials.
- ◆ Take a minute to look it up, so you don't have to live it down. Keep your dictionary handy. Spell names correctly. We all wince when an educator misspells or misuses a word: "between you and I"…or, "And, then I go…" These misuses cause people to say, "And these people are teaching our children?"

Frenchtown Elementary School principal Jacqueline Norcel's student job application (shown on the facing page) uses an interesting technique to get students to apply for various jobs at her Connecticut school. The tone of her message is positive and reflects her desire to have students indicate their interest in helping at the school.

Dr. Lindsay sets a more serious tone with the request for parental interest and acknowledgment of the receipt of the "Student-Parent Handbook" (p. 110) and the "Behavioral Expectations" (p. 110) of students. Both the student and parent signatures are required in order for the form to be accepted.

(Text continues on page 111.)

Ridgefield High Signature Packet Form

RIDGEFIELD HIGH SCHOOL
Ridgefield, Connecticut

12th GRADE SIGNATURE PACKET

PLEASE DO NOT SEPARATE THESE FORMS.

The attached information is important. Please take a moment to read, complete, and sign each form. This package must be returned prior to the opening of school or to your Grade Level Administrative Assistant during the first week of school.

Required Signatures:

Handbook Receipt	Student and Parent
Behavioral Expectations Form	Student and Parent

Please contact the Grade Level Administrative Assistant, Paulette Zaccagnino, if you have any questions.

Student Name _____ Grade _____

One form must be completed for each child in a family. Forms must be returned before attending any social events.

Frenchtown Elementary Job Application

Frenchtown Elementary School   JOB APPLICATION 2003-04

PLEASE FILL OUT ALL QUESTIONS AND RETURN TO MRS. NORCEL.

Date _____ Name _____

Teacher _____ Room # _____

I am applying for the position of _____

I feel I can do this job because _____

_____

I know I must be responsible and complete all my schoolwork in a quality manner if chosen for this job.

_____
Student Signature

FROM: Mrs. Norcel

**Your job will be: _____

_____

Ridgefield High Handbook Receipt

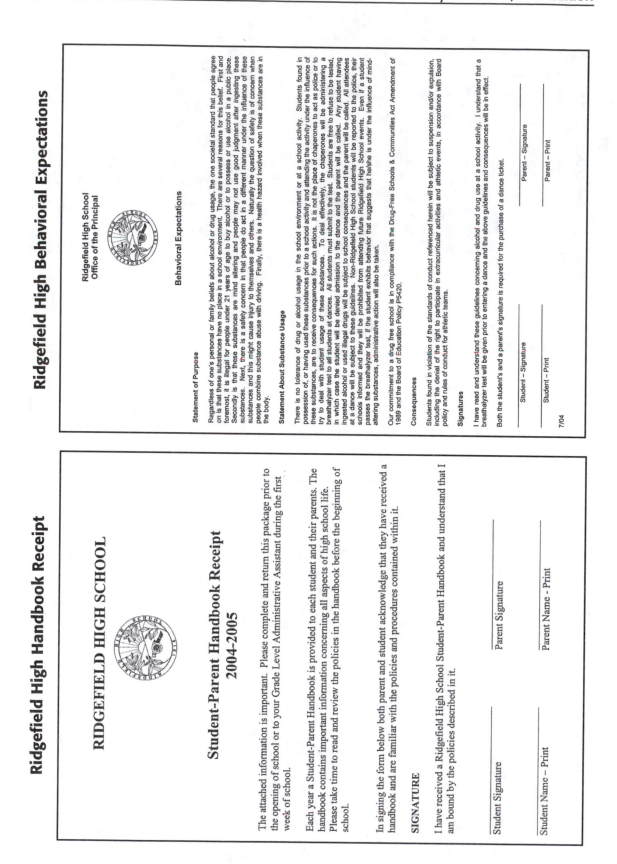

RIDGEFIELD HIGH SCHOOL

Student-Parent Handbook Receipt
2004-2005

The attached information is important. Please complete and return this package prior to the opening of school or to your Grade Level Administrative Assistant during the first week of school.

Each year a Student-Parent Handbook is provided to each student and their parents. The handbook contains important information concerning all aspects of high school life. Please take time to read and review the policies in the handbook before the beginning of school.

In signing the form below both parent and student acknowledge that they have received a handbook and are familiar with the policies and procedures contained within it.

SIGNATURE

I have received a Ridgefield High School Student-Parent Handbook and understand that I am bound by the policies described in it.

_____   _____
Student Signature   Parent Signature

_____   _____
Student Name – Print   Parent Name – Print

Ridgefield High Behavioral Expectations

Ridgefield High School
Office of the Principal

Behavioral Expectations

Statement of Purpose

Regardless of one's personal or family beliefs about alcohol or drug usage, the one societal standard that people agree on is that these substances have no place in a school environment. There are several reasons for this belief. First and foremost, it is illegal for people under 21 years of age to buy alcohol or to possess or use alcohol in a public place. Secondly is that these substances are mind altering and people may not use good judgment after ingesting these substances. Next, there is a safety concern in that people do act in a different manner under the influence of these substances and this might cause injury to themselves and others. Naturally the question of safety is of concern when people combine substance abuse with driving. Finally, there is a health hazard involved when these substances are in the body.

Statement About Substance Usage

There is no tolerance of drug or alcohol usage in the school environment or at a school activity. Students found in possession of, or having used these substances prior to a school activity and attending the activity under the influence of these substances, are to receive consequences for such actions. It is not the place of chaperones to act as police or to try to deal with student usage of these substances. To deal effectively, the chaperones will be administering a breathalyzer test to all students at dances. All students must submit to the test. Students are free to refuse to be tested, in which case the student will be denied admission to the dance and the parent will be called. Any student having ingested alcohol or used illegal drugs will be subject to school consequences and the parent will be called. All attendees at a dance will be subject to these guidelines. Non-Ridgefield High School students will be reported to the police, their schools informed and they will be prohibited from attending future Ridgefield High School events. Even if a student passes the breathalyzer test, if the student exhibits behavior that suggests that he/she is under the influence of mind-altering substances, administrative action will also be taken.

Our commitment to a drug free school is in compliance with the Drug-Free Schools & Communities Act Amendment of 1989 and the Board of Education Policy P5420.

Consequences

Students found in violation of the standards of conduct referenced herein will be subject to suspension and/or expulsion, including the denial of the right to participate in extracurricular activities and athletic events, in accordance with Board policy and rules of conduct for athletic teams.

Signatures

I have read and understand these guidelines concerning alcohol and drug use at a school activity. I understand that a breathalyzer test will be given prior to entering a dance and the above guidelines and consequences will be in effect.

Both the student's and a parent's signature is required for the purchase of a dance ticket.

_____   _____
Student – Signature   Parent – Signature

_____   _____
Student – Print   Parent – Print

7/04

Faculty agendas are an important communication link between the principal and the school's family members. In many cases, the items to be discussed at these important gatherings are solicited prior to the meetings. The order of the presentation of items is usually left to the discretion of the principal. Note the similarities of the agendas from Friendly Lakes Elementary School and Sumter Middle School—each indicated the date, location, and starting and ending times of the meetings (p. 112). Also note that food was provided. One of the major differences between the two agendas is that the person responsible for presenting the information is identified at one of the schools but not the other. However, both are very comprehensive and will lead to the successful sharing of information. One strategy many principals use is adding the last item, "For the good of the order," which is an effective way for faculty members to share thoughts or to ask for information that might otherwise not have been discussed.

The extensive research work done by Edgar Dale and Jane Chall at Ohio State University resulted in the Dale-Chall Formula. Their formula measured reading ease by taking into account the average sentence length and the number of words that do not appear on the "Dale List of 3,000 Words Most Commonly Used" (Cutlip et al., 2000). The "write-ability" of everyone can be further developed if the Write-Ability Enhancers listed on page 113 are used.

Good writing is good writing regardless of the subject. Six key points to keep in mind for all written communications sent from the principal and the school are the following:

- Use the plain word rather than the fancy word.
- Use the familiar word instead of the unfamiliar word.
- Never use a long word when a short one will do as well.
- Never use two (or more) words when one will do as well.
- Master the simple declarative sentence and use it—often.
- Cut out needless words, sentences, and paragraphs.

> **Writing is for reading. Better writing makes better reading, and better reading makes better writing.**
>
> *– Edgar Dale*

SMS Faculty Meeting Agenda

SMS FACULTY MEETING
August 6, 2004 9:00 am – 11:00
Cafeteria

I. Welcome Back! - Icebreaker – Who Did What This Summer ?

II. Introduce New Faculty Members and Staff

III. School Safety

  a. CIRT – Critical Incident Response Team (Handout)
  b. CIRT Board – Green Cards/Maps/etc. (Handouts)
  c. Evacuation Drills (Handout)
  d. Student Accident Reports (Handout)

IV. Student Forms (Emergency, Acceptable Use Policy, Insurance, Free/Reduced Lunch, Student Record Information, & Student Rules)

V. Lunch Numbers

  a. Teachers
  b. Students

VI. Performance-Based Pay (Handout)

VII. Duties

  a. General
  b. Supervision at Doors, 7:45 – 3:15, Bathrooms
  c. Work Hours – Appointments
  d. Supervision of Students
  e. All First Week/Last Week

VIII. Other

  a. Tardy Policy
  b. Dress Code
  c. Bus Numbers – Get Numbers from Every Student and Compile List
  d. West Bus Loop – Now in PM has Buses going to Western Part of County (Bushnell, Lake Panasoffkee, & Sumterville)

IX. Lunch Served (Cold Cuts, Fruit, Salad, and Dessert.)

Friendly Lakes Elementary School Agenda

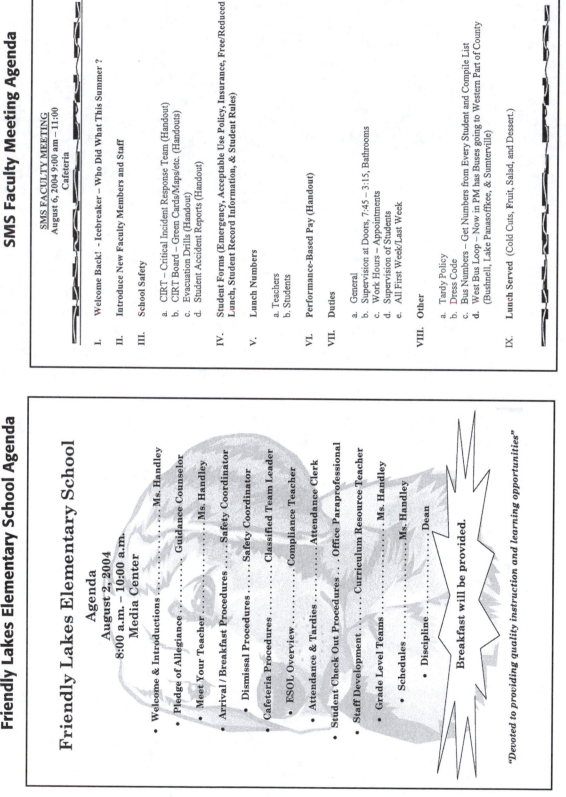

Friendly Lakes Elementary School

Agenda
August 2, 2004
8:00 a.m. – 10:00 a.m.
Media Center

- Welcome & Introductions . . . . Ms. Handley
- Pledge of Allegiance . . . . Guidance Counselor
- Meet Your Teacher . . . . Ms. Handley
- Arrival / Breakfast Procedures . . . . . Safety Coordinator
- Dismissal Procedures . . . . . . Safety Coordinator
- Cafeteria Procedures . . . . Classified Team Leader
- ESOL Overview . . . . Compliance Teacher
- Attendance & Tardies . . . . Attendance Clerk
- Student Check Out Procedures . . . . Office Paraprofessional
- Staff Development . . . . . . Curriculum Resource Teacher
- Grade Level Teams . . . . Ms. Handley
- Schedules . . . . Ms. Handley
- Discipline . . . . Dean

Breakfast will be provided.

"Devoted to providing quality instruction and learning opportunities"

Write-Ability Enhancers

- Define your audience and purpose. Ask these two questions while you write:
  - What do they want to know?
  - What do they need to know?
- Catch the reader's attention quickly. Use a short introduction to make quite clear what is coming and the questions to be answered.
- Make key points visible. A reader should be able to skim a story or article, see quickly what it says, and decide whether to read it.
- Use subheads, italics, boldface, or numbering to make it easier for the reader to see the main points.
- Spread out the printed material to make it less dense. Smaller, shorter paragraphs create reading ease for the reader.
- Aerate the material, let it breathe; let the white paper show up more.
- Use relevant examples to simplify and clarify an article.
- Simplify the vocabulary.
- Watch the structure of sentences. It is the complexity of sentences and not their length that is the cause of their reading difficulty.
- Use visual materials such as drawings, bold print, and charts to sharpen the message. Do not, however, use visual materials just for the sake of using them.
- Repeat and summarize thoughtfully. As the end of the article is approached, focus on answering the reader's question: So what?
- In other words, confine your messages to what the readers want and need to know. By putting yourself in the reader's shoes, you will be more apt to share important information in such a fashion that more people will receive important benefits.

Robert Gunning's research resulted in a readability formula that measured reading difficulty by the average sentence length, number of simple sentences used, verb force, proportion of familiar words, proportion of abstract words, percentage of personal references, and percentage of long words. What results is known as the "Fog Index" (Cutlip et al., 2000). The Fog Index reduces everything to a number that approximates the grade level at which a person must read to comprehend the material. For example, writing with a Fog Index of 10 is aimed at those who read at or above the 10th-grade level.

Gunning's formula can also be applied to the reading complexity of various popular magazines. Some examples are: *Harper's* is 12, *Time* and *Newsweek* are 11; *Reader's Digest* is 10; Ladies Home Journal is 8; and comic books are 6.

In applying the Fog Index to any writing, it might be wise to take note of the following:

- The average American reads at the ninth-grade level. However, many people read below that level.
- Most readers feel more comfortable reading at one or two levels below their maximum.

Eschew Obfuscation!

What? You don't know what that means? In some cases, parents have had the same reactions to messages they have received from their child's school principal or teachers. The use of jargon, gobbledygook, educationese, or edubabble has caused educators to be called consistent…they don't want others to understand them. The consistency, unfortunately, can be traced to the communication gap—using diamond-studded words when gold-filled ones will do. So, be aware of the use of words noneducators don't use and understand and work to eliminate them. Remember the KIS (keep it simple) guidelines mentioned earlier as you work to keep your written communication understandable, acceptable, and read.

> **Those who write clearly have readers, those who write obscurely have commentators.**
>
> *– Albert Camus*

Marquee or Sign Board

One specific area where effective written communications are important can be seen in the messages that are displayed on a school's marquee or sign board. Review the messages presented in Chapter 4, on page 93, to see how important information was conveyed. The basic details of events or activities are presented and spelled correctly. Although misspelled words can be used by business establishments in their advertisements or on their signs, either intentionally or unintentionally, there is absolutely no room for incorrect spelling on a school's marquee or sign board.

Newsletters

As has been stated many times throughout this book, regular, informative communication from the principal's office helps build local support for a school. And one of the best and most cost-effective forms of one-way communication is the school newsletter from the principal or the parent–teacher–student association.

When done properly, a school newsletter is a valuable public relations tool that generates not only interest but good will. Parents, community members, business partners, members of the media who report on school events, and others can supply information to include in the newsletter about school programs and events, to highlight individual student and teacher achievements, and also to provide generally useful information to everyone in the community.

In contrast to most printed material, a school newsletter is read when it reaches home. Studies have shown that parents rate the school newsletter as their second most important source of information about the schools. The most important source is what their children say about the school. The school newsletter is an important instrument to

- build support for the school program;
- keep accurate information before the people who "own the schools";
- increase community involvement, participation, and attendance at school functions;
- make citizens aware of the importance of public education in relation to the quality of life in the community;
- contribute to the improvement of the school's educational program; and
- assist parents in helping their children learn.

In addition, a school newsletter reflects some important details about the principal:

- It may be the only regular contact a principal has with most of the parents. Therefore, the newsletter is a prime way to convey what kind of person the principal is and what kind of school he/she has developed.
- It is a strategy that implies that contact with the parents is valued and that the principal is willing to extend herself/himself to gain the parents' interest.
- It contains news, which implies the principal believes the readers are entitled to know what is happening. Also, it reflects the fact that the principal enjoys sharing school news and information with them.

So, then, a carefully planned, well-thought-out newsletter may have several objectives while serving as a major communication link with people outside of the school.

Newsletter Objectives

- *Informing*—What important things have taken place or will take place that the readers should know about? Are there any changes in curriculum, staff organization, programs, policies, procedures, or services for students or staff? Remember that the purpose of a newsletter is to inform, never to preach or push a particular cause. Parents do appreciate knowing the rules and information concerning new decisions and the programs of the school.

- *Educating*—Is there information that would help the readers in their role in the educational process? Keep language simple. Remember that some parents may be poorly educated. Avoid academic language and education jargon.

- *Promoting*—Newsletters can be an excellent way to promote activities such as workshops and seminars or special events, to gain support for education, or to develop good human relations. If photographs are used, make certain they are clear and meaningful to the readers. Label and identify all photos. Black and white prints reproduce best.

Remember to keep the objectives of the newsletter *realistic* and *achievable*.

What to Include in a Newsletter

Once the audience and the objectives of the newsletter have been determined, the next task is to determine what the content of the newsletter will be. Principals who have developed effective newsletters have established a regular formula for sharing details in their newsletter. For instance, most of them include a few significant comments from themselves. Also, student and faculty accomplishments are featured, along with important details about upcoming events. A calendar of events, encouraging parental support in solving problems at the school such as traffic problems related to dropping off and picking up students (parents are relieved to know the school is aware of the situation and is working on it) and other seasonal happenings should also be included. These can become regular features of the newsletter and should appear in the same general location of the newsletter each month. In addition, other topics to include in the newsletter are the following:

- School activities, especially classroom activities
- Opportunities for parents and others to help at school, such as volunteering, serving on the principal's advisory committee, room parents, or other jobs
- Personality sketch of the teachers, secretary, support staff members, food service employees, custodians, counselor, school crossing guards, bus drivers, and school administrators
- How staff development programs on early release days better prepare teachers—what specific activities they participate in on those days
- Awards, special recognition, unusual leadership of students, perhaps even a "student of the month" for outstanding citizenship
- Awards, recognition, advanced degrees earned by teachers and other school employees
- What is being done to challenge outstanding students
- How the instructional program is meeting the individual needs of all students
- Brief summaries of important parent group business
- Reminder news items, such as school hours, morning arrival time of students, follow-up communications when a student has been tardy or absent, and changes in the cost of breakfast or lunch
- Thoughts for the day
- Poems or other inspirational messages (Mother's Day, Father's Day)

Notice the format and information that are presented in the newsletters from schools at different levels. Junella Handley developed the "Friendly Lakes News" (p. 118) for Friendly Lakes Elementary School as an end-of-the-year newsletter. This was an assignment for a course on school–community relations. The newsletter is one item she developed for a resource file of items that all principals will need to use as they work to become effective communicators. Although Friendly Lakes is an imaginary school, Ms. Handley incorporated information from her real school into the newsletter. Note her personal message, information about contacting the school, and related information from all areas of the school's learning program.

Friendly Lakes News Newsletter

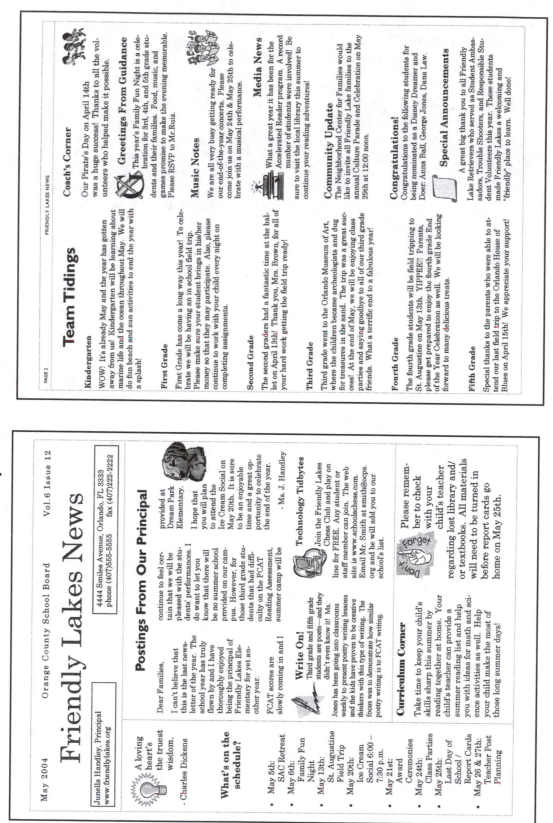

May 2004   Orange County School Board   Vol. 6 Issue 12

Friendly Lakes News

Junella Handley, Principal
www.friendlylakes.org

4444 Smiles Avenue, Orlando, FL 3333
phone (407)555-5555   fax (407)222-2222

A loving heart's the truest wisdom.

- Charles Dickens

What's on the schedule?

- May 5th: SAC Retreat
- May 6th: Family Fun Night
- May 13th: St. Augustine Field Trip
- May 20th: Ice Cream Social 6:00 – 7:30 p.m.
- May 21st: Award Ceremonies
- May 24th: Class Parties
- May 25th: Last Day of School / Report Cards
- May 26 & 27th: Teacher Post Planning

Postings From Our Principal

Dear Families,

I can't believe that this is the last newsletter of the year. The school year has truly flown by and I have thoroughly enjoyed being the principal of Friendly Lakes Elementary for yet another year.

FCAT scores are slowly coming in and I continue to feel certain that we will be pleased with the students' performances. I do want to let you know that there will be no summer school provided on our campus. However, for those third grade students that had difficulty on the FCAT Reading Assessment, summer camp will be provided at Dream Park Elementary.

I hope that you will plan to attend the Ice Cream Social on May 20th. It is sure to be an enjoyable time and a great opportunity to celebrate the end of the year.

- Ms. J. Handley

Write On!

Third grade and fifth grade students are poets—and they didn't even know it! Ms. Jones has been going into classrooms weekly to present poetry writing lessons and the kids have proven to be creative thinkers with this type of writing. The focus was to demonstrate how similar poetry writing is to FCAT writing.

Technology Tidbytes

Join the Friendly Lakes Chess Club and play on line for FREE. Any student or staff member can join. The web site is www.schoolschess.com. Email Mr. Smith at smith@ocps.org and he will add you to our school's list.

Curriculum Corner

Take time to keep your child's skills sharp this summer by reading together at home. Your child's teacher can provide a summer reading list and help you with ideas for math and science activities as well. Help your child make the most of those long summer days!

Don't forget Please remember to check with your child's teacher regarding lost library and/or textbooks. All materials will need to be turned in before report cards go home on May 25th.

PAGE 2   FRIENDLY LAKES NEWS

Team Tidings

Kindergarten

WOW! It's already May and the year has gotten away from us! Kindergarten will be learning about marine life and the ocean throughout May. We will do fun beach and sun activities to end the year with a splash!

First Grade

First Grade has come a long way this year! To celebrate we will be having an in school field trip. Please make sure your student brings in his/her money so that they may participate. Also, please continue to work with your child every night on completing assignments.

Second Grade

The second graders had a fantastic time at the ballet on April 13th! Thank you, Mrs. Brown, for all of your hard work getting the field trip ready!

Third Grade

Third grade went to the Orlando Museum of Art, where the children became archeologists and dug for treasures in the sand. The trip was a great success! At the end of May, we will be enjoying class parties and saying goodbye to all of our third grade friends. What a terrific end to a fabulous year!

Fourth Grade

The fourth grade students will be field tripping to St. Augustine on May 13th. YIPPEE!! Parents, please get prepared to enjoy the fourth grade End of the Year Celebration as well. We will be looking forward to many delicious treats.

Fifth Grade

Special thanks to the parents who were able to attend our last field trip to the Orlando House of Blues on April 15th! We appreciate your support!

Coach's Corner

Our Pirate's Day on April 14th was a huge success! Thanks to all the volunteers who helped make it possible.

Greetings From Guidance

This year's Family Fun Night is a celebration for 3rd, 4th, and 5th grade students and their families. Food, music, and games promise to make the evening memorable. Please RSVP to Mr. Ruiz.

Music Notes

We are all very busy getting ready for our end-of-the-year concerts. Please come join us on May 24th & May 25th to celebrate with a musical performance.

Media News

What a great year it has been for the Accelerated Reader program. A record number of students were involved! Be sure to visit the local library this summer to continue your reading adventures!

Community Update

The Neighborhood Center for Families would like to invite all Friendly Lake families to the annual Culture Parade and Celebration on May 29th at 12:00 noon.

Congratulations!

Congratulations to the following students for being nominated as a Disney Dreamer and Doer: Anna Ball, George Jones, Dana Law.

Special Announcements

A great big thank you to all Friendly Lake Retrievers who served as Student Ambassadors, Trouble Shooters, and Responsible Student Volunteers this year. These students made Friendly Lakes a welcoming and "friendly" place to learn. Well done!

Christopher Davis, also a graduate student in the school–community relations course, developed the "Woodland Compass" (p. 120) for his school, Woodland Lakes Middle School. Mr. Davis chose, as his newsletter for the course assignment, the first one he would distribute to parents and students. Again, notice the care he used to include details about contacting the school, important dates for the first month of the school year, a calendar reflecting the events, a summary of service club news from the past year and a look to the future, along with his messages to parents and students. Gina Pirozzi, another graduate student, developed her newsletter (p. 121) as if she was the principal of the school where she was assigned as a teacher. Note the care and concern she showed in her newsletter to include her message and the updates on activities related to math, language arts, reading, and other subjects at the three grade levels of the school.

Many high school principals use other strategies in the newsletters they mail home to parents. Most of these newsletters are 6–12 double-sided pages. To help defray the costs of developing and mailing the newsletters, most contain advertisements. Note the details in the comments from the principals at three Central Florida high schools. David Bordenkircher, principal at South Lake High School in Lake County, Florida, includes his words of optimism and encouragement as the students, teachers, and parents prepare for the upcoming state achievement tests (p. 122). Dr. Mark Rendell, principal at Titusville High School in Brevard County, Florida, and Eugene P. Torchinski, principal at Dr. Phillips High School in Orange County, Florida, have each summarized their thoughts about the school year as it came to a close; they also sounded words of optimism for the new school term (pp. 123–124). The final newsletter of the school year, from Ridgefield High School in Connecticut (p. 125), contains principal Dr. Dianna M. Lindsay's end-of-the-year thoughts on page two. She reserved the importance of front-page news for recognition of the school's teacher of the year and top students for the third marking period, as well as a major emphasis on the three students who were awarded National Merit Scholarships.

(Text continues on page 126.)

Woodland Compass Newsletter

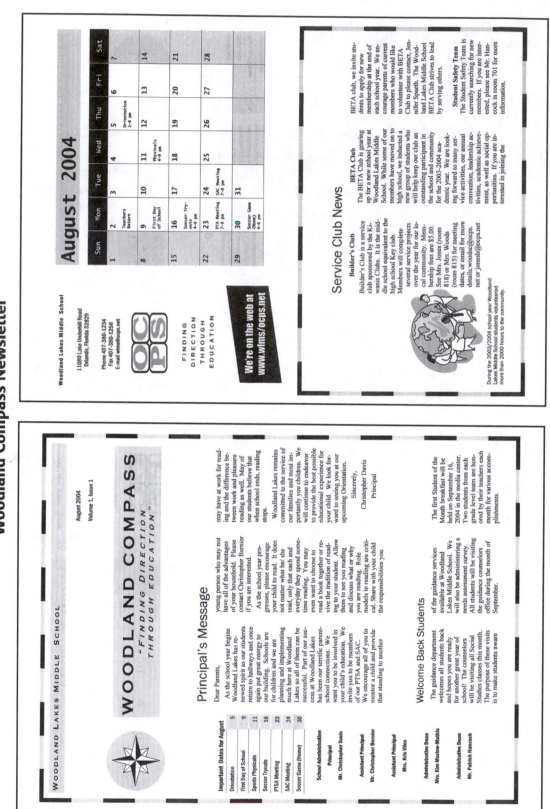

Dolphin Daily Newsletter

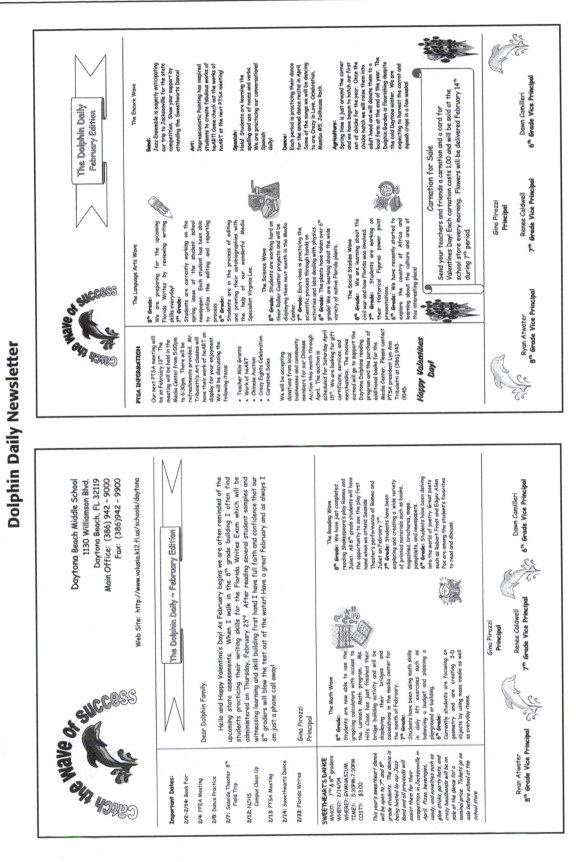

Flight Patterns Newsletter

For The Parents, Students, Staff, & Community Of South Lake High School

March 2004
Volume 5, Issue 3

Flight Patterns

SOUTH LAKE HIGH SCHOOL

South Lake High School
15600 Silver Eagle Road
Groveland, FL 34736

Non - Profit Organization
U.S. Postage Paid
Permit # 2346
Orlando, FL

Who's Who at South Lake

Principal .... David Bordenkircher

Assistant Principals .... Mike Haack
....Herman Durias

Assistant Principals II .... Billy Skelton
.... Cathy Slack

Director of Student
Services/CS .... Dr. Doris Green

Guidance Counselors .... Gail Adams
.... Robyn Campos
.... Dr. Doris Green
.... Barney Ritchen
.... PaulWheeler

School Resource Officers .... Richard Light

Telephone 352/394-2100

Fax 352/394-1972

Letter From The Principal

Dear Eagle Community,

It is game time! All year I have been updating you on the progress toward accomplishing our Action Plan for Academic Improvement. The plan grew out of extensive research and planning this past summer, and called for the implementation of many strategies that were categorized under five headings (curriculum, extra-curricular, organization & structure, attendance, and technology). I am proud to say that the staff and students of South Lake High School have worked very hard on these strategies and that each and every step has been successfully implemented.

At the writing of this letter, we have already completed the administration of the FCAT Florida Writes! We tested over 98% of our tenth graders, which is approximately 5% more than last year. The test was given in homerooms of about 18 students each, rather than in the auditorium with 400 students. By all accounts it was a very successful effort. We are currently preparing to administer the reading, math, science and NRT portions of the FCAT on March 2-11.

When you read this letter most, if not all, of that will be accomplished as well. We are currently building the momentum of preparation and *"peparation"* in order to have each student fully focused, both academically and attitudinally, for optimum performance on the test. Through the efforts of the staff, and the talents and abilities of our students, I believe that South Lake High School and the community that it serves will be well represented with pride and dignity and prove once again that South Lake High School is a great place to be. On behalf of the students and staff of South Lake High School I feel confident in saying that, more than ever before, we are ready...bring it on!

Dave Bordenkircher
Principal
South Lake High School

Please visit South Lake High School's website:
http://www.lake.k12.fl.us/school-slh/

Terrier Tales Newsletter

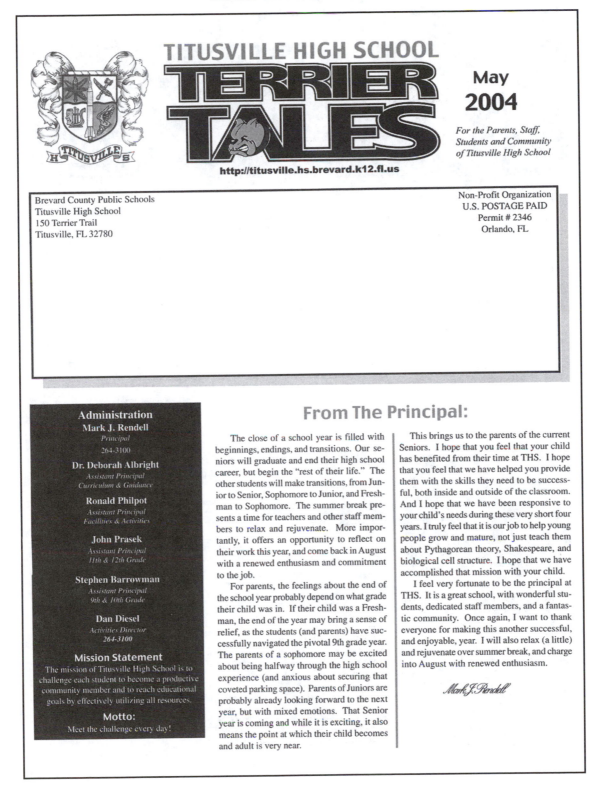

TITUSVILLE HIGH SCHOOL
TERRIER TALES

May 2004

For the Parents, Staff, Students and Community of Titusville High School

http://titusville.hs.brevard.k12.fl.us

Brevard County Public Schools
Titusville High School
150 Terrier Trail
Titusville, FL 32780

Non-Profit Organization
U.S. POSTAGE PAID
Permit # 2346
Orlando, FL

Administration

Mark J. Rendell
Principal
264-3100

Dr. Deborah Albright
Assistant Principal
Curriculum & Guidance

Ronald Philpot
Assistant Principal
Facilities & Activities

John Prasek
Assistant Principal
11th & 12th Grade

Stephen Barrowman
Assistant Principal
9th & 10th Grade

Dan Diesel
Activities Director
264-3100

Mission Statement

The mission of Titusville High School is to challenge each student to become a productive community member and to reach educational goals by effectively utilizing all resources.

Motto:
Meet the challenge every day!

From The Principal:

The close of a school year is filled with beginnings, endings, and transitions. Our seniors will graduate and end their high school career, but begin the "rest of their life." The other students will make transitions, from Junior to Senior, Sophomore to Junior, and Freshman to Sophomore. The summer break presents a time for teachers and other staff members to relax and rejuvenate. More importantly, it offers an opportunity to reflect on their work this year, and come back in August with a renewed enthusiasm and commitment to the job.

For parents, the feelings about the end of the school year probably depend on what grade their child was in. If their child was a Freshman, the end of the year may bring a sense of relief, as the students (and parents) have successfully navigated the pivotal 9th grade year. The parents of a sophomore may be excited about being halfway through the high school experience (and anxious about securing that coveted parking space). Parents of Juniors are probably already looking forward to the next year, but with mixed emotions. That Senior year is coming and while it is exciting, it also means the point at which their child becomes and adult is very near.

This brings us to the parents of the current Seniors. I hope that you feel that your child has benefited from their time at THS. I hope that you feel that we have helped you provide them with the skills they need to be successful, both inside and outside of the classroom. And I hope that we have been responsive to your child's needs during these very short four years. I truly feel that it is our job to help young people grow and mature, not just teach them about Pythagorean theory, Shakespeare, and biological cell structure. I hope that we have accomplished that mission with your child.

I feel very fortunate to be the principal at THS. It is a great school, with wonderful students, dedicated staff members, and a fantastic community. Once again, I want to thank everyone for making this another successful, and enjoyable, year. I will also relax (a little) and rejuvenate over summer break, and charge into August with renewed enthusiasm.

Mark J. Rendell

Dr. Phillips High School Newsletter

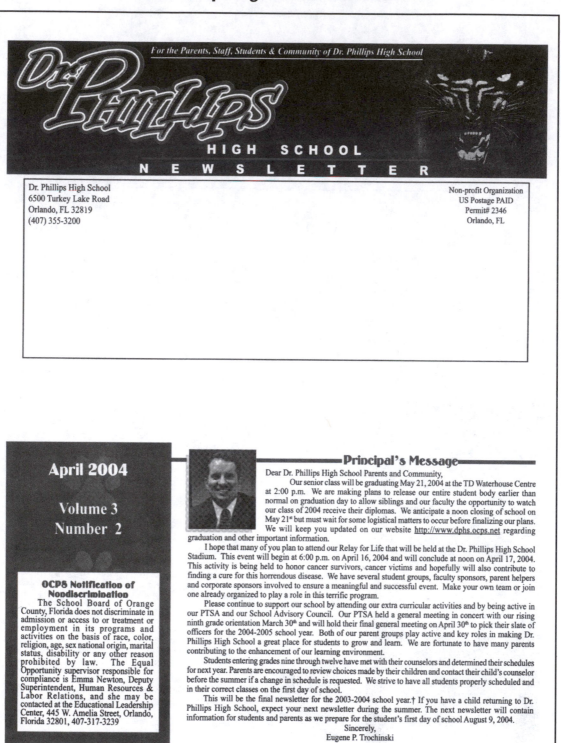

For the Parents, Staff, Students & Community of Dr. Phillips High School

Dr. Phillips
HIGH SCHOOL
N E W S L E T T E R

Dr. Phillips High School
6500 Turkey Lake Road
Orlando, FL 32819
(407) 355-3200

Non-profit Organization
US Postage PAID
Permit# 2346
Orlando, FL

April 2004

Volume 3
Number 2

OCPS Notification of Nondiscrimination

The School Board of Orange County, Florida does not discriminate in admission or access to or treatment or employment in its programs and activities on the basis of race, color, religion, age, sex national origin, marital status, disability or any other reason prohibited by law. The Equal Opportunity supervisor responsible for compliance is Emma Newton, Deputy Superintendent, Human Resources & Labor Relations, and she may be contacted at the Educational Leadership Center, 445 W. Amelia Street, Orlando, Florida 32801, 407-317-3239

Principal's Message

Dear Dr. Phillips High School Parents and Community,

Our senior class will be graduating May 21, 2004 at the TD Waterhouse Centre at 2:00 p.m. We are making plans to release our entire student body earlier than normal on graduation day to allow siblings and our faculty the opportunity to watch our class of 2004 receive their diplomas. We anticipate a noon closing of school on May 21st but must wait for some logistical matters to occur before finalizing our plans. We will keep you updated on our website http://www.dphs.ocps.net regarding graduation and other important information.

I hope that many of you plan to attend our Relay for Life that will be held at the Dr. Phillips High School Stadium. This event will begin at 6:00 p.m. on April 16, 2004 and will conclude at noon on April 17, 2004. This activity is being held to honor cancer survivors, cancer victims and hopefully will also contribute to finding a cure for this horrendous disease. We have several student groups, faculty sponsors, parent helpers and corporate sponsors involved to ensure a meaningful and successful event. Make your own team or join one already organized to play a role in this terrific program.

Please continue to support our school by attending our extra curricular activities and by being active in our PTSA and our School Advisory Council. Our PTSA held a general meeting in concert with our rising ninth grade orientation March 30th and will hold their final general meeting on April 30th to pick their slate of officers for the 2004-2005 school year. Both of our parent groups play active and key roles in making Dr. Phillips High School a great place for students to grow and learn. We are fortunate to have many parents contributing to the enhancement of our learning environment.

Students entering grades nine through twelve have met with their counselors and determined their schedules for next year. Parents are encouraged to review choices made by their children and contact their child's counselor before the summer if a change in schedule is requested. We strive to have all students properly scheduled and in their correct classes on the first day of school.

This will be the final newsletter for the 2003-2004 school year.† If you have a child returning to Dr. Phillips High School, expect your next newsletter during the summer. The next newsletter will contain information for students and parents as we prepare for the student's first day of school August 9, 2004.

Sincerely,
Eugene P. Trochinski

Ridgefield High School Newsletter

Gathering Newsletter Story Ideas

Finding enough material to fill the newsletter on a regular basis can be a relatively easy task. Stories can be found all around if you look and listen. Some principals gather newsworthy items as they practice managing by walking around (MBWA). Items of interest to many people can be remembered by jotting them down on 3 × 5 index cards. Including the important facts to answer the five Ws (Who? What? Where? Why? When?) makes it easy to transfer the details later into an article for the newsletter. The dated 3 × 5 cards can be kept in a manila pocket folder until they are needed for the writing of the newsletter.

Handheld tape recorders are useful devices to record items to be used in newsletters. Some principals record details (the five Ws) when they see a news item. The school secretary can listen to the verbal message and details and convert them to items for a future issue of the school newsletter. Some principals record information in their PDAs for future use.

Other principals who publish effective newsletters supplement their sources of information for stories by involving members of the school's faculty and staff. These people often see and hear newsworthy items that the principal sometimes misses. Once they see their "news tip" appear in the newsletter, they are often encouraged to seek out future stories on a regular basis. It is best to credit their news contribution not in the newsletter but rather with a personal note or happy gram.

Publication Information

Another major consideration of newsletters is when and how often to publish the newsletter. The first rule of thumb is to publish it on a regular basis. How frequently the newsletter is published will depend on the following:

- ♦ How frequently you need to get news out
- ♦ How lengthy you plan to make it
- ♦ How much money you have to cover printing and distribution costs

Let's look at each of these items in more detail.

Newsletter Distribution

Most effective school newsletters are distributed on a monthly basis. The exact day of the month can be determined by the individual school's schedule. By distributing a newsletter at the start of the school year, parents will be informed of important details as another school year begins. This simple suggestion is compounded by the adoption of year-round school calendars in many school districts, because for the most part there is no one set starting date of a school year for all students, parents, and faculty. But that should not be seen as a reason not to publish a newsletter; rather, it is an opportunity to develop a creative way to communicate with the school's community.

In any case, once the distribution schedule is determined, it should be communicated in the newsletter so parents and other readers will know when to expect the newsletter to arrive in their homes. Remember how Dr. Phillips High School principal Eugene P. Trochinski alerted the parents that they would be receiving the next newsletter during the summer if their child was returning to the school? He even told them the newsletter would "contain information for students and parents as we prepare for the student's first day of school on August 9, 2004." For instance, having the delivery date set as the first Tuesday of every month is better than saying the first day of each month, because November 1 could occur on the weekend. Thus, having a set day of the week is better than a date, which fluctuates. At the elementary school level Tuesdays and Wednesdays are better than other days of the week because the newsletters probably won't get mixed in with other papers. Brief newsletters are better than long ones. The more frequently the newsletter is published, the fresher the news is. The *news package* is smaller, and the newsletter has a better chance of being read. A general rule is to publish at least monthly.

In the elementary schools, the method of getting the newsletters home will be through the efforts of the children. Some principals give every student a copy of the newsletter to take home. Parents who have several children in the school are encouraged to share extra newsletters with neighbors who don't have children in the schools. This seems to be an effective way to get the school's news shared with community members because, according to Harold Hodgkinson, about one home in four in America has a child attending public schools (Elam, 1993). Other elementary school principals find that younger students are more reliable couriers of the newsletters and are therefore assigned the responsibility. Middle and high school principals find it worth the money to mail the newsletters home rather than sending them home with students and the ads that are included in these newsletters help to defray the mailing costs. Newsletters qualify for bulk mailing rates. The local post office will have specific details and rates.

Check periodically on the efficiency of the distribution system. Consider making telephone calls to parents to see if they received the last newsletter and if they have any comments or questions. Another approach the author used successfully was to have a clip-and-return slip with every newsletter. Every elementary student received a newsletter to take home to the parents (extras were to be shared with neighbors who did not have children in school). Parents were to complete the requested information and clip the form for the student to return to the respective homeroom teacher. A time limit was imposed, with the homeroom(s) (check-in teacher) that had the highest percentage of returns receiving a special treat (e.g., a large cookie with their lunches). This approach was effective because it caused the students to work together to receive a reward as a group and for individual students to be rewarded. Here is an example of a clip-and-return slip used at an elementary school.

Clip/Return Slip

Clip/return to your child's check-in teacher by THURSDAY, SEPTEMBER 15, 2 ___.

STUDENT'S NAME _____

CHECK-IN TEACHER _____

PARENT'S SIGNATURE _____

HAVE YOU RETURNED YOUR
WRAPPING PAPER ORDER?

Don't Forget!!

Another approach used successfully by some principals was to have all the returned slips placed in a large container with some of them drawn as monthly winners. Identified students receive individual prizes or awards. This approach has the potential of rewarding a limited number of students, and perhaps some students would be luckier than others by being recipients of the rewards more than others, whereas a cooperative, collaborative effort is not stressed.

Newsletters on the School's Web Site

Many school principals also are making their school's newsletter available on the school's Web site. The newsletter is posted the same day that paper copies are sent home with the students or are mailed. Removing the previous edition from the Web site, but adding a link to it on the site, to make room for the latest edition becomes a task for someone to remember to do. The advantages outweigh the disadvantages to this strategy but still require paper copies to be sent to each family because of the unreliable nature of parents remembering to access the electronic version. Remember, in Chapter 4, how North Carroll High School principal Dr. Gary Donkleberger effectively updates and uses his lists of parents' e-mail addresses to communicate with them? His ongoing request for updates on new e-mail addresses allows him to constantly stay in touch with parents through his listserv strategy. His repeated requests for e-mail information in every newsletter allows him to remind parents to send in theirs or to update them when necessary.

The success stories of schools that have developed Web sites were presented in an article on educationworld.com. Specifically, the article "Share the Pride: Create a School Web Site" contains a wealth of information about developing a Web site and features several examples of school Web sites. Additional links to those sites and online resources are included.

The Length of the Newsletter

One consideration of the length of the newsletter is to determine what size paper to use and how many pages to include in each issue. Most newsletters are prepared on standard 8.5" × 11" paper with printing on both sides of the page. At the elementary school level, the number of sheets of paper for each issue can vary from two to five or six sheets. Important decisions to make when deciding the length of the newsletter relate to the information shared in other chapters of this book. Some school principals use two sheets of 11" × 17" paper folded to the 8.5" × 11" size for their newsletters. (When I was an elementary school principal, I used two sheets of 8.5" × 14" canary-colored paper printed on both sides for monthly newsletters.) Another special consideration, if the newsletters are to be mailed: Make certain the final size meets all postal regulations. The trick to successful acceptance of the newsletter is to present the items in an attractive format, with the focus on the people and activities of the school.

Financial Resources to Support Newsletters

How much money there is to spend on this important part of a school's total communications program will have an impact on the frequency of distribution and length of the newsletters. The financial considerations that impact the final cost include the total number of copies to be printed; the number of sheets per issue; the size of paper used; the color of the paper; printing costs (sometimes a school or business partner or advertisements will cover these expenses); folding, assembling, and stapling costs (volunteers can be used to reduce these costs); and mailing costs.

To Be Successful, a Newsletter Must Be...

♦ Meaningful
♦ Attractive

A newsletter should stand out from all other material competing for the reader's attention.

Decisions, Decisions, Decisions

Some important considerations to develop reader appeal are shown next.

Newsletters That Have Reader Appeal

- Make certain the masthead is clear, easily recognizable, and consistent.
- Use generous margins.
- Make the type clean and readable.
- Coordinate the headline typeface or style with the type used in the newsletter—12-point font—courier or times roman.
- The best color of paper is white; other light colors may be acceptable. (The author used canary-colored paper and was told many times by readers that they found it a comfortable color and easier to locate if the newsletter became mixed up in a stack of papers.)
- The best color of ink is black; other dark colors may be acceptable but will be more expensive.
- Always try to keep stories on the same page from start to finish.
- Use graphic elements frequently, but—
  - Don't use too many graphics on a single page, because it confuses the reader.
  - Leave enough space between items.

The first item that catches a reader's eye should be the masthead or nameplate. If it is unique and presented in an uncluttered way, it will be more easily recognized and identified as a source for school news. Note the nameplates on the following newsletters:

Each of the nameplates or mastheads on these newsletters meets the four main topics listed earlier—each is legible, distinctive, appropriate, and attractive. Special notice should be made of the fact that each newsletter, except the Port Malabar School newsletter, also has important details about the school:

- The name of the school principal—Clark School's principal's name is missing.
- The school's mailing address, telephone and fax numbers, e-mail address, and Web site URL are found on some but not all.

Twain Tales

Mark Twain Elementary

Twain Tales
April, 2004

Mark Twain Elementary School
Lori Kinney, Principal
6901 S. Franklin St.
Centennial, CO 80122
303-347-4700

Absence Reporting Line- 303-734-5825
http://twain.littletonpublicschools.net
For LPS job information please visit our
district website:
www.littletonpublicschools.net

Sandy Sullivan, Secretary- 303-347-4711
Jill Brogdon, Secretary- 303-347-4710
Kim LeCavalier, PTO Pres.-303-347-5850
Michael Donegan, TAC Chair -303-734-0203
District Security-303-347-3420
LPS Bond Info-303-347-3490
Board of Education Information Line- 303-347-3515
FAX-303-347-4720
Lunch Line- 303-347-4706
Charlotte Krieg (Twain Tigers)- 303-347-4900

Vision Statement
Littleton Public Schools. Exceptional community,
extraordinary learning, expanded opportunity, and
success for all students.

Mission Statement
To educate students for the future by challenging every
individual to continuously learn, achieve, and act with
purpose and compassion.

School Hours

Office	8:00 am-4:30 pm
Kindergarten am	9:05 am-11:55 am
Kindergarten pm	12:55 pm-3:40 pm
KED	12:45 pm-3:40 pm
Grades 1-5	9:10 am-3:40 pm
SACC	6:30 am-9:00 am &
	3:40 pm—6:00 pm

Twain's Peak Performance Character
Traits are:
Mission
Team work
Character
Confidence
Knowledge
Self-Discipline
Growing
Creativity

Dear Twain Community,

Change is constant—this we know for sure. One change about to take place at the end of this school year involves the transition of students from one grade level to another. Emotions run high, with parents and students wondering what the next year will be like. All of our staff members are highly-qualified, capable, professional educators, who work hard to help students learn. They act with purpose and compassion. Students can learn from each and every one of them.

Littleton Public Schools and Mark Twain Elementary honor choice in many ways. One way that Twain honors choice is in welcoming parental input about teacher preference for their student(s). Twain continues to honor that input. Parents may complete a "Student Transition Information" sheet (available in the main office), which provides an opportunity to describe your student's strengths and challenges. If you so desire, you may prioritize your selection of next year's teachers for your student(s) on that sheet. All information comes to me and assists me in the scheduling of students into the class that has the "best fit." Please note that many parents never participate in selecting teachers throughout their student(s) K-12 school years. It is not a necessary part of the education process. Again, Twain honors parental input, and in so doing, continues to offer this selection opportunity.

Sincerely,
Lori Kinney
Principal

Clark's Wednesday Express

Clark's Wednesday Express

Growing Through Excellence

Clark Elementary School
5764 E 700 N
Franklin, IN 46131
School: 535-8503
Fax: 535-5521

Transportation: 535-7255
Voice Mail/Homework Hotline: 535-5025
Safe School Helpline: (800)418-6423 ext. 359
Web Site: http://cpcsc.k12.in.us/ces
PTO Voice Mail Ext. 4040
Weather Hotline: 535-2025 ext. 8000

Newsletter Date
March 10, 2004

Volume 1, Issue 23

Upcoming Events
- Fri. March 12—
Spaghetti Dinner 5:00-
8:00 P.M.
- Tues. March 16 - PTO
Skating Party-6:00 -
8:30 P.M.
- Wed. March 17—
Report cards go home.

PTO NEWS

Reminder that the Spaghetti Dinner is this Friday, March 12th, from 5:00-8:00 P.M. You can still purchase advance tickets tomorrow (Thursday) during lunch. The cost is $5.00 for adults and $2.50 per child (12 and younger). Tickets will be sold at the door Friday for $5.50 per adult and $3.00 per child (12 and younger).

Also, please bring in donations for desserts on Friday, March 12th, to the school Office. Thank you!

5TH GRADE TALENT SHOW INFO

The 5th Grade Talent Show will be during the Spaghetti Dinner on Friday, March 12th at 7:00 P.M. The kids have been working so hard at perfecting their talents! **ALL** students in the Talent Show should be at school **no later** than 6:30 that evening in order to be in costume and in the correct seating order by the time the show starts. Please come to the gym when you arrive and check in with Mrs. Forey. We look forward to seeing you there!

UPCOMING NEWS & INFORMATION

Individual Spring photographs will be taken on March 26th. Every child will be photographed and proofs will be sent home for you to order pictures from. You are under no obligation to purchase any pictures.

Parents of Pre-schoolers! Kindergarten Roundup is coming soon. April 20th from 1:00-6:00 P.M. is the date for this exciting occasion. Please share this news with friends or neighbors who might not receive the Wednesday Express. **There will be no kindergarten that day. PLEASE NOTE IN THE PREVIOUS WEDNESDAY EXPRESS THE TIME WAS PUT IN WRONG (1-7:00 P.M.) IT SHOULD BE 1:00-6:00 P.M. SORRY FOR ANY INCONVENIENCE. THANK YOU!**

On Thursday, March 11, 2004, well-known columnist and speaker, John Rosemond, will be visiting our Corporation. He will address parents on Thursday evening from 7:00 p.m. to 8:30 p.m. in the Whiteland High School Auditorium and all staff on Friday afternoon. I have personally read Mr. Rosemond's columns for years and respect his common sense approach to parenting. I would urge all parents to attend this special event. There will be an opportunity to purchase many of Mr. Rosemond's books at the same time. Please come early so you have a good selection.

April 16th is now a "whole" school day. The "half" staff development day has been changed to **April 29th**. Please make a note of this change. Also, dismissal will be at 12:35 and there will be no afternoon kindergarten.

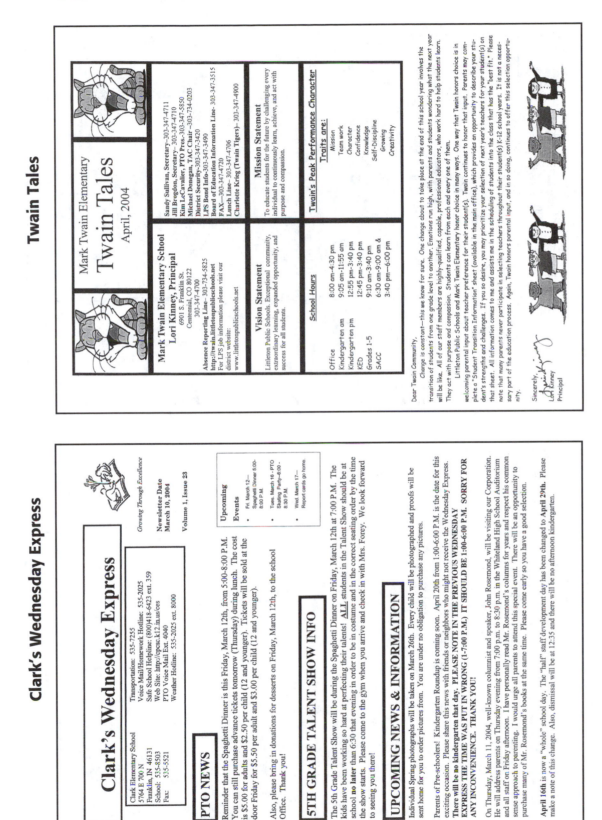

Pelican Post

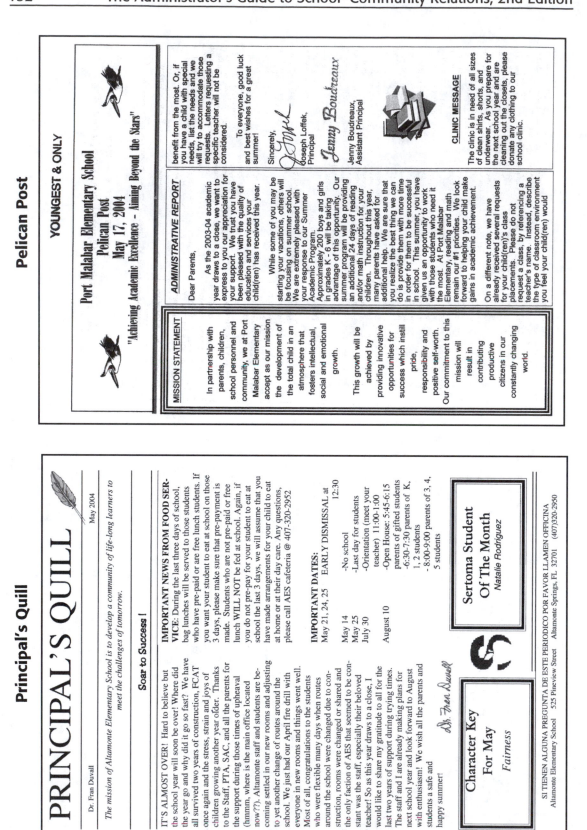

Principal's Quill

PRINCIPAL'S QUILL

Dr. Fran Duvall   May 2004

The mission of Altamonte Elementary School is to develop a community of life–long learners to meet the challenges of tomorrow.

Soar to Success !

IT'S ALMOST OVER! Hard to believe but the school year will soon be over! Where did the year go and why did it go so fast? We have all survived two years of construction, FCAT once again and the stress, strain and joys of children growing another year older. Thanks to the Staff, PTA, SAC, and all the parents for the support during those times of upheaval (hmmm, where is the main office located now??). Altamonte staff and students are becoming settled in our new rooms and adjusting to yet another change of routes around the school. We just had our April fire drill with everyone in new rooms and things went well. Most of all, congratulations to the students who were flexible many days when routes around the school were changed due to construction, rooms were changed or shared and the only faction of AES that seemed to be constant was the staff, especially their beloved teacher! So as this year draws to a close, I would like to share my gratitude to all for the last two years of support during trying times. The staff and I are already making plans for next school year and look forward to August with enthusiasm! We wish all the parents and students a safe and happy summer!

Dr. Fran Duvall

IMPORTANT NEWS FROM FOOD SERVICE: During the last three days of school, bag lunches will be served to those students who have pre-paid or are free lunch students. If you want your student to eat at school on those 3 days, please make sure that pre-payment is made. Students who are not pre-paid or free lunch WILL NOT be fed at school. Again, if you do not pre-pay for your student to eat at school the last 3 days, we will assume that you have made arrangements for your child to eat at home or at their day care. Any questions, please call AES cafeteria @ 407-320-2952

IMPORTANT DATES:

May 21, 24, 25   EARLY DISMISSAL at 12:30

May 14   -No school
May 25   -Last day for students
July 30   -Orientation (meet your teacher) 11:00-1:00
August 10   -Open House: 5:45-6:15 parents of gifted students
-6:30-7:30 parents of K, 1, 2 students
- 8:00-9:00 parents of 3, 4, 5 students

**Character Key
For May**

Fairness

**Sertoma Student
Of The Month**

Natalie Rodriguez

SI TIENEN ALGUNA PREGUNTA DE ESTE PERIODICO POR FAVOR LLAMEN OFFICINA
Altamonte Elementary School   525 Pineview Street   Altamonte Springs, FL 32701   (407)320-2950

- The logo, slogan, or mascot for the newsletter or school (e.g., Wednesday Express, Twain Tales, Principal's Quill, and Pelican Post) are included.
- The issue date, volume number, and issue number of the newsletter are all shown.
- Some interesting information about the school, such as "growing through excellence," "soar to success," or "achieving academic excellence—aiming beyond the stars," is in the newsletters.
- Vision and mission statements are included on some of the newsletters.

Format

The format refers to the size of the newsletter and the number of columns to be used. As was mentioned earlier, most newsletters are printed on 8.5" × 11" or 8.5" × 14" sheets of paper, flat or folded. Note the format examples of sizes of paper and the ways each may be folded or presented. The newsletters from the high schools discussed earlier in the chapter use the booklet format C. Some elementary schools use this approach too, but format A with a staple in the upper left-hand corner is the most frequently used. The example reflects three commonly used approaches to presenting information to the readers. The number of columns used will be determined by the size of the page. If the page is 8.5" × 11", two or three columns are best. An 8.5" × 14" sheet folded to 7" × 8.5" can handle one or two columns effectively. Note how the four newsletters presented on page 134, and those described earlier in the chapter, have been developed in a variety of formats.

With the availability of computers and various software programs, including desktop publishing, there are now a variety of type styles, sizes, fonts, and graphics that add to the versatility and attractiveness of newsletters.

The focus of the newsletter should be on students, faculty, and other members of the school's family, not on the school administrators. The focus on students can be on their accomplishments, organizations, honors, and interests. An attempt should be made to include all levels of students. Although it is good to focus on academic honors of students and examples of students' volunteering in the community (community service projects), attempts should be made to include honors of lesser importance and students' hobbies, too. These types of stories are good human interest stories.

The newsletters naturally are shared with parents, stepparents, and guardians. Many principals include the superintendent of schools, school board members, school district community relations coordinator, and other members of the school district's central office staff—especially the person responsible for evaluating the principal—on their distribution list. Provisions should be made to expand

Newsletter Formats

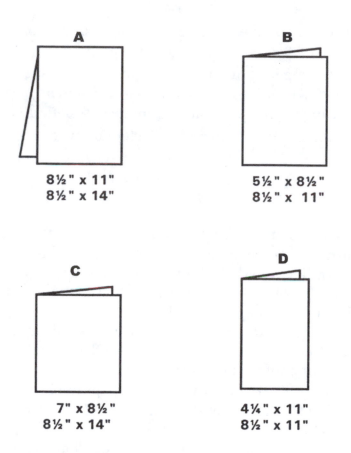

A

8½" x 11"
8½" x 14"

B

5½" x 8½"
8½" x 11"

C

7" x 8½"
8½" x 14"

D

4¼" x 11"
8½" x 11"

the distribution to include retirees (including retired teachers and administrators), key communicators, community leaders, local businesses (including real estate offices), churches, and, at the high school level, alumni. Some principals encourage all school employees to take copies of the school's newsletter to their barber and beauty shops and doctors' and dentists' offices on a regular basis.

It is important to let parents know the frequency of distributing newsletters. Most principals share that information in the first newsletter sent home. Notice the messages from the principals in the newsletters that follow. In the first one, the distribution schedule is announced. The second one contains a principal's message that tells why a particular newsletter was late in arriving. The principal's message in the third newsletter relates that no additional newsletters will be sent for that year. These three principals were proactive and used initiative to inform their readers about the publishing schedule of their monthly newsletters—they didn't leave anything to guesswork.

(Text continues on page 138.)

Leaphart Elementary Newsletter

The Principal's Piquant Partner

LEXINGTON COUNTY SCHOOL DISTRICT FIVE
George E. Pawlas, Principal
Leaphart Elementary School
120 Piney Gorve Road
Columbia, South Carolina 29210
(803) 798-0030

ENROLLMENT: 767

VOLUME 2	10 SEPTEMBER 1984	NUMBER 1

A THOUGHT

"When we are confused by the world, we can gain a renewed feeling of security from seeing the light in the eyes of a happy, trusting child." — Harry Hepner

----

HELLO!

We certainly have seen lots of light shining brightly in the eyes of your children. Although we did have a short, fun-filled summer vacation, everyone seemed to be back to the serious business of education on the first day of school. We thank you for entrusting us with the responsibility of educating your children. We will do our individual, and combined, professional best to reach that objective. Your interest and support will ensure success.

CHILDREN ARE NATURAL LEARNERS

These monthly newsletters, written by the principal and guest writers, will be carried home by each student on the first Monday of each month. You've noted this is an exception . . . watch for the October issue on October 1st.

Each learning unit will also develop an update of activities which have been occurring in that unit. Each of these unit publications will be included with the report cards. The first of the six updates will be sent with the Oct. 10th report cards. This great project is being spearheaded by MRS. PATSY TOWERY.

NEW ADULT LEPRECHAUNS

WE NEED...
· 48 oz. MARGARINE CONTAINERS
· MAGAZINES
· OLD JEWELRY
· LACE, TRIM
· RIBBON
· COTTAGE CHEESE CONTAINERS.
SEND TO: ART ROOM

While MRS. MARGARET CAMERON, Pixie Unit, awaits the arrival of her first child, her duties have been assumed by MS. VALERIE RASH.

MRS. BRENDA COOKE and MRS. GAIL PAULK have joined our staff as aides in the Compensatory Education program and Developmental Therapy Program, respectively.

Welcome

You'll want to say "HELLO" to them, and all of the rest of the Leaphart staff at the P.T.O. meeting TOMORROW NIGHT. We'll look for you in the Little Theater at 7:30 p.m. NOTE: Because of the nature of the meeting, we are requesting students not attend this night.

Also joining our fine arts teaching staff is MRS. COBY BOWERS and MS. DEBRA HALL. MRS. BOWERS will be teaching music classes and helping with school productions and chorus presentations.

Everyone will meet in the Little Theater. We hope you will be in attendance to meet your child's teacher and receive information about the spring testing program.

School Pictures

MARK THE DATE: FRIDAY, SEPTEMBER 21, 1984

More details will follow. Instead of group photos, we will be developing a school annual. If you would be interested in helping us, please call the school office. (798-0300)

CONGRATULATIONS TO:

ALLISON CARTER, Shamrock Unit, for winning a Hoola Hoop contest. ALLISON received a $25 gift certificate.

CHRIS McCLURE, Emerald Isle Unit, won a trophy for his outstanding tennis play in the Junior Tennis League. RICK BAXLEY, Emerald Isle Unit, earned Boy Scout merit badges for cooking and first aid this summer. KATY GETTINGER, Emerald Isle Unit, earned three medals in the State Swim Championship meet.

At the City Swim meet REED MORTON, Shillelagh Unit, earned a high point trophy for boys eight years and under. He set two records — in the backstroke and the butterfly. The backstroke record had stood for 10 years.

Lake George Elementary Newsletter

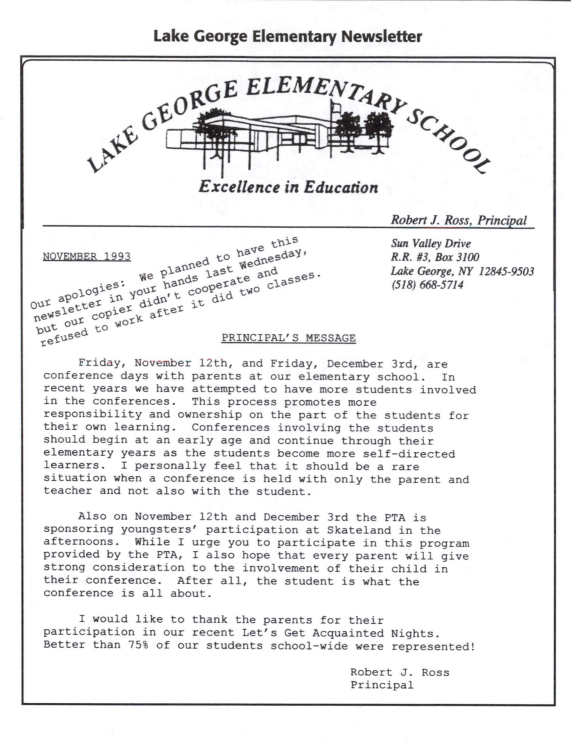

LAKE GEORGE ELEMENTARY SCHOOL

Excellence in Education

Robert J. Ross, Principal

NOVEMBER 1993

Our apologies: We planned to have this newsletter in your hands last Wednesday, but our copier didn't cooperate and refused to work after it did two classes.

Sun Valley Drive
R.R. #3, Box 3100
Lake George, NY 12845-9503
(518) 668-5714

PRINCIPAL'S MESSAGE

Friday, November 12th, and Friday, December 3rd, are conference days with parents at our elementary school. In recent years we have attempted to have more students involved in the conferences. This process promotes more responsibility and ownership on the part of the students for their own learning. Conferences involving the students should begin at an early age and continue through their elementary years as the students become more self-directed learners. I personally feel that it should be a rare situation when a conference is held with only the parent and teacher and not also with the student.

Also on November 12th and December 3rd the PTA is sponsoring youngsters' participation at Skateland in the afternoons. While I urge you to participate in this program provided by the PTA, I also hope that every parent will give strong consideration to the involvement of their child in their conference. After all, the student is what the conference is all about.

I would like to thank the parents for their participation in our recent Let's Get Acquainted Nights. Better than 75% of our students school-wide were represented!

Robert J. Ross
Principal

Johnson Junior High Newsletter

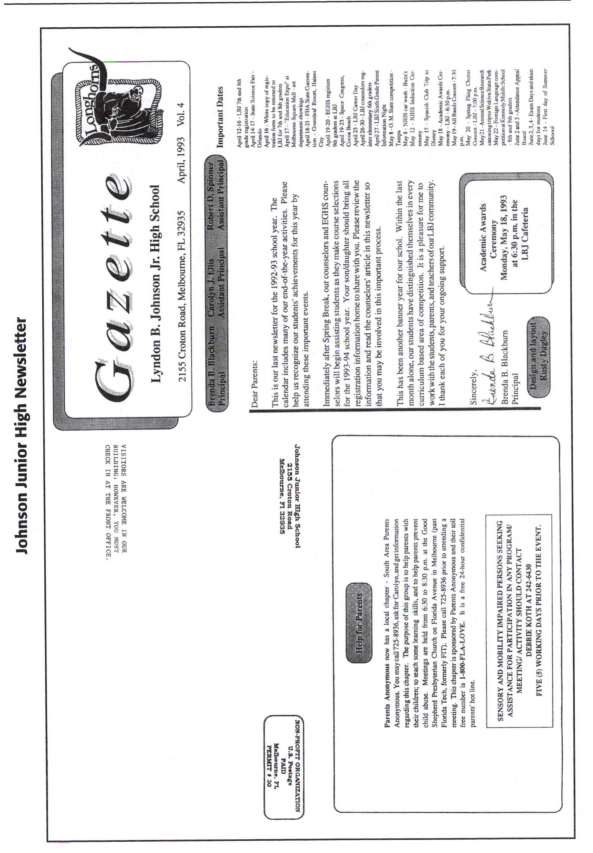

Gazette

Lyndon B. Johnson Jr. High School

2155 Croton Road, Melbourne, FL 32935   April, 1993   Vol. 4

| Brenda B. Blackburn | Carolyn J. Ellis | Robert D. Spinner |
| Principal | Assistant Principal | Assistant Principal |

Dear Parents:

This is our last newsletter for the 1992-93 school year. The calendar includes many of our end-of-the-year activities. Please help us recognize our students' achievements for this year by attending these important events.

Immediately after Spring Break, our counselors and EGHS counselors will begin assisting students as they make course selections for the 1993-94 school year. Your son/daughter should bring all registration information home to share with you. Please review the information and read the counselors' article in this newsletter so that you may be involved in this important process.

This has been another banner year for our school. Within the last month alone, our students have distinguished themselves in every curriculum based area of competition. It is a pleasure for me to work with the students, parents, and teachers of our LBJ community. I thank each of you for your ongoing support.

Sincerely,

Brenda B. Blackburn

Brenda B. Blackburn
Principal

Important Dates

April 12-16 - LBJ 7th and 8th grade registration
April 14-17 - State Science Fair - Orlando
April 16 - White copy of registration form to be returned to LBJ for 7th and 9th graders
April 17 - "Education Expo" at Melbourne Square Mall - art department showings
April 18-21 - FHA State Convention - Greenleaf Resort, Haines City
April 19-20 - EGHS registers 9th graders at LBJ
April 19-23 - Space Congress, Cocoa Beach
April 23 - LBJ Career Day
April 26-30 - LBJ counselors register elementary 6th graders
April 27 - LBJ Sixth Grade Parent Information Night
May 8 - O. M. State competition - Tampa
May 8 - NHS car wash - Buzz's
May 12 - NHS Induction Ceremony
May 15 - Spanish Club Trip to Disney
May 18 - Academic Awards Ceremony - LBJ - 6:30 p.m.
May 19 - All Bands Concert - 7:30 p.m.
May 20 - Spring Fling Chorus Concert - LBJ - 7:00 p.m.
May 21 - Annual Science Research canoeing trip to Wekiva State Park
May 22 - Foreign Language competition at Kennedy Middle School - 8th and 9th graders
June 2 and 3 - Attendance Appeal Board
June 2, 3, 4 - Exam Days and short days for students
June 14 - First day of Summer School

Academic Awards Ceremony
Monday, May 18, 1993
at 6:30 p.m. in the
LBJ Cafeteria

Design and layout
Rusty Dagley

VISITORS ARE WELCOME IN OUR BUILDING; HOWEVER, YOU MUST CHECK IN AT THE FRONT OFFICE.

Johnson Junior High School
2155 Croton Road
Melbourne, Fl 32935

Help for Parents

Parents Anonymous now has a local chapter - South Area Parents Anonymous. You may call 725-8936, ask for Carolyn, and get information regarding this chapter. The purpose of this group is to help parents with their children; to teach some learning skills, and to help parents prevent child abuse. Meetings are held from 6:30 to 8:30 p.m. at the Good Shepherd Presbyterian Church on Florida Avenue in Melbourne (past Florida Tech, formerly FIT). Please call 725-8936 prior to attending a meeting. This chapter is sponsored by Parents Anonymous and their toll free number is 1-800-FLA-LOVE. It is a free 24-hour confidential parents' hot line.

SENSORY AND MOBILITY IMPAIRED PERSONS SEEKING ASSISTANCE FOR PARTICIPATION IN ANY PROGRAM/ MEETING/ ACTIVITY SHOULD CONTACT
DEBBIE KOTH AT 242-6430
FIVE (5) WORKING DAYS PRIOR TO THE EVENT.

Classroom Teacher Newsletter

Many elementary schools have found that a weekly newsletter from a primary-level classroom teacher is an effective way to communicate about curriculum and the class's progress. Some other schools have found that a weekly letter directly from each child to the parents is also an effective way to share information about classroom activities. If all of the students did the same type of work, all of the responses can be written on the whiteboard or chalkboard by the teacher for the children to copy. The main headings, or categories, can be set up on a template for easy reproduction and completion by students each time. The exception might be the last item, where every response will be different. A sample newsletter, "The Week's News from Classroom 213," indicates that a newsletter doesn't have to be complicated and polished to communicate effectively. The main point is to be proactive in sending information on a regular basis from the school to the supporters of the school.

Parents who believe that the other significant people in their children's lives are dedicated to providing the children with a quality education will support those special people. A definite way to let parents and others know what is happening in the school is through the use of a school newsletter.

Meyers and Pawlas (1987) and Pawlas and Meyers (1989) identified specific dos and don'ts for producing a top-flight newsletter. Many of their suggestions can also be applied to other forms of communications sent from the school. Their suggestions are found on page 140.

A few years ago, when Ken Meyers and I were both elementary school principals, we participated in a monthly principals' newsletter exchange. I was the originator of the exchange network, which developed after I made a presentation at one of the annual conventions of the National Association of Elementary School Principals (NAESP). Joining the exchange group was easy: as long as I received your newsletter, you received one of mine in return. At one time there were more than 100 members of the exchange network sharing newsletters with each other. Today the task can be even easier through the use of school Web sites. Hopefully some principals will pick up on this suggestion and start the "Electronic Principals' Newsletter Exchange Network."

One of the members of the newsletter exchange had to drop out of the exchange because of reduced financial support for the schools. In removing himself from the exchange, Dr. Allan Vann, the principal of James H. Boyd Elementary School in New York State, included a letter with a copy of his newsletter when he sent them to his colleagues. His message presented the value he placed on the newsletter exchange. See paragraph two of Dr. Vann's letter on page 141.

(Text continues on page 142.)

The Week's News From Classroom 213

Mill Creek Elementary School
The Week's News from Classroom _213_

This is what we did in Mrs. Kerr's classroom during the week of _October 1-5_.

Dear _Mother and Dad_,

In math we are studying:
addition and some regrouping of numbers when adding. We took a test today.

These are examples of the kinds of problems we worked on this week:

```
  49          13          15
 +26         +57         +77
```

In reading I
read to Mrs. Kerr and worked on homonyms

In social studies we are learning about
continents and bodies of water

In science we are studying
about what to eat to stay healthy

Some interesting things I did this week were:
I read about some unusual animals and I wrote a story about them.
A man from the animal shelter visited us too.

Love,
Bonnie

- -

(Parents, please clip and have your child return this slip on _____.)
Thanks, Mrs. N. Kerr

I have read my child's comments   ☐ Check here if you would
                                             like to meet with me.

_____   _____ Parent's Tel. No.
       Parent Signature and Date

21 Dos and Don'ts for Producing
a Top-Flight School Newsletter

- Be positive.
- Mention lots of people (staff members, students, parents); and mention them by name.
- Be selective about the material that's included.
- Don't use your newsletter as a soapbox.
- Use the newsletter to keep community residents informed of upcoming school events.
- Don't be afraid to interject humor.
- Make your newsletter easy to read.
- Use colorful, lively writing.
- Use a consistent writing style throughout the newsletter.
- Have several people proofread your newsletter to be sure it is free of errors.
- Don't assume you need lots of color printing in your newsletter.
- Keep the format lively.
- Collect interesting quotations, pictures, and short articles that can be used as fillers.
- Give the newsletter a strong, attractive masthead that runs in each issue.
- Decide on a yearly publication/distribution schedule—and meet it.
- Devise some way to verify that parents see each issue.
- Ask for parent volunteers.
- Involve local businesses.
- Look at other schools' newsletters for ideas.
- Don't give up.

Newsletter Exchange Letter

ELWOOD PUBLIC SCHOOLS
JAMES H. BOYD ELEMENTARY SCHOOL
286 CUBA HILL ROAD
HUNTINGTON, NEW YORK 11743-4865

MICHAEL A. MAINA
SUPERINTENDENT OF
SCHOOLS

ALLAN S. VANN, Ed.D.
PRINCIPAL
516 266-5430

May 31, 1994

Dear Colleague:

I've enjoyed exchanging newsletters with you these past few years but, unfortunately, district budget cuts are causing me to cut back on postage. So . . . next month's issue of the **BOYD BANNER** will be the last one I mail to you.

Thank you so much for sharing information about your school through your newsletters. I have found this one of the most rewarding experiences I have ever participated in. I've been amazed to learn that, regardless of geographical location or any other factor, we all keep saying pretty much the same things to parents. Big school, small school, urban, rural, or suburban . . . we're all telling our parents how important it is that they read with their children each night, or we're reminding them not to park in our bus circles!

I've used many of your articles, as you know, in my own issues of the **BANNER**, and have used them in other forums as well. For example, I recently reproduced an article from one colleague's newsletter to reinforce my math presentation at a PTA meeting. It was helpful to show that even across the country, principals were seeking to inform parents about similar curriculum changes!

Enjoy a great summer, and if your budget will allow you to continue to send copies of your newsletters, please do so. If you do stop, I'll understand . . . but it's been a great ride!

Sincerely,

Allan Vann
Principal

Where to Find Items of Interest

Other methods of learning about newsletters include reading professional journal articles, attending state and national conference or convention sessions that focus on the production of newsletters, asking other local principals to exchange with you, and joining the National School Public Relations Association (NSPRA) to keep current on developing ideas and trends. Perhaps the best final suggestion to be offered on writing your first newsletter is, "Just do it."

> **If you wish to become a writer, write.**
>
> **– Epictetus**

Most principals who have effective newsletters will tell you that their newsletters have evolved over the years. Practice makes perfect, and your preferred style of writing and presentation will develop as you write more and more newsletters.

Another suggestion that many principals have heeded is to keep all of the newsletters from one academic year in a folder for reference the following years. Although most of the information would be different for the following year, some details or ideas would be similar. In any case, the yearly collections of newsletters serve as visual evidence of the evolution that should take place from year to year. Previous newsletter items can serve as reminders of events that might recur from one year to another.

One vehicle through which these relationships can be fostered is through newsletters and other written communications from the school.

> **Society is held together by communication and information.**
>
> **– James Boswell (Dale, 1984)**

Summary

The impact written communications have on the support of parents and other people who interact with the school cannot be stressed too much. Therefore, the need to keep the communications relevant, upbeat, and accurate cannot be overstressed. Former superintendent Joseph L. Davis of the Columbus, Ohio, Public Schools suggests that all school communications should be focused on 9 *P*s: people, programs, performance, policies, problems, plans, priorities, progress, and praise (Bainbridge, 2002).

Case Problem

Consider your present school assignment as the source for your information as you think up 10 story ideas that you could use in a newsletter. Using the information from this chapter as a guide and the 10 story ideas as the information to share, prepare a newsletter from your school that you would share with parents. If a desktop publishing program is available, use it instead of writing out your stories. Include the important facets of an effective masthead, headlines, format, paper, and graphics as you complete the task.

Newsletter Software and Related Materials

http://educationworld.com/a_admin/admin/admin357.shtml

"P.R. Ideas for Principals" and "Share the Pride: Create A School Web Site" The educationworld.com site and article, "P.R. Ideas for Principals," also has newsletter templates

http://office.microsoft.com/en-us/templates/default.aspx (good source for newsletter templates)

Microsoft Publisher (2000 and subsequent editions) is an effective source for newsletter designs

The Educator's Quotebook (Dale, 1984)

Phi Delta Kappa

The Forbes Scrapbook of Thoughts on the Business of Life, 1992 edition

http://www.triumphbooks.com (Triumph Books, Inc., 601 S. LaSalle St., Suite 500, Chicago, IL 60605)

References and Suggested Readings

Bainbridge, W. L. (April, 2002). Why we must "decommit" to gobbledygook. *The School Administrator, 59*(4), 34–35.

Cutlip, S. M., Center, A. H., & Broom, G. M. (2000). *Effective public relations* (8th ed.). Upper Saddle River, NJ: Prentice Hall.

Dale, E. (1984). *The educator's quotebook.* Bloomington, IN: Phi Delta Kappa Educational Foundation.

Elam, S. Ed. (1993). *The state of the nation's public schools: A conference report.* Bloomington, IN: Phi Delta Kappa Educational Foundation.

http://www.educationworld.com/a_admin/admin/admin357.shtml (Article entitled P.R. Ideas for Principals).

http://office.microsoft.com/en-us/templates/default.aspx

Meyers, K., & Pawlas, G. (1987). Be an old news pro when you put out that newsletter. *The Executive Educator, 9*(2), 25–26.

Pawlas, G., & Meyers, K. (1989). #3: *The principal and communication.* Bloomington, IN: Phi Delta Kappa Educational Foundation.

Yerkes, D., & Morgan, S. (1991). *Strategies for success: An administrator's guide to writing.* Reston, VA: National Association of Secondary School Principals.

6

Effective Parent Involvement in Schools

Why Study About Effective Parent Involvement in Schools?

♦ Sharing information about the progress of students has been, and still is, a major responsibility of teachers and administrators.

♦ The number of homes with school-age children is less than 25% of all homes in the United States.

♦ Successful conferencing requires the effective use of empathetic listening.

♦ What information to share, how to share that information, and how to follow up after the conferences are the keys to getting and maintaining support.

Although parent and community involvement tend to drop off after the elementary school years, more effort must be put forth to convey the message that the middle school years are a crucial time to stay involved. Middle school is a time to set high expectations for students in all subject areas. It is a time for families and communities to stay involved in a student's learning activities.

By the same token, studies for many years have shown that students have a need for greater independence but the families of high school students remain important influences. A 1994 study of parents, teachers, and students in the urban, two suburban, and two rural high schools in Maryland, conducted by the Center for Families, Communities, Schools, and Children's Learning, focused on learning more about parental communities at the secondary level. The results yielded these results:

- The stronger a school's program to involve parents (423 responded in the survey), the higher they rated its overall quality.

- The programs that helped parents work better with their children on learning activities at home were rated high.

- When parents were involved, they later became volunteers to share their time and talents with students.

- The parents began to serve on committees on high school curriculum, safety, climate, and other school improvement topics.

- Students (1,300 shared their thoughts) who had family members involved in their education since ninth grade reported they were more willing to collaborate with them later.

- When students saw their teachers, counselors, and administrators working to involve their parents, they were more ready, willing, and able to participate in student–parent interactions.

- Teachers' attitudes (150 teachers responded) about parent involvement were primarily influenced by their perceptions of whether other teachers, administrators, the superintendent and school board, parents, and the community supported it.

- On average, high school teachers reported they contacted few parents, about half, with notes or memos; about one-third via phone; about one-fifth in meetings or conferences; and fewer at events, report card pick-ups, home visits, or community meetings.

Harriet A. Coleman, principal at Hunter's Creek Middle School in Florida, includes information in her newsletter about programs that depend on parent support and involvement to succeed. One, the School Advisory Committee (SAC) is a group of parents, teachers, community members, and administrators who provide input for the development of policy, procedures, and programs of the school. Involvement in the PTA allows parents to help with decisions in student recognition, student activities, and fund raising. A national program, Partners in Education, is designed to involve the business world directly in education. The last way Hunter's Creek Middle School parents can be involved is through the ADDitions Program, which is the school's and school district's volunteer program.

Dr. Dianna M. Lindsay, principal at Ridgefield High School in Connecticut, has included suggestions in her newsletter and in the student/parent handbook on ways parents can be involved in the school. She stated, "Effective schools encourage parental and community involvement in schools. Research studies show that high student achievement and self-esteem are closely related to parental participation in their children's education. In addition, support of the schools comes from a community that is aware of the accomplishments of its schools. We subscribe to the belief that the success of a school is a cooperative effort among students, parents, staff, and community." Her school features grade-level advisory meetings for interested parents to discuss academic and social issues of common interest and concern. The evening meetings are held each semester, with follow-up meetings scheduled as needed. The usual parent–teacher conferences are scheduled with daytime and evening hours provided.

Newsletters and other techniques described in the preceding chapters are effective ways to communicate with groups of parents, guardians, and others. (Many children live with adults other than their parents. Acknowledgment is given of the other categories of adults who serve in a parental role; however, for the continued discussion of this chapter and others, they will all be referred to as parents.) There are, however, many more times and occasions when it is necessary to communicate with parents individually on some or all of these issues:

- The child's academic progress or deficiencies
- Classroom behavior
- Attendance problems
- Personal or family situations that impact school work
- Homework issues
- Attitudes toward self, school, and peers
- Screening or testing for student placement
- Disciplinary matters
- Scheduling
- High school graduation requirements
- Postgraduation plans

The opportunities to communicate with individual parents or guardians on a one-to-one basis can occur in face-to-face encounters, via telephone calls, with comments on report cards, in interviews, on home visits, over the Internet, and during parent conferences. A teacher, parent, counselor, or administrator may originate these individual communication opportunities.

For years, elementary schools have offered parents opportunities to meet with teachers and administrators to discuss their children. In more recent years, many of those schools are holding family literacy nights where they train parents to reinforce reading strategies the children learn in school. In addition, other schools are having learning sessions for parents about the use of computers and other forms of technology. To lure parents to these sessions, some schools provide pizza meals or give out door prizes and offer extra credit to students whose parents come.

Middle school Web sites offer homework hotlines to keep parents informed about their children's assignments. Principal Dan Jeffers of Mudock Middle School in Port Charlotte, Florida, and his staff plan to operate an automated phone system that will leave school news on parents' phones.

Within the same school district, but at Lemon Bay High School, assistant principal Marcia Louden indicated that they tailored their outreach program to help boost student achievement while giving parents what they feel they want and need. An example of a specific event is the offering of parental training in Stephen Covey's (1989) *7 Habits of Highly Effective People.* In addition, the school is offering parent meetings focused on specific topics, such as students taking advanced placement classes and those who are at risk of failing a class. The attitude of cooperation between parents and school personnel is seen as the way of better supporting students.

Engaging More Parents

Many parents tend to be more involved in their children's education in elementary school because they can spend the day helping at the school and having greater access to the teachers. That changes in middle school, where children are not so quick to talk about school, and thus the burden shifts to parents to find out what's going on. There are more teachers to keep track of, and the homework is more complicated. Principal Donna diGracia of Punta Gorda Middle School insists that parents need to be more involved because the middle school years are the most important and impressionable time of their children's lives. Like many of her middle school administrator colleagues, she and her teachers keep parents updated by writing comments to them in response to what the parents have written in their children's assignment books. To engage more parents, diGracia schedules meetings around events that showcase students. Some examples used at Punta Gorda Middle School are band concerts and choral presentations. Principal Kathleen Bohlander of L.A. Ainger Middle School and her teachers realized the annual fall open house orientation was an effective event but was not getting the parents as informed and involved as they had hoped. So, she expanded the school newsletter to five issues. They include more details about school activities and added a section on parenting tips. The progress reports sent out today include more detailed information about the student's grades for tests, quizzes, and class assignments.

Some middle and high school officials indicate that they have attempted to involve parents, but these attempts only brought in a small number of parents. Other administrators have said they met with more success by organizing and scheduling informative events more than once and at times more convenient to parents. To accomplish that, Charlotte High assistant principal Maria Gifford surveys parents to see what they want to learn about and the best times to do that learning. Gifford and her colleagues are also working on making high school parents feel welcome at the school. One of the most popular classes offered at the school was a student presentation on the history of Florida through music. As the result of the parent survey responses, the school plans to offer pottery classes for parents.

Hence the actions of the school administrators in the Charlotte County Public Schools in Florida should serve as the direction others should take to get parents more involved—especially at middle and high schools. Parents need to feel welcome at the schools; they need to be surveyed to see what they feel they need and want regarding information about the learning programs and how they might help their children; and sessions should be offered at various times because of their busy lives. The leaders of the schools in Charlotte County recognize that they need to offer parents something that answers their question, "What's in it for my child and me?" These school administrators and teachers realize they need parents now more than ever.

Parent conferences still remain one of the most frequently used forms of communicating with parents. Those who are most successful using the approach indicate that their success is built in the foundation of the plan they have devised to carry out the mission.

Parent Conferences

Success in school often results from the combined efforts of the most important people in a student's life: parents and teachers. The face-to-face parent conference is a widely used method of individual communication at the elementary and secondary levels. Parents of elementary-age students are more apt to participate for all of the reasons listed. However, parents of secondary-level students tend not to participate unless there is a special problem.

Conducting an effective conference with parents requires the use of sophisticated communication and listening skills. The aim of every conference with parents should be to accurately share information, both from school personnel and the parents, which will be in the best interest of the child being discussed. In the past, many parents felt overwhelmed when they were requested to come to the school to participate in a parent conference because in many instances they were not involved in positive ways. No conference should conclude with parents feeling that their questions and concerns have fallen on deaf ears. And more important, parents should never be left with the feeling that their thoughts, ideas, and approaches do not have any value—that only school personnel know what is best for a specific child.

Every conference situation is unique. Parents come to a conference with different questions and concerns and in different emotional states (Pawlas & Meyers, 1989). Carefully planned conferences yield results that are longer lasting and more successful. There is no better way to gain parental support than through the private meetings with parents during conferences with them.

Although teacher preparation programs contain opportunities for teacher candidates to become aware of the need to conference with parents or guardians, not all of them provide opportunities for the students to actually practice a conference situation. Almost every student teacher or intern has had an opportunity to participate, as an observer or peripheral participant, in a conference with parents. Most of the new teachers with whom I have spoken (and that number is in the hundreds) have indicated that one of their greatest fears is conferencing with adults. They saw how the process was handled by a veteran teacher, their mentor or supervising teacher, but the fact they had to handle the task alone was viewed as "awesome."

In fact, after more than 30 years of educational experiences, I can still vividly remember my first parent conference. Even though I had thoroughly prepared for the conferences, my first one was with a parent my colleagues assured me would "break me in right!" The experience was memorable. I learned a lot; I believe the mother did, too, because she became a big supporter of our class and all of the activities we attempted.

Good parent–teacher conferences should have several purposes of which educators should be aware. First, conferences should establish a good working relationship between teacher and parents, which assists the school and home in effectively meeting the needs of the child. Second, conferences have become a routine procedure regardless of whether the child is having extraordinary problems, to serve as a means of updating the parents about the child's progress in school. A third purpose of the conference can be to serve as a time for parents to share information with the teacher that could help the child meet with even more success in school.

For the most part, parents, teachers, and administrators have common goals with regard to students.

Parents', Teachers', and Administrators' Goals for Students

- All students to succeed
- All students to progress at the rate best for each of them
- All students to know that learning takes place at school, at home, and elsewhere
- All students to feel that the standards at home and at school complement each other

Principals play a key role in setting the teachers' thoughts on several key points regarding conferences with parents. In past years, many school districts expected teachers to have two regularly scheduled conferences with parents. The traditional-calendar schools selected one conference during the fall semester, usually around the time of the first nine-week marking (grading) period. The second scheduled parent conference usually coincided with the third nine-week marking period in the spring semester. With the explosion of year-round schools around the country at the elementary level, along with the switch to six-week marking periods, some changes have occurred in the timeline of these scheduled meetings with parents. In any case, as plans are made for face-to-face meetings with parents, teachers' thoughts should be focused on these topics:

♦ Why parent conferences are desirable and necessary

♦ The main purposes of the conferences

♦ The kinds and types of evidence that would give valid proof of the meeting's success or failure

♦ The extent to which the parent's child should be a part of preparing for, participating in, and helping to evaluate the conference

The reasons for conferring with parents can be reduced to these three:

♦ *To get* information

♦ *To give* information

♦ *To find* solutions to academic or behavioral problems

Scheduling Conferences With Student Involvement

The first scheduled conference with parents is a *very* important meeting for several reasons. First, the fall, or first, conference is a good time to have the parents share information about the child. Second, this is an appropriate time to establish goals to be worked on, with progress indicated in follow-up discussions with parents or at the next report card period. Third, it is a perfect opportunity to share examples of the student's work with the parents. Often, the items being assembled in student portfolios can be presented for discussion and review by the parents at these conferences. Bob Ziegler, retired principal at New Hope Elementary School of New Hope, Minnesota, reminded parents in one March newsletter that each child will conduct part of the conference using school work collected in his or her student portfolio. Parents and teachers use the last half of the conference time to discuss concerns or related issues. But by including a student in the conference, trust, the student's self-image, and responsibility will be improved. A fourth reason would be that the first scheduled conference with parents is a great opportunity to share *positive* information about a student's work.

Getting Parents Focused
on Key Questions to Ask

The National Education Association's (NEA) Web site, http://www.nea.org/parents/ptconf.html, offers a useful publication, "How to Make Parent–Teacher Conferences Work for Your Child." Written in a parent-friendly manner, the publication contains suggestions for parents to consider as they are getting ready for the conference, while at the conference, and after the conference. The suggestions offered are useful for parents to consider no matter at what level their children are in school. The items presented by the NEA could easily be added to school newsletters prior to the time of the year when the first set of conferences is scheduled.

Some principals include in their newsletters key questions for parents to consider before coming to the conference. This preparation can make the parents more effective participants in the conferencing process. The principal's newsletter is a great publication to remind parents of when conferences are going to be scheduled. For example, principal Bob Ziegler used this as his lead article in one spring issue of the *New Hope Elementary StarLine* when he wrote, "Spring conferences will be scheduled for all parents and students to be held during the late afternoon and evening of Thursday, March 10 and March 17. Conferences will also be held on Friday, March 18." He concluded by writing, "We encourage you to attend this important event in the school life of your child(ren)." Conderman, Hatcher, and Ikan (1998) described the positive results from the eighth grade student-led conferences at Prairie Middle School in Cedar Rapids, Iowa. The successful approach combines authentic assessment via portfolios with greater student involvement, ownership, and empowerment. Some suggestions for parents to use that may prove helpful to making the parent–teacher conference a meaningful experience for them are listed on the facing page (*top*).

Parents should be viewed as valuable contributing participants in the conferencing process. Some things parents can contribute to the conference are shown on the facing page (*bottom*).

Suggestions for Parents to Consider
Before Coming to a Conference

- First, decide what it is you want to ask the teacher. Ask your child if there is anything he/she wants you to discuss with the teacher (of course, it is better if the student is a participant in the conference.

- Second, decide what it is that you can tell the teacher about your child. Remember, teachers see only the school side of each student. There may be some information about your child that will aid the teacher to better understand each child and make for better school adjustment and progress.

- Third, do not forget the conference when you leave the school. The most important aspect of the conference is discussing the results of the conference with your child. Point out the child's strong points, then talk about those areas where improvement is needed. Start immediately on any action mutually agreed on between you and the teacher.

- Fourth, follow up or call the school if you want to check on your child's progress, or if you think another conference is needed. Communication is considered an ongoing process.

What the Parents Can
Contribute to the Conference

- The child's reaction to the school
- The child's previous school experiences, both negative and positive
- The parent's reaction to the school
- The child's home responsibilities
- The child's response to rules and regulations at home
- The child's reactions to changes in the family or household
- The child's relationship with family and neighbors
- The child's interests or hobbies outside of school
- The child's special needs, such as medication, nutrition, allergies, or health aids

Successful retired elementary principals Harryette Baker, at Ellisville Elementary School, Ellisville, Missouri, and Dr. Thomas Gramitt, at Urbin T. Kelley School in Southington, Connecticut, added a list of questions in their parent newsletters for the parents to actually ask at the parent–teacher conferences:

Questions Parents Should be Encouraged to Ask at a Conference

- "What steps can I take to help my child at home?"
- "What is the daily schedule in the classroom?"
- "What are my child's strengths and weaknesses?"
- "What are your homework grading policies?"
- "How is discipline handled in the classroom?"
- "How does my child get along with others?"
- "Have any changes in vision, hearing, or behavior been noted?"
- "What is the best way to contact you if I have concerns or questions during the year?"
- "What are ways I can support school experiences at home?"
- "Would you be willing to meet with me before or after school hours because I have to leave for work before school starts?"
- "Can we develop a system for communicating such as passing an assignment notebook back and forth to ask and answer questions?"

When Rex Vogel, now retired but once the elementary principal at Fraser School in Edmonton, Alberta, and the principal at Lee Ridge School in the same school district, worked with his teachers in developing an eight-page invitation (pp. 155–158) to parents and their children to participate in a conference at the school. The publication helped to focus the parents' thoughts on what would be discussed at the conference.

(Text continues on page 159.)

Edmonton Public Schools Invitation
(pp. 1–2)

An **Invitation**

to you and your child

A PARENT–TEACHER–STUDENT CONFERENCE

is confirmed for _____

on _____, November _____

from _____ to _____

in Room # _____ at Lee Ridge School.

PLEASE BRING THE STUDENT PROGRESS REPORT TO YOUR CONFERENCE.

If an emergency or illness arises requiring cancellation of your appointment, please call the school immediately at 462–3230. The teacher(s) will gladly arrange for another time.

Your child's teacher(s),

_____

_____

EDMONTON PUBLIC SCHOOLS

The parent-teacher-student conference we have planned is an important part of our school's reporting and evaluation process. We hope this booklet will assist you in preparing for your conference with us. Please read it carefully, and list any questions you may wish to ask.

During the past few months, we have been preparing information and materials to share with you about your child's progress. We will discuss your child's social, emotional, physical, and academic growth. We are sure this will be beneficial to you and your child.

PARTNERS IN EDUCATION

Edmonton Public Schools Invitation
(pp. 3–4)

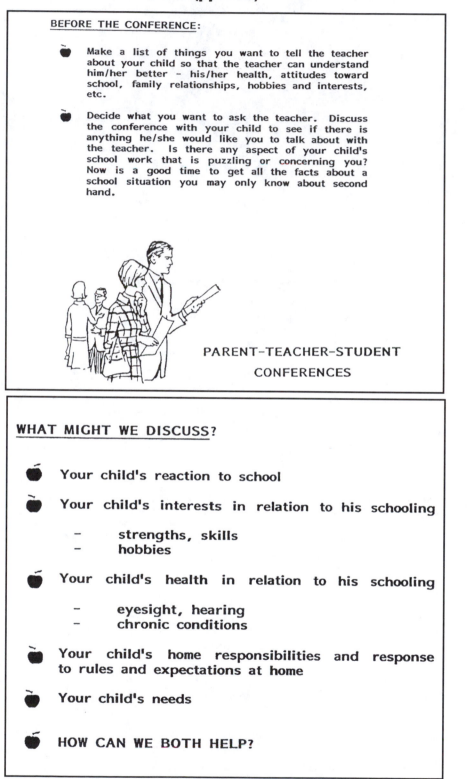

BEFORE THE CONFERENCE:

🍎 Make a list of things you want to tell the teacher about your child so that the teacher can understand him/her better – his/her health, attitudes toward school, family relationships, hobbies and interests, etc.

🍎 Decide what you want to ask the teacher. Discuss the conference with your child to see if there is anything he/she would like you to talk about with the teacher. Is there any aspect of your child's school work that is puzzling or concerning you? Now is a good time to get all the facts about a school situation you may only know about second hand.

PARENT–TEACHER–STUDENT
CONFERENCES

WHAT MIGHT WE DISCUSS?

🍎 Your child's reaction to school

🍎 Your child's interests in relation to his schooling

 - strengths, skills
 - hobbies

🍎 Your child's health in relation to his schooling

 - eyesight, hearing
 - chronic conditions

🍎 Your child's home responsibilities and response to rules and expectations at home

🍎 Your child's needs

🍎 HOW CAN WE BOTH HELP?

Edmonton Public Schools Invitation
(pp. 5–6)

DURING THE CONFERENCE:

- Please arrive a little early. This helps the teacher to begin your conference on time and gives you the full time.

- Start the conference on a positive note. Let the teacher know you and he/she are on the same TEAM. Establish a mood of cooperation so that the conference becomes a joint effort.

- Have a list of questions ready. What specific information do you want from the teacher? Ask such questions as: Is my child's performance satisfactory? Is my child's behaviour a problem? How does my child do socially?

- Expect the teacher to speak plainly. If you don't understand a particular term, if you are unfamiliar with an aspect of the program, or if you find the report confusing, ask the teacher to explain it.

- Offer the teacher the benefit of your expertise. No one knows your child as well as you do. Tell the teacher how your child acts at home. Compare notes to help each other understand your child better. Exchange learning techniques that work.

- Ask to see samples of your child's work. Do they show improvement? Are they consistently neat? Has your child missed a large number of assignments? You can get a good idea of how much progress your child is making by comparing samples of his work.

- IDENTIFY TWO OR THREE OF YOUR CHILD'S CURRENT STRENGTHS AND WEAKNESSES. PUT THEM IN WRITING FOR FUTURE REFERENCE; THEN MAKE PLANS TO REINFORCE THE STRENGTHS AND TO HELP IMPROVE THE WEAKNESSES. SPECIFY WHAT YOU WILL DO AT HOME, WHAT THE TEACHER WILL DO AT SCHOOL, AND WHAT YOUR CHILD WILL DO TO ACCOMPLISH THIS GOAL. SET A DATE WHEN YOU WILL CHECK BACK WITH THE TEACHER TO EVALUATE PROGRESS.

- Keep lines of communication open for future contact.

WORKING TOGETHER WE CAN MAKE OUR CONFERENCE THE BEST EVER!

AFTER THE CONFERENCE:

If you forget the conference when you leave school, it isn't likely to have positive results. Follow-up actions include:

- Discuss the conference with your child.

  FIRST POINT OUT STRENGTHS.

  Then talk about areas that need improvement.

- Start immediately on any action you have decided to take. Did the teacher recommend books for you or your child to read? Is there a better arrangement for studying at home? Is outside help needed in a special area? Begin at once to follow through with the plan you and the teacher decided upon.

- Feel free to call the school if you wish to check on your child's progress or if you think another conference is needed. Teachers value such interest on the part of parents.

- Make certain your child understands that you and the teacher are working together; that you and the teacher are in PARTNERSHIP with the sole aim of helping him/her get the best education possible.

**Edmonton Public Schools Invitation
(pp. 7–8)**

YOUR CHECK LIST:

_____ I've decided on some specific questions I want to ask the teacher.

_____ I'll arrive on time (there may be other appointments after mine).

_____ I'll leave promptly when my time is over.

_____ I'll express appreciation for the help and interest of the teacher(s).

_____ After I reach home, I'll jot down notes of the important points that were discussed.

_____ I'll plan definite action and get started right away.

_____ I'll check with the teacher in a few weeks to discuss my child's progress since the meeting.

for better results
let us
join forces

NOTES

THINGS I WOULD LIKE TO DISCUSS:

Preparing Teachers for
Parent–Student–Teacher Conferences

On the other hand, parents have a right to expect specific information about their child from the teacher. Care must be exerted to share information about the student, the school, and other related details in language that parents can understand. Some general contributions teachers should make are described next.

What the Teacher Can Contribute to the Conference

- The child's academic and social progress in school
- The child's work habits
- Specific evidence of responsibility: effort and initiative
- The child's relationships with other children
- Evidence of health problems
- Evidence of special interests and abilities
- The child's ability to listen and to concentrate
- Areas of needed improvement
- Ideas to enhance the educational partnerships of teacher/student/parent

In addition to these items, teachers should inform parents that there may be occasions when it becomes very important that a parent contact the school and arrange for a conference with the teacher, guidance counselor, or school administrator. Some situations are examples of learning or behavior that call for immediate attention.

The school should be contacted when the student

- doesn't want to go to school;
- is upset about something that has happened at school or at home;
- has behavior problems in the community (problems with police or courts);
- has sudden changes in behavior, such as becoming moody, aggressive, or belligerent, or has sudden changes in sleeping patterns.

Preparing for the Conference

Preparing for each individual conference is a necessity, for, as the old saying indicates, "If you fail to plan, you can plan to fail." Plans for parent conferences fall into preconference planning, conference day preparations, conducting the conference, and postconference suggestions.

Preconference Planning

Earlier in the chapter, information was shared to give to parents before they come to a conference. These suggestions can be sent home with an invitation letter from the teacher. The letter approach works effectively at the elementary school level. (At the junior high or middle school level, contacts with parents to schedule conferences are handled more effectively by telephoning the parents to establish the date and time.) One such letter, which I prepared and duplicated on the school's letterhead, was used to prepare the parents to be active participants in the process. If possible, the letter to the parents and guardians should be personalized by using their names and the name of their child. The technology available to most teachers should make this a rather easy task, which, if used, should make the parents realize how important you feel their conference is. A sample form letter is shown on the opposite page.

In some cases, parent–teacher conferences at the junior high or middle school and high school levels are generally scheduled on an as-needed basis. That is, either a teacher or the parents may request a face-to-face meeting. Dr. Rose Kish, former principal of Neptune Middle School in Kissimmee, Florida, included information on how parents would be kept informed about each child's progress and how to arrange a conference with a teacher in the *Neptune Middle School Student Handbook and Calendar*. For example, this former principal of the U.S. Department of Education 1992–1993 Blue Ribbon School offered parents these ways of learning about their child's progress. The methods offered were the following:

- The school newsletters
- The PTSO Open House and the open house held each Thursday afternoon
- Midterm progress reports that are sent home with each student during the fourth week of each nine-week grading period
- Report cards which parents receive at the end of each grading period
- Teacher phone calls and conferences
- Postcards sent by teachers
- The parents' active involvement in the school

Dr. Kish offered the parents opportunities to schedule lengthy discussions with the child's team of teachers by calling the school's guidance office (Kish, 1993).

Conference Letter

Lexington County School District Five
LEAPHART ELEMENTARY SCHOOL
120 Piney Grove Road • Columbia, South Carolina 29210
(803) 798-0030

George E. Pawlas, Principal   Janis S. O'Cain, Assistant Principal

Dear (Mr./Ms.) _____:

You and I are going to talk about someone very special next week. That someone special, of course is __(child's name)__ .

When we meet next week, __(date)__ , __(starting/ending times)__ , I'll be talking about these things:
1. How your child is doing.
2. What we have done . . . and plan to do in our class.
3. How you and I can work together as partners to provide the best possible education for __(child's name)__ .

We will look at specific examples of your child's work.

You probably have some things you would like to discuss, too—like homework, how you can help at home, and school procedures and policies. It helps if you write down the things you want to discuss before you come to the conference. The space below, and the back of this letter, can be used to write down questions and comments you have. Please bring this letter with you to our meeting.

Questions you want to ask at the conference:
_____
_____
_____
_____

After our conference, we will develop a plan to ensure __(child's name)__ has a successful school term. You will receive a copy of my comments, your comments, and the plan we develop.

Please notify me as soon as possible if you are unable to keep this conference time by either sending a note with __(child's name)__ or by calling the school, __(telephone number)__ .

Thanks for helping me help __(child's name)__ .

Sincerely,

__(your name)__
__(child's name)__ 's Teacher

Some additional ideas for teachers to consider in the preconference planning process follow.

- The invitation letter should be sent home early enough to allow for parent planning and an affirmative response and offer an opportunity for them to request another day or time for the conference.

- Within a school, try to schedule consecutive conferences for parents with several children. At the middle school level, involve all of the teachers the student has, but designate one as the lead teacher for the conference.

- Schedule each conference (especially the ones that might be more difficult) with enough time to cover all the topics you want to discuss and leave time for the parents to ask their questions.

- Post a conference schedule outside the classroom or near the conference area (a reminder to parents that you do have a schedule to follow). Give the school secretary a copy of your schedule so office personnel can give assistance to those who call or go by the office area.

- Decide whether you want the child to participate in the conference. The child is the perfect person to explain what he/she did when completing the assignments that are being discussed. The growth of authentic assessment procedures requires the student to discuss and explain what was done to complete the assignment. As more and more schools are using other forms of assessment, such as portfolios, the students play an increasingly more important role in the process.

- Make certain each example of the child's work contains the date when the assignment was completed so that progress can be observed. If the child helps select the materials, it should increase his/her understanding of the purpose.

- Evaluate the child's work and choose the points you wish to discuss.

Conference Day Preparations

On the day of the conference, additional arrangements must be made to ensure the success of each conference. Some preparations to consider for those times are listed:

- Use an "In Conference—Please Be Seated" sign, which should be prepared and posted to avoid unnecessary interruptions.

- Have the books and related instructional materials used in the classroom available as their use is explained for the parents.

- Technology used in the teaching and learning process should be up and ready to go so that a brief demonstration can be made, if necessary.
- Have several chairs placed outside the classroom, but near the door, for early-arriving parents. Provide reading material for the parents to use if they arrive early for the conference.
- Conference seating should be provided away from the door to prevent distractions. Experts advise that one should try to avoid an across-the-desk arrangement. Hold conferences at a *table*, round if possible; a desk, especially the teacher's desk, seems to set up an invisible wall between parents and teachers. Have three adult-sized chairs available, if possible—one for each parent and yourself. Have an appropriate student-sized chair ready, too.
- Have test data available for easy reference.
- Have paper, pencils, and pens available at the table for note taking.
- Gather samples of the student's work in key areas such as math, reading, writing, spelling, homework assignments, tests, and classwork to show the parents how the child is doing in each of these areas.

The student's participation in the parent conference can be decided by the teacher, the parents, and the student. Whether or not the child should assume responsibility for presenting all or part of the information during a conference with parents is a question for the teacher and student to answer jointly. Certainly it is a growth experience for a student to have the opportunity to tell the parents about his/her assets and liabilities, successes, and strategies for future accomplishments. Reporting can also be a tension-producing experience, requiring maturity and objectivity that could be beyond the present capabilities of some learners.

Conducting the Conference

When the day of the conference arrives, it is important that some special considerations be met.

- Set the climate. Parents should be greeted cordially and in a relaxed manner.
- Express appreciation for the parents' participation in the conference.
- Begin and end each conference on a positive note. No matter how many problems a student has, some good points need to be reported.
- If the teacher schedules the conference, care must be made to balance the presentation between discussing strengths and weaknesses. A conference planning sheet will help and is provided in the chapter.

- Maintain momentum and focus. Because most parent–teacher conferences are conducted on specific days, with a specific number of conferences on each of those days, time is important. Write down specific parental concerns to discuss in greater detail if time permits, or as the focus of a follow-up conference.

- Use the conference planning sheet as the guide for the topics to discuss. Add parents' comments and suggestions to those already written by the teacher.

- Wrap up the conference. By recapitulating the goals, conclusions, or actions as they relate to each student, an organized record of the conference will be developed. Allow parents an opportunity to request an additional conference, and attempt to schedule it.

- Extend thanks to the parents. Many teachers send a follow-up thank-you note home to parents a few days after the conference in addition to extending these thoughts as the actual conference ends.

- Keep the principal informed. Some elementary and middle school principals review all of the conference planning sheets after the scheduled parent–teacher conferences have been completed. They indicate that this allows them to be updated on the plans that have been made for each student. In addition, teachers are encouraged to share specific important details about plans to meet the needs of difficult students.

- Evaluate the conference. By adding a few anecdotal notes about each conference, the teacher will develop a valuable resource for future reference.

Two Key Words of Communication

- Honesty

- Openness

Report of Parent–Teacher Conference

Child's Name _____ Grade _____ Teacher _____

Date _____ Parent(s) Who Came _____

YOUR CHILD AS A PERSON (Suggested areas to be included in discussion)

      Attitude
      Citizenship
      Cooperation
      Receptiveness
      Respect for people, ideas
      Respect for property
      Self-discipline
      Social interaction

YOUR CHILD AS A STUDENT (Suggested areas to be included in discussion)

      Able to make decisions
      Applies skills he/she knows
      Completes work
      Does critical thinking
      Has pride in achievement
      Is motivated
      Organizes
      Thinks creatively
      Works independently

EFFORTS RELATED TO ACHIEVEMENT

YOUR CHILD AS A GROWING PERSON (Goals for the year or progress on goals set)

SUMMARY

Parent Signature _____   Teacher Signature _____

Student Signature _____

White Copy: Parents   Yellow Copy: Teacher

Parent Conference Sheet

Name _____

Assets _____

Things to work on _____

_____

_____

Subjects

Reading _____

_____

_____

Writing (Composition) _____

_____

Math _____

_____

Social Studies _____

_____

Science _____

_____

Careers _____

_____

Other _____

_____

Attitude _____

_____

Outcome of Conference _____

_____

Reading Level _____

_____
                                        Parent's Signature
Math Level _____

_____
Date _____   Teacher's Signature

Many elementary schools are becoming year-round schools or magnet schools, or use multiage grouping of students. Dr. Jenell Bovis, former principal at Windy Ridge Elementary School in Orange County, Florida, involved the faculty and parents in the development of several student progress assessment forms. Students attending Windy Ridge were grouped into multiage classrooms based on their abilities. The assessment form for kindergarten-first grade (p. 168) was prepared and discussed at two required conferences with parents.

To reinforce the cooperative spirit of school and home collaboration, parents were given a bumper sticker to display on their automobiles. The message is a strong one that the school personnel respected and appreciated the cooperation and working relationship that was established with the parents.

Windy Ridge Bumper Sticker

Some parents find themselves in a quandary as to whether or not to call the school with a problem. Most parents say they don't want to bother the school with trivial complaints, yet they are concerned when their child is upset. Most principals would urge the parents to call to let them know if there is a problem. By combining efforts, the principal and the parents can determine whether or not any action is needed.

Bob Ziegler, retired principal of New Hope, Minnesota, Elementary School, developed some guidelines for parents to consider when they were concerned about their child's academic or social progress. These six guidelines, shown on page 169, when included with the four offered earlier, should give parents concrete ideas of when a meeting with school personnel may be the correct move to make. Many times parents don't view their child's behavior, moods, or actions as out of the ordinary when in reality the problem has existed and is on a road to an unpleasant future.

Teachers and administrators have seized the captive nature of back-to-school nights or open houses to share these guidelines in written format with the parents. A follow-up mention in a teacher or principal newsletter is a useful technique, too. Still other principals convey the message and guidelines in the parents' handbook and on the school's Web site.

Student Progress Assessment

ORANGE COUNTY, FLORIDA PUBLIC SCHOOLS	WINDY RIDGE ELEMENTARY SCHOOL
DONALD SHAW, SUPERINTENDENT	JENELL M. BOVIS, PRINCIPAL

STUDENT PROGRESS ASSESSMENT

KINDERGARTEN FIRST GRADE KINDERGARTEN/FIRST GRADE

Name _____ Teacher _____

Year _____ Term: 1 2 3 4 Days Present _____ Days Absent _____ Days Tardy _____

Personal Development:

Code: Satisfactory – S Working/Developing – W Needs Improvement – N

Independence _____ Follows Directions _____

Listening _____ Completes work on time _____

Self-Confidence _____ Functions in a cooperative group _____

Positive Attitude _____

FINE MOTOR SKILLS:

Can write name _____

LANGUAGE ARTS:

Letter Recognition		Letter Sounds
_____	Aa	_____
_____	Bb	_____
_____	Cc	_____
_____	Dd	_____
_____	Ee	_____
_____	Ff	_____
_____	Gg	_____
_____	Hh	_____
_____	Ii	_____
_____	Jj	_____
_____	Kk	_____
_____	Ll	_____
_____	Mm	_____
_____	Nn	_____
_____	Oo	_____
_____	Pp	_____
_____	Qq	_____
_____	Rr	_____
_____	Ss	_____
_____	Tt	_____
_____	Uu	_____
_____	Vv	_____
_____	Ww	_____
_____	Xx	_____
_____	Yy	_____
_____	Zz	_____

Has understanding of and can identify:

Compound words _____   Contractions _____

Synonyms _____   Antonyms _____

Homonyms _____   Rhyming words _____

Main Idea _____   Cause & Effect _____

Directional words _____   Plurals _____

Right & Left _____   Draws pictures _____

Labels pictures _____   Comprehension _____

Long and short vowels _____

Beginning, middle, end _____

Attempts spelling approximations _____

Writes complete sentences _____

Uses capital letters _____

Uses ending punctuation _____

Consonant blends _____

MATH:

Identifies numbers to: **Can count by:**

_____ 10   Ones to _____

_____ 20   Twos to _____

_____ 50   5's to _____

_____ 100   10's to _____

Place Value _____   Money Skills _____

Attempts to estimate _____   Addition _____

Subtraction _____   First-Twelfth _____

Colors (words) & shapes _____   Fractions _____

Tell time to hour/half hour _____

Identifies number words _____

Guidelines for Parents Concerned About Their Child's Academic or Social Progress

Here's How to Know If It's Time to Call the Teacher

- You suspect your child is having a problem in school. Should you call the teacher? Or should you say nothing and hope for the best?

- Most teachers say they want to know what's going on in their students' lives. Chances are, if you've noticed a problem, your child's teacher has observed it, too. By working together, you may be able to come up with a solution that's right for your child.

Here Are Some Times When You *Definitely* Should Call Your Child's Teacher

- You see a dramatic change in your child's behavior. A happy child becomes withdrawn. A friendly child wants to be alone.

- Grades drop. This may be in one subject—or all of them.

- You suspect your child may be telling you things about school that aren't true. He or she may say there's no work or assignments.

- There's been a change in your family. A new marriage, a separation, a divorce, or a new baby all can affect school work.

Principal Involvement in Parent Conferences

Principals are often involved in conferences with parents, both in the presence of teachers and without them. In fact, one of the most important functions a principal plays as the center of communication is the role played in parent conferences. In many cases, the suggestions offered earlier in this chapter for teachers to consider as they prepare for conferences with parents were probably practiced by many principals when they were teachers. However, the position of principal carries with it higher levels of ability and understanding and expectations from parents and the public.

Most principals, the author included, made certain that, before they met with parents about a student-teacher problem, the teacher had been involved in a conference with the parents. Some parents choose to go to the top with their concerns when oftentimes the solution can be found at the classroom level. In some cases, where there is a conference between the parents and the teacher, the principal can serve as an intermediary when parents, teacher, and principal meet. I remember one such incident when a sixth-grade student's math grade fell from an A in the second grading period to a C in the third grading period. The policy was for the teacher to send home an interim report alerting the parents to the drop in the grade. That interim report had not been sent home; the parents were concerned and met with the teacher. She explained she forgot to send home the interim report but insisted the student's third grading period math scores necessitated the lower grade. The parents did not accept those comments and reasons, and they came to see me. After hearing their concerns and explanation of what happened, I assured them I would meet with the teacher to discuss the situation and then get back in touch with them. At the meeting I had with the teacher, I asked to see the student's grades for the entire school year. As the grades for the third grading period were shared, it became apparent a mistake had been made because, at the worst, his grades were a B+ average. The error in the grade resulted because the teacher had used the grades from the student below the student in her grade book. A simple mistake, but one that was a serious one in the eyes of the parents. In those days the grades were handwritten on the report cards; changing the grade with "white out" was not the solution—preparing a whole new report card was the only solution. That was followed up with a handwritten apology from the teacher.

Principals participating in parent conferences, in the role of principal, may have a few new lessons to learn. Parents often come to today's principal with concerns ranging from student problems to community concerns. A principal must stand ready to *listen, take notes,* and issue a *prescription,* just as most doctors do. Principals are expected to have the answers or know where they can be found.

Occasionally, a parent may be overly concerned, overindulgent, oblivious, and, in some cases, overanxious when he or she comes to a conference. The principal has to shape the conference from destructive to constructive, from pessimistic to optimistic. Some principals have found the 10 conference techniques listed on the facing page useful as they develop their skills in conferencing with parents.

Although there are many stereotypes of parents, a few of the types a principal may encounter are the overanxious parent, the irate parent, and the critical parent. Included with a brief description of each of these types are a few suggestions and strategies that might be useful.

Before meeting with any parents, many principals contact the child's teacher to gain that person's perspective about why the parent would want to meet with the principal and to verify that the parents and teacher have met. (In some cases, parents may request that the principal not inform the teacher(s) because of repercussions against their child. Respect those requests if you feel it is in the best interests of the child.)

10 Conference Techniques for Caring Principals

1.   Begin and end each conference with a positive comment.

2.   First, listen carefully and attentively. Write notes sparingly and explain that the notes will help you keep the important details in perspective.

3.   Hear criticisms and concerns *fully.* Ask for suggestions to solve problems. Let parents get their frustrations out in the open and then you can both deal with them.

4.   Be truthful, and combine truth with tact.

5.   Don't inquire or probe if the parent is reluctant. Allow parents to be self-expressive; listen.

6.   Avoid educationese. Use clear, descriptive statements.

7.   Offer suggestions that a reasonably prudent parent would be expected to follow. Ask the question, "Did I plan *with* the parent and not *for* the parent?"

8.   Respect a parent's confidence. Parents often reveal some of their innermost feelings in talking with the school principal.

9.   Follow up a conference when appropriate with a telephone call or some other type of communication. Try to give parents a perspective for their own problem by sharing comparable experiences with them.

10.   Let the parents know they are not alone, that many before have "survived" the situation they are in.

The Overanxious Parent

This parent comes to the principal's office concerned about either academic or emotional developmental problems. The child may be underachieving and may not be getting along with peers. Some strategies for a principal to use in this situation include the following:

♦ Listen carefully.

♦ Offer some type of perspective—give the parent the teacher's perspective, the school counselor's perspective, and perhaps the school nurse's.

♦ Make a plan for some type of action, too.

♦ Include, as part of the plan, a schedule of regular follow-up contacts with the parents.

- Be sympathetic, but have directions in mind, and give them.
- List alternatives. The parents should realize that a number of options should be considered when dealing with problems. Work with the parents in selecting the options that should yield the best results for everyone.
- Mark in your calendar book or PDA the name, telephone number, and reasons for contacting the parents on the agreed-on dates and times. (Educators, overall, get bad marks from the tax-paying public for their lack of follow-through on this issue.)
- Keep written, dated notes and summaries of future contacts as a running log of actions taken.
- Keep the teacher or teachers impacted by your involvement informed about what you have done, unless there are some reasons not to do so.

The Irate Parent

This parent is by far the most serious type of person to deal with. For the most part, this parent comes to school with some type of built-in frustration factor plus some emotional fuse that has set it off. Some principal strategies for this problem include the following:

- Listen very carefully. Maintain eye contact. Keep body language in an open manner.
- Tell the parent you are going to be writing brief notes to help you capture the key points of concern.
- Let the parent talk himself/herself out before you start speaking.
- Don't mount a counteroffensive.
- Plan and study your response. Be sure the parent is ready to listen.
- Try to stay with the issue of the conference. Stay away from the anger or tears. Acknowledge the emotionalism, but don't rationalize any decisions toward either.
- Plan for any follow-up contacts or conferences that might be needed. Make certain these obligations are met.

The Critical Parent

This parent comes to the school armed with "expert" opinions on how to teach children. The main goal is to have the child taught the three Rs and nothing else. Some principal strategies to use with this type of parent are the following:

- Listen attentively.
- Don't argue; disagree without being disagreeable.

- Use facts to inform the parent and also to appeal to the parent's emotions.
- Admit that you don't know all the answers, but be willing to seek out and provide additional information.
- Make plans for any additional future contacts or conferences. Make certain these obligations are met.

Odds and Ends

In the world of school administration, the goal of successful administrators is to have as many contacts as possible with parents and the various publics end up in win-win situations. Covey (1989), in his book *The 7 Habits of Highly Effective People*, presents in habit 5 the notion of "Seek First to Understand…Then to Be Understood." This involves being an *empathetic listener* and using the highest form of listening. Covey maintains many people practice only *selective listening*—hearing only certain parts of what others are saying. Some may practice *attentive listening*—focusing energy on the words that are being said. An administrator who practices empathetic listening listens with the intent to understand. Empathetic listening gets inside a person's frame of reference. Empathy is not sympathy or that you agree with someone. Rather, it is the overt sign that you fully understand that person emotionally as well as intellectually.

A few miscellaneous items that serve as examples of communications developed to improve conferences between parents and teachers follow. The first item included is a letter from a high school teacher (p. 174). Who could resist the chance to meet such a dedicated teacher? The second item, a letter to a mom and dad from a child (p. 175), has appeared in several elementary school principals' newsletters. Most of the principals send this home in a newsletter when dates and times of the parent conferences are mentioned. The third item is a list of suggestions for the teacher conducting a parent conference (p. 176).

> **Any child can tell you that the sole purpose of a middle name is so he can tell when he's really in trouble.**
>
> **– Dennis Fakes**

Eau Gallie High School Letter

EAU GALLIE HIGH SCHOOL

1400 COMMODORE BOULEVARD MELBOURNE, FLORIDA 32935-4199

TELEPHONE (407) 242-6400

FAX (407) 242-6427

A State Merit School

Dear Mrs. Suleski,

The fall semester of the 1993-94 school year has finally come to a close. It has been a very challenging and rewarding semester. Having your son in ecology has really made my teaching that much more rewarding. Dan has received an A as well as honors credit in ecology for the fall semester of this year. This level of performance reflects a great concern for achievement and a high standard of values. The leadership and ability to work independently displayed by Dan is commendable.

You, as a parent, deserve a pat on the back for a job well done. Dan's performance is a direct reflection on the values taught at home. My job as a teacher becomes that much easier and more rewarding when I have people like you supporting and reinforcing the values of a good education.

Thanks again for being the kind of parent Eau Gallie High School can be proud of!

Sincerely,

Steve Allgeyer
Chemistry/Ecology Teacher
Eau Gallie High School

THOMAS A. SAWYER, PRINCIPAL
TERRY HUMPHREY, ASSISTANT PRINCIPAL • CHUCK KEENER, ASSISTANT PRINCIPAL
R. LEE RUFFNER, ASSISTANT PRINCIPAL • KATHLEEN L. TEOREENE, ASSISTANT PRINCIPAL
AN EQUAL OPPORTUNITY EMPLOYER

"Dear Mom and Dad" Letter

September 8, 2004

Dear Mom and Dad,

At conferences, you will receive a "snapshot" of me. This picture will be a time exposure of me that's been developing during the past 9 weeks. Considering my many likes and dislikes, my mood changes from day to day, I think it's a pretty good likeness of me.

When you see my snapshot, remember this is a report of someone near and dear to you. So please don't get too up tight if you see a blemish. I hope you will accept me as I am.

Please do not picture me as being better than all the other children. Remember that all children do not learn to talk or walk at the same time, nor do they learn math and reading at the same rate. I ask you not to compare me with my brother, my sister, or the kid next door. You can set realistic goals for me but please be careful not to push me to succeed at something that is beyond my ability.

I want you to understand that my report card is a picture of my school progress. When you meet with my teacher, you will learn many things about my life at school, even some things that might surprise you.

My teacher knows me as I am at school. You know how I am at home. The "real" me is somewhere in between. When these two pictures become blended with acceptance and understanding, I hope my "snapshot" will be a shining portrait.

Your Child

Parent–Teacher Conferences

- ◆ Start early

  Make contacts with parents early in the school year.

- ◆ Look at the problem

  Decide what the main issues of the overall problems are.

- ◆ Listen, listen, listen

  Be a careful, empathetic listener before you begin to share information.

- ◆ Think positively

  Sandwich negative comments between positive comments. Stress that the solution to the problem can be shared by everyone involved.

- ◆ Cover ground

  Be in control of the time. Thirty minutes per conference is appropriate. Summarize the discussion, keep promises, follow up with a phone call, note, or another face-to-face meeting.

- ◆ Keep the principal informed

  No surprises!

Using the Internet to Boost Parent–Teacher Relationships

It has been proven through many research studies that student success is linked with parental involvement. The Internet can become a vital tool to enhance communication between the school and homes. With the increasingly complicated lives of teachers and parents, it is becoming more and more difficult for parents and teachers to communicate by telephone or through handwritten messages. The "use of e-mail can establish an alternative, ongoing mode of communication between teachers and parents. According to the Pew Internet and American Life Project (Fallows, 2002), more than 57 million American adults use e-mail on the job. More than 80% of these adults feel the use of e-mail helps them with their daily work tasks and saves them time—working parents and teachers should use this time-saving tool" (Hernandez & Leung, 2004).

Other Proven Parent Involvement Ideas

Dr. John H. Wherry, president of The Parent Institute, compiled a list of "The Best Parent Involvement Ideas of the Past 10 Years." A few of the many relevant suggestions are presented here:

- Help parents understand why they are so important to their children's school success.
- Give parents specific things they can do to help their children.
- Remember that research shows parents often feel their concerns have been solved once they have been heard.
- Set up a parent center of information and support services to let parents know the school recognizes the vital role parents play in the child's education.
- Find ways to get dads involved, such as attending school events and/or reading with the children at home.
- Make efforts to understand the culture of parents. Provide school communications in parents' native language.
- Find other ways to break down the language barrier by using parent translators.
- Try to avoid making judgments about parents' lack of interest in their children's education because you will probably be wrong.
- Contact parents quickly whenever there is a problem with their child, or even a misunderstanding with a teacher.
- And finally, remember the 3 Fs for success: food, family, and fun.

Principal Lori Kinney at Mark Twain Elementary School in Colorado and her school colleagues have developed several activities to get parents involved above and beyond the ways already mentioned. At The Night of the Arts, parents and their children can enjoy the children's artwork that is displayed in multiple galleries throughout the school. Also, the Twain choir performs in the gym while books and authors of the Twain Publishing Co. share information about their works in the school's atrium. Ice cream is even served in the cafeteria! At the school's Parent Education Nights, parents learn about how children start to read and write, use technology and math skills, and how parents can learn skills and methods to use at home. Principal Kinney also capitalizes on another sure way to get parents to the school and make some money, too—the spaghetti dinner. Some additional events that are used at this parent-friendly school are the Field Days, where students compete in outdoor sporting events and games, and the Micro-Marathon, an event where students, staff, teachers, parents, babies in strollers, and toddlers race for fun and self-esteem. Another event that is special to that school is Twain Day. This is a day for the entire school to celebrate Mark Twain's life. Musical, cultural, and art activities focus on this historic period.

The adaptability of each of these events for all elementary schools is apparent because, after all, what works at one school should work at another school—all that is needed is the creativity of those involved and the willingness to make it happen.

In the mid- to late 1990s, Central East Middle School in Philadelphia, Pennsylvania, incorporated a Family Math, Science, and Technology Night into its fall schedule of activities. The inner-city school of more than 1,000 students began the event under the leadership of principal Julio Feldman. He worked with the Coalition of Essential Schools and incorporated the coalition's Ten Common Principles among the staff. The Central East's Family Nights began at 5:30 p.m. sharp and focused on math, science, and technology. Entire families cycled through three areas of interactive displays. They spent 30 minutes at each display, trying short experiments, making predictions, sampling software, and playing math games. Participants received handouts at each station to extend the learning once they got home. At 7:00 p.m. the principal invited everyone to the cafeteria, where supper was served. Before thanking those in attendance at 7:30 p.m., the principal announced the winners of several door prizes. As parents left, many asked, "When's the next one?"—a sure sign that they enjoyed the experiences they had. Each year the number of families that participated increased, but new principal John Frangipani, at the school in recent years, indicated the event was discontinued because the funding stopped.

A new concept, *e-parenting,* is allowing parents who must travel as a result of their work responsibilities to check every night on how their children did in school that day as well as what's coming up the next day. Camera phones, digital cameras, PDAs, and family and school Web sites are all ways many cyber-savvy travelers use to stay in touch while they are away.

A Closing Thought

Meeting with parents and guardians has been a major responsibility all educators have. Knowing what to say and how to say it, while also hearing and understanding the information being shared by the parents are important parts of the process. School leaders must provide the necessary training and establish the expectations for all members of a school to carry out as these responsibilities are completed.

Summary

Face-to-face meetings with parents are effective times to discuss the progress their children are making in school. One of the keys to the success of these conferences can be traced back to the planning that occurred before the meetings. With the increased use of alternative assessments, the involvement of students as participants in conferences is on the rise. Today, education is being evaluated, scrutinized, and overseen like never before. For one reason or another, many segments of the population are "experts" on educating children. School principals are often called on to support teachers, especially when the parent participants are overanxious, irate, or critical.

The January 1998 *Education Update* from the Association for Supervision and Curriculum Development contained nine tips for fostering successful school-parent partnerships:

Tips for Fostering Successful School-Parent Partnerships

- ◆ Make families a priority in this school.
- ◆ Make the school inviting, friendly, informal, and not bureaucratic.
- ◆ Provide an inservice program for teachers and staff that addresses parental involvement.
- ◆ Strategize ways to involve parents in schools—many do not know how to become involved or feel intimidated because they haven't been in school since they were students themselves.
- ◆ Provide training programs for parents on how to become involved in the school.
- ◆ Make parents equal partners with educators by allowing them a voice in school decisions.
- ◆ Avoid education jargon. School staff need to be aware of cultural and language barriers.
- ◆ Schedule meetings at times convenient for parents, even if those meetings are not convenient for educators.
- ◆ Show respect for parents' perspectives.
- ◆ Cultivate an open and civil atmosphere in which the principal is the facilitator.
- ◆ Keep parents well informed and encourage effective two-way communication.
- ◆ Make sure that there are clearly defined policies regarding parental involvement and homework in the school.
- ◆ Celebrate participation.

Case Problem

Using the information and forms featured in this chapter as guides, develop a conference invitation letter to parents, reminder announcements for a principal's newsletter, or a feedback sheet you would use after you had reviewed your teachers' conference summary sheets.

> **What the best and wisest parent wants for his own child, that must the community want for all of its children.**
>
> **– John Dewey**

Perhaps the *Florida Today* editorial staff had John Dewey's words in mind as they wrote the back-to-school editorial shown on the facing page. In any case, the words of the editorial suggest the need for parents and the entire community to be involved in the schools—one way or the other.

> **The purpose of a parent...**
>
> **is not to raise children easier, but to raise them better.**
>
> **is not to make money, but to make lives.**
>
> **is not to criticize the home, but to raise its standards.**
>
> **is not to ignore poor schools, but to secure good ones.**
>
> **is not to operate schools, but to cooperate with them.**
>
> **is not to find fault, but to find facts.**
>
> **is not to make every child a prodigy, but to give him a chance.**
>
> **– Anonymous**

Florida Today **Editorial**

Our Views

Back to school

Classroom success requires community effort from parents, teachers and elected officials

Public schools around Brevard County open their doors today, with an expected enrollment of 75,000 students.

Most head back to schools that consistently receive high scores by statewide FCAT standards, but too many students still aren't working at grade level.

It's always easy to blame teachers or the school district for problems. But troubles often happen because parents have forgotten that education begins in the home.

That means parents must take responsibility for classroom success in a way that goes beyond packing lunches and putting kids on the bus.

They must teach children the difference between right and wrong, and provide the moral compass so necessary in life.

They must enforce proper standards of behavior — including respect for teachers, fellow students and obeying rules — with discipline.

They must help children with their homework every day — not just now and then or not at all.

They must attend parent-teacher meetings, listen to what teachers say and then followup the instructions with work at home.

They must, in sum, be full and leading participants in the education process.

That said, teachers and other school personnel are obviously essential as well. And Brevard is lucky to have hundreds of dedicated educators who go the extra mile day after day.

Teachers at Sherwood Elementary, for example, jumped in to paint classrooms in July when a budget glitch meant money to pay painters was unavailable.

Still, parents can find contact with schools intimidating, especially as children transition to middle and high

File photo

Class starts. A crossing guard helps Sherwood Elementary students cross Post Road in 2003.

school where course work is more difficult and concerns about drug and safety increase.

That's why school counselors, teachers and all staff must respond promptly to parents' inquiries. Happy parents who feel their concerns are taken seriously support schools more readily than disgruntled ones.

The larger community also shares the duty of ensuring a positive school year for all Brevard's children. That means driving with caution in school zones, or volunteering time and talent to schools.

It should also mean more community groups partnering with schools to boost learning, as Florida Tech and Harris Corporation have done at University Park Elementary in Melbourne by providing mentors.

And — since state legislators have refused to do so — the community must shoulder an increasingly large portion of the financial burden to keep education standards high, as the county's school population continues to grow.

That means providing money to build the new schools that growth requires, and it's why we reiterate our call for Brevard County commissioners to approve an impact fee on new housing construction when they meet today.

Commissioners must not let this moment pass, but act in the best interests of our children's future — and the future of the Space Coast — and put their unanimous support behind the measure.

UNITY

I dreamt I stood in a studio
And watched two sculptors there.

The clay they used was a young child's mind
And they fashioned it with care.

One was a teacher—the tools he used
Were books, music and art.

The other, a parent, worked with a guiding hand,
And a gentle loving heart.

Day after day, the teacher toiled with touch
That was deft and sure.

While the parent labored by his side
And polished and smoothed it o'er.

And when at last, their task was done
They were proud of what they had wrought.

For the things they had molded into the child
Could neither be sold nor bought.

And each agreed they would have failed
If each had worked alone.

For behind the teacher stood the school
And behind the parent the home.

– Anonymous

References and Suggested Readings

Conderman, G., Hatcher, R. E., & Ikan, P. (1998). Why student-led conferences work. *Kappa Delta Pi Record, 34*(4), 132–134.

Covey, S. (1989). *The 7 habits of highly effective people: Restoring the character ethic.* New York: Simon and Schuster.

Eiseley, L. (1978). *The star thrower.* New York: Harcourt Brace Jovanovich.

Faber, A., & Mazlish, E. (1974). *Liberated parents/liberated children.* New York: Avon Books.

Faber, A., & Mazlish, E. (1980). *How to talk so kids will listen & listen so kids will talk.* New York: Avon Books.

Hernandez, S., & Leung, B. P. (2004). Using the internet to boost parent–teacher relationships. *Kappa Delta Pi Record, 40*(3), 136–138.

Kish, R. (1993). *Neptune Middle School 1993–94 student handbook and calendar.* Kissimmee, FL: Neptune Middle School.

Pawlas, G., & Meyers, K. (1989). *#3: The principal and communication.* Bloomington, IN: Phi Delta Kappa Educational Foundation.

7

Working With the News Media

Why Learn About Working With the Media?

- ◆ The news media represent an important channel for communication in the community.

- ◆ The ability to communicate effectively with many important publics, including the news media, is a mark of leadership.

- ◆ Whenever you are involved with a media person, you will have an opportunity to share information, clear up a misunderstanding, clarify a situation, use your intellectual leadership, and demonstrate your integrity and ethics.

- ◆ They will come to your school, whether you want them to or not.

An important part of a principal's job is telling the school's story to the community. Working constructively with the media is a vitally important way to do that. The effective use of the media can be the key to success in today's educational environment. A principal must make media relations a part of the school's overall communication plan. Opportunities abound to use media power to your advantage. Principals and others unwilling to participate are woefully behind the times. The art of communicating, using the media, continues to be an important key to success in the education climate.

Unfortunately, many school administrators put a low priority on media relations. However, there are some compelling reasons to use the media. Ninety-eight percent of America's households have televisions, and an even higher percentage have radios. More than half of all Americans regularly read general interest or trade magazines or newspapers, either in print format or online. One reason may be the lack of trust or, in some cases, hostility on both sides. Many school people believe that newspaper and television reporters are "out to get them" and will play up the bad news about education while playing down the good. Rather than foster that mindset, school leaders must develop the correct mindset about the media. Developing the right mindset is essential. It requires enthusiastically embracing the challenge of dealing with the media. Also, understanding the basis for success is a continuous dedication to thorough preparation. Members of the media—print and electronic—must all be treated as equally important. Never underestimate how much media exposure could benefit or harm you and your school. Also, the school leader should not be intimidated by members of the media. They have a job to perform, and you are a part of the process. Success will be realized by those who remain positive, informed, and confident.

This chapter focuses on establishing positive relations with members of the news media. Dealing with the media in crisis situations is the focus of Chapter 9.

Reporters, however, frequently complain that educators are defensive and uncooperative, either unprepared to give relevant background information on a specific story or shrouding that information with educational jargon. In many large school districts, all contacts with the media must be conducted through the office of the district's public information officer.

Because of such distrust, some school leaders believe that the only media relations are no press relations. But when an unfavorable story is reported—and it happens, even in the best of schools—that kind of attitude spells trouble.

But it doesn't have to be that way. There is no mystery about developing and maintaining positive relations with the local media. It is really just a matter of following some basic principles. Working with the media is only a small part of the total picture of a school–community relations plan. By including it in the school's total approach to sharing a school's story, the foundations for consistent, accurate reporting of school issues and activities will be laid.

It is vital to keep both the media and the public at large well informed about what is going on in the schools, who is doing it, and why and how the stories are being made. Because the media constitute a basic communications channel to the rest of the community, school public relations experts make it a practice to provide background information to reporters on a regular basis. This information gives reporters a frame of reference in which to interpret news stories.

Large school districts have a public relations, public information, or community relations person to coordinate the system's communications efforts. It is this person's job to get to know the people who report educational news for the local newspapers and radio and television stations. They keep in close touch with these reporters by calling them to find out what issues and topics they and their editors are most interested in. In smaller school districts, the responsibility of sharing information with members of the media may rest with the school principal.

If you are in a school district where a community relations office exists, the people in that office might be able to help you by discussing possible questions you can expect to be asked, or they might be able to help you explain the background or a new angle of the story. They might provide information about the reporter, too. If you are in a smaller district, these items might be ones you want to consider as you prepare your news releases.

Having someone at the central office who maintains media contacts and arranges press coverage is a nice advantage to have. However, even with the help of a district PR person, the school principal is still the one responsible for getting an individual school's story shared.

Print News Media Representatives— What's Their Line?

The members of the news media are professionals, too—just as principals are in the field of education. Theirs is a life of one deadline after another. It is helpful, both to school principals and news reporters, to develop one-to-one relationships with media contacts. Get to know, on a first-name basis, the reporters who cover school news. In some cases, education reporters don't have an understanding of the education system. Some of them have been assigned the school beat because it was available, no one else wanted it, or the reporter was the last one to be hired. They can learn, though, if the principal takes the time to work with them on a personal basis. Reporters who cover the education beat usually do not remain in those positions for a long period of time, but the efforts a school administrator puts forth to know who the education reporter is will pay great dividends even in the short run. The personal relationships made through the proactive efforts of the school principal can lead to favorable coverage of relevant school issues.

One elementary school principal who had moved from one region of the United States to another wanted to get his school's story into the local newspaper. The school secretary helped him to identify the education reporter for the newspaper. The principal wrote an introduction letter to the reporter in which details about the school, curriculum, and special news activities the principal planned to implement were outlined. An open invitation for the reporter to tour the school; talk with students, faculty, and staff; and experience the learners in action was also part of the letter. The reporter called the principal to schedule a visit to the school. That first visit resulted in a newspaper story about a learning incentive program that was begun at the school. Its purpose was to get students to memorize, internalize, and correctly use basic math facts. For each math operation a student mastered, he or she received a wallet-sized Math Hall of Fame membership card. The news reporter liked the story and included it as a feature item.

That first story was well received by the community, and telephone calls and letters came to the school. Parents supported the program—they had read about it earlier in the principal's newsletter—and confirmed their children's enthusiasm to their neighbors. The principal called the newspaper reporter to thank him for the article and also to share some details about other possible newsworthy sto-

When the news reporter received the principal's thank-you note, he called to set up a time to visit the school again.

This true story reveals the power of being *proactive* in sharing information about a school's learning program. These actions of the principal fit into a deliberate plan to send information to the media on a regular basis. Also, the principal recognized that the reporter didn't have an unlimited number of hours to do his job. All reporters have deadlines to meet, and they must become experts on various topics as they develop their story ideas. For the most part, reporters don't have the luxury of time to develop a story line as extensively as most educators would want them to. That's why it is important for school principals to aid members of the media as much as possible.

Be *polite, cooperative,* and *factual* when dealing with representatives of the media. Remember that reporters represent the public. Because the public has a right to know what is going on in the schools, the school principal has a responsibility to help the reporter deliver the story. Upcoming events are usually more newsworthy than events that have already happened. A dozen helpful tips from Ordovensky and Marx (1993) to develop and maintain positive relationships with the media are provided on the facing page.

Just as a school principal should use the dozen tips to enhance relationships with the media, so should care be taken to avoid certain behaviors, seven of which follow.

When Dealing With Reporters, Don't…

- Clam up. Silence is at best an invitation for a more in-depth investigation of a situation in question. This can lead to more speculation and development of rumors.
- Be afraid to point out serious errors, but avoid the impulse to gripe about small details.
- Submit stale or old news. Reporters want details in advance of the event, not after it has occurred.
- Attempt to keep reporters out of a school, although they should be viewed as visitors to the school and be expected to adhere to rules established for all visitors.
- Make statements on which you are not willing to be quoted.
- Attempt to gloss over a situation. By not being honest and forthright in all of your encounters with members of the media, you will destroy your credibility.
- Speculate. If you don't know the answer, don't guess. Say you don't know but that you will get back to the reporter with the answer.

12 Helpful Tips for Building
Positive Relationships with the Media

- Get to know the members of the media on a first-name basis. Find out what their interests are and the deadlines they face.
- Be readily available to reporters. Return telephone calls promptly.
- Be honest, sincere, and straightforward in giving reporters the facts. Never say, "No comment." If you don't know the answer, offer to find out and call the reporter by the deadline. Protect your credibility.
- Give the same courtesies to reporters as you extend to any other visitors.
- Avoid educational jargon—always!
- Help the reporter get the story, but don't try to suggest how it should be reported.
- Make the faculty, staff, and students available to reporters. (If students' names or photos are to be used, be sure to obtain the parents' permission first.)
- Give the media advance notice of a newsworthy event (preferably in writing, by fax, or via e-mail) so they can work it into their schedule. Unexpected events require telephone notification.
- Piggyback stories whenever you can. Pointing out another story besides the one the news media are there to cover may pay off in two stories rather than one.
- Nothing is "off the record." A reporter is not engaging in private conversation.
- Never ask a reporter to show you the story before it is published or to return photographs.
- Take time to say thank you when your school gets good coverage. The time spent making a telephone call or writing a note is money in the bank.

Now that you know the strategies to use and those to avoid as you develop and foster your relationship with the media, you should keep two important concepts in mind. In talking with reporters and editors, they unanimously shared with me their two most common complaints about unsolicited stories:

- Not enough information has been given to them (and because of time constraints they can't call you).

♦ The news item arrived too late to use. (If it happened in the past, it's not news to most working journalists—it's history!)

Some other thoughts to consider when you are deciding whether the information you want to publicize is really news. Ask yourself: If I were a member of this school, would this information interest me? If the answer is no, forget it; if the answer is yes, consider how wide an audience will be interested: national, area, county, employees, or your school community. That decision will dictate to whom you send the release, or whom you call with the tip.

Story Ideas

Trying to decide what would make a newsworthy story for parents and community members to read should be the principal's number-one concern. A newsworthy story fits one or more of the following categories:

♦ Unusual

♦ Timely

♦ An illustration of progress

♦ Understandable to the average person

♦ From an impressive source

♦ Human interest

Although this list is not inclusive, it is offered to generate some ideas for further consideration. Alert school administrators have always known that the best news stories concern the students who attend the schools that local citizens pay taxes to support. Instructional activities—the heart of education—are always a potential source of news stories that inform the public about educational programs and services. Classroom teachers should be viewed as a direct source of information for stories about education. The challenge to school administrators is to develop a program for organizing and developing a news-making operation along with an open working climate so that the local daily or weekly newspaper will work in the best interest of the school.

Some story ideas actually have more specific meaning at certain times of the year. The news releases that need to be developed are those that help to get the school's story out to the public, and the more timely they are, the better. The items listed on pages 191–193 are suggestions for what can be written about and when the impact would be the most effective.

(Text continues on page 194.)

News Releases:
What to Write About and When

July/August

- New programs to be introduced
- Safe walking tips
- Registration/health requirements
- Getting buses ready
- Goals for the next year
- Next year's school calendar—holidays, teacher work days, and exam and testing dates
- Items needed to support the schools
- Summer maintenance
- Getting the names and addresses of new families for later communication efforts
- Bus routes and schedules
- School opening days and times
- Videorecording the first day of school and continuing to record throughout the school year
- Annual report wrap-up
- School lunch menus and costs
- Bad weather procedures (tornadoes, hurricanes)

September

- Opening enrollment numbers
- School lunch calendar
- School lunch nutritional information
- Back-to-school nights, open houses
- The questions most often asked of school secretaries
- What it's like to be a kindergartner
- New employee profiles
- School bus safety
- Homework policies
- District and school goals
- Bad weather procedures and reminders
- Preparations for state-sponsored standardized testing in some states

October

- Homecoming plans
- Parent–teacher conferences
- Report card dates
- November holidays
- Enrollment changes
- Continue video recording school activities
- Return to Standard Time…in most states

November

- American Education Week plans
- Capital improvements planned or underway
- November holiday reminders

December

- Holiday programs
- Cold weather school closings
- Winter holiday reminders

January

- Midyear roundup
- Care and Share Month…involving staff and students to do something special for senior citizens
- January holiday reminders
- Long-range planning activities
- Preparations for state-sponsored standardized tests, in most states, due in the next few months

February

- February holiday reminders
- Have a Valentine Appreciation Day for school volunteers
- Spotlight on history curriculum (Black History Month)

March

- Spotlight on
  - Special education (National Mental Retardation Month)
  - Music curriculum (Music in Our Schools Month)

- School lunches and nutrition (Nutrition Month)
- Art (Youth Art Month)
- Return to Daylight Saving Time (first Sunday in April), in most states
- Budget needs for the next fiscal year

April

- Spotlight on school media centers
- Spotlight on school secretaries (third week of April is Administrative Professionals Week)
- Arbor Day
- Bicycle safety tips
- Taking orders for video of activities from the past year

May

- Graduation plans
- Survey of the graduating class (5th, 8th, 12th graders) to get their comments and suggestions for improving school programs
- Volunteer appreciation
- Scholarship and academic awards ceremonies
- A list of summer educational activities for students
- Spotlight on the history of your district (May 4 is Horace Mann's birthday)
- Teacher appreciation activities

June

- Graduation/promotion activities
- Scholarship recipients
- Report cards
- Honor rolls
- Staff retirements
- Summer school
- Summer reading/learning activities

Note: Many of these activities will have to be adjusted if year-round schools are in operation in the school district.

From the ideas listed here, you can see that the creativity of the school principal can be an asset in identifying story ideas to submit to the media. Events that happen in all schools, such as graduation and assemblies, must have a fairly unusual aspect to interest the media because these activities occur at all schools.

Looking at sources for feature stories from another perspective should lead you to these five areas:

- *In the classroom*—Unusual ideas, techniques, or approaches being used by teachers are relevant sources for news items. The uniqueness of the activity will set it apart from other items shared with reporters.

- *In the curriculum*—The use of technology to enhance learning and how the community can help through tutoring programs—but, again, those uses must present the information in ways that update past procedures or strategies.

- *In the students*—Awards and accomplishments of students, above the expected or ordinary, how students with special needs are being served, make for interesting reading, too. Also, their extended positive relationships and efforts with community organizations make for worthy reading for citizens who do not have children in the schools.

- *In the teachers*—Conversations with teachers who have earned special recognition and awards for their efforts help to alert the public to the positive role teachers play each day. Interviews and feature stories about school and district teachers of the year also make citizens aware of accomplishments of effective teachers. Another popular article for the mass media to consider could focus on teachers or administrators who are retiring. Their thoughts about students, teaching, and education usually update the public to education *now* compared to education *way back when*.

- *In the nonteaching staff*—The new cafeteria dietitian or school custodian's approach to solving past problems can be useful for citizens to know. Especially relevant would be a feature entitled, "The Day in the Life of a School Secretary, or Custodian, or Cafeteria Supervisor."

In some school districts, the superintendent of schools writes articles for the local newspapers on a regular basis. In others, such as the Brevard County District in Florida, the superintendent of schools usually delegates the community relations person to be the district's spokesperson. Dr. Richard DiPatri prepared a guest column for the newspaper as part of the school district's Teacher Appreciation Week efforts. Notice how he highlighted the successes of the district while also giving the credit for those accomplishments to the teachers.

"Three Cheers for Teachers"

FLORIDA TODAY

COLUMNS

Three cheers for teachers

Brevard instructors the reason that schools so good

Teachers spend eight or more hours a day with our children. Teachers provide the knowledge to help our students become successful in life and business.

They're the reason why airplanes fly, computers compute, cancers are researched, ballets are danced, novels are written, skyscrapers are built, and fine "art" decorates so many parents' refrigerator doors.

This is Teacher Appreciation Week, which makes it a great time for us to give tribute to all hard-working teachers for being the best they can be in our classrooms. It is because of our teaching staff that our results in Brevard County schools are so remarkable.

Results are the numbers that are important to many people from Washington to Tallahassee. Being accountable is part of our responsibility to our students. It is what we do in our business.

Our great results occur because of the quality teachers in each and every school building in this district. As a result, we have much to be proud of this year:

■ Brevard boasts 70 A schools,

Richard DiPatri

Guest Columnist

or 88 percent of all public schools along the Space Coast. In all, 96 percent are A or B schools.

■ Brevard is in the top nine districts in the state in Florida Comprehensive Assessment Test scores in grades 3-10 for both reading and math.

■ Under Gov. Jeb Bush's A+ Plan, the results of the 2003 district report cards were announced a few months ago, and Brevard is second in the state behind only Okaloosa County.

■ 27 of 33 of our Title I schools, those with the highest concentration of students in poverty, are A schools.

■ There are only two school districts out of 67 districts in Florida that have fewer students not proficient in reading or math in grades 3-10.

What does the sum of all these results mean for our school system?

Student performance is our

No. 1 priority. It is the essence of our strategic plan. But some of us may have become immune to great results because the performance of our district has been increasing every year.

It's really about our teachers, and the time and effort they put into their jobs each and every day.

Our teachers are the reason we have such great results. Through teachers' talents and the belief that all students can learn, these educators help to bridge the achievement gaps, inspire young students to dream, and help our students experience success in our schools.

Brevard employs more than 4,500 quality teachers who put their heart and soul into the education profession and get results.

They care about our children and their future success, and are to be commended for their hard work and dedication.

So take the time to reach out and thank your child's teacher during this special week in which we honor our schools system's greatest asset. ■

DiPatri is superintendent of Brevard County public schools.

Sometimes stories about schools take on a negative slant. Five likely stories with a negative slant about which the media might show an interest are outlined on page 196.

Reporters—Your Allies

The most effective way to deal with reporters is to be available, open, and honest. By following those suggestions, a rapport—even a trust—will evolve between reporters who cover the schools and the person responsible for a school's public relations efforts. Reporters will learn that the responses they receive are straight, not loaded with obfuscation or presented in such a way as to be misleading.

Five Likely Stories With a Negative Slant

- *"Good News" Stories*—These are stories on the unique, amazing, and positive side of education and differ from the following four types.
- *Police/Emergency Matters*—These are stories that might focus on fires, assaults, drugs, or illness. Some things to remember are:
  - The safety of students, faculty, and staff is the number-one priority. Students can't learn if they don't feel safe.
  - Be familiar with your district's crisis plan or emergency plan and use it.
- *Job Actions/Labor Problems*—These stories focus on pickets, strikes, and work stoppages. Things to remember:
  - Keeping school operations running smoothly comes first.
  - Never give a personal opinion.
  - Be familiar with your district's plan for responding to a situation like this.
  - The safety of students, faculty, and staff who report to school is very important.
- *The School as an Illustration of a National Issue or Problem*— These could be stories about safety issues, discipline problems, violence, guns, and sex education.
- *The Personal Gripe*—This type of story would be the result of a parent or a community member bypassing the established district policy and procedures and talking directly with the media.

Things to remember

- Many complaints are against people.
- Know the rights of employees.
- Know how to not make a comment without saying "no comment."

As in other instances, the personal touch can be the deciding factor in developing positive relationships with members of the media. Reporters have expressed positive reactions when they received visits from school principals who were personally delivering important written news releases. They related how this personal touch added importance to the news releases delivered. That favorable consideration allowed for more positive news about those schools being shared with the community.

Maintaining a healthy relationship with reporters is essential. Establishing good relationships can be traced to "the proper care and feeding of news to reporters." Remember, good reporters have many sources within your school. Dishonesty will be discovered. Some guidelines to consider are the following:

- *Help the reporter meet the deadlines.* A reporter is rushed because news is not only perishable but also must be written to meet specific deadlines. If you miss the reporter's contact, return phone calls promptly. By giving the reporter advance notice of special events or projects, you also will be helping to create a flow of potential news articles. Written background or information on stories that otherwise might require hours of research on the reporter's part should reduce the time the reporter would need to develop the story.

- *Understand the job of the reporter.* Don't blame reporters for things they don't control. Others on the newspaper's staff decide how much of the story to run or whether to use it at all. Remember, the reporter almost never writes the headline on a story.

- *If you have a good story, a follow-up, or a complaint, go directly to the education reporter.* Although you may wish to talk with an editor, you should first let your regular reporter in on your thoughts.

- *Avoid giving out information that is difficult to interpret or understand.* To avoid the possibility of having a story rejected, keep the information and data present in terms noneducators can understand. As *Dragnet*'s Sergeant Joe Friday did, you should focus on the facts. Be honest! Tell the truth, but don't release confidential information or offer personal opinions. Use caution in choosing words, phrases, and examples. Report only facts, not rumors. It is credible to state that all information is not in and you are working to complete it.

Looking for the news story, and reporting the details, takes time. To expedite the process and ensure that the necessary details are contained in the news tip, a standardized format should be used. A samples of one school district's news coverage request is displayed on page 198.

In this school district, every school principal and faculty had the responsibility of supplying the information on the form before submitting it to either the news gatherer at the school or at the school district office. The information provided was verified, and in some cases clarified, before it was sent to the media.

Berkeley County News Coverage Request

News Coverage Request

_____   _____
                                     DATE SENT

_____   _____
     NEWS COORDINATOR   SCHOOL

Phone Number: _____   Best Time to Call: _____

Who: _____

What: _____

When: _____
                        (date and time)
Where: _____

Why: _____

_____

_____

_____

Best Time to Visit: _____

Possible Subjects For Photographing/Filming: _____

_____

_____

Person To Contact Other Than News Coordinator: _____

_____   Phone _____

News Releases

This school district identified a news coordinator at each school whose responsibility it was to channel school news items to the appropriate media persons. This news coordinator served as a liaison to the media, while being the recipient of articles and ideas from members of the school faculty. Newsworthy items sponsored by the school's parent–teacher organization should be shared with the contact person. Although the principal was not the person identified as the news coordinator, the principal reviewed the news items before they were sent from the school. From the relationship developed with members of the media, an understanding was achieved on matters such as these:

- The kinds of school events considered newsworthy—or just the opposite
- The preferred format for press releases
- The deadlines for the media
- Whether it was okay to suggest photo possibilities or whether to request a photographer to cover the school event

From the information provided by the teacher, the school's public relations person would develop a news release with the answers to the four items identified above. An important consideration to remember is to include information about the five Ws and one H:

- Who
- What
- When
- Where
- Why
- How

For instance, consider the press release shown on the opposite page. Notice how this release included the standard five Ws:

- Who: Johnson Middle School seventh and eighth graders
- What: A concert
- When: 1 P.M., Tuesday, September 16
- Where: Cedar Oaks Retirement Community Center
- Why: To help senior citizens celebrate Grandparents Day

Concert Press Release

Johnson Middle School
Margaret Cameron, press contact
Tel. No. 555-4267
Date: September 1, _____

Concert

Seventh and eighth graders from Johnson Middle School will help brighten Grandparents Day for local senior citizens with a musical concert scheduled for 1 p.m. Tuesday, September 16, at Cedar Oaks Retirement Community Center.

The concert will feature songs from an era gone by, and will include "You Are My Sunshine," plus other favorites of the seniors. The students have a few surprises, too.

The concert is free and open to the public. The students will serve refreshments after the performance.

#   #   #

Note that the press release was sent out more than a week before the event. This would allow reporters the opportunity to decide if the event will fit into their work schedules and also to get the stories in the media so that readers will have time to participate.

The best news release headlines are *newsy*—of interest to readers. A quality headline should express a single newsworthy story in eight words or less. The headline should answer the question, "What happened?" or, better, "What will happen?," as shown in the Charter Technical Center news release on page 201.

The news releases should be *typed, double-spaced*, and prepared on one side of a sheet of paper. In writing, use the third person. Keep words, sentences, and paragraphs short and uncomplicated. Try to limit the news release to no more than two pages. If the release is longer than one page, type "MORE" at the bottom of the page. Don't worry about writing a finished story. Use plain English, avoid educational jargon, and concentrate on the important facts. If possible, use the school's masthead or other distinctive masthead so that the reporters will be able to identify your school easily. Type headlines in capital letters. Be sure the news release has a date on it. Use the complete name of each person, and be sure to double-check the spelling of the names for accuracy. Use the exact date(s) and time(s) of the event, being sure to include a.m. and p.m. to avoid confusion. At the end of the news release, use either "# # #" or "–30–" to signal that the news release is

Charter Technical Center News Release

NEWS RELEASE
Volusia County Schools

For Immediate Release
May 8, 20 _ _

First Meeting Set for Charter Technical Career Center

DAYTONA BEACH—The governing board for the Charter Technical Career Center will hold its first meeting on Thursday, May 20. The meeting will be held from 9:30–11:30 a.m. at Daytona Beach Community College, Building 16, Room 232, Daytona Beach. Attached is the meeting agenda.

The Charter Technical Career Center is operated by the Partnership for Workforce Development, Inc. through a charter with Daytona Beach Community College, Flagler County Schools, and Volusia County Schools.

A series of updates will be presented to the governing board, which is responsible for establishing school policy for the Charter Academy for Career Education. The public is invited to attend.

For more information, contact _____, community information director, at _____.

–30–

NH

Attachment

An Affirmative Action/Equal Opportunity Employer

done. Another important part of a news release is the school's contact person. This information will expedite the process if the reporter has any questions.

Dr. Fred Anderson learned to use his positive relationships with the media to keep his school in the news. The press release he wrote to promote an upcoming activity at his school is shown on page 202. Note that he provided lead time for the media representative to get the item into the paper. He kept his messages simple, to the point, and focused.

Be sure of the facts and that quotes, if used, are accurate. Cover all the important facts of an event, but be as brief as possible. Because time and deadlines are two important facts of life for reporters, they will eliminate any padding or irrelevant information you include.

Use News Conferences

Some school districts have found that news conferences, which are planned by the superintendent's office, are effective ways to release information about new programs, student test scores, and building projects, and they should have districtwide implications. Members of the media give added attention when the

**Custer County Freshman
Orientation Picnic News Release**

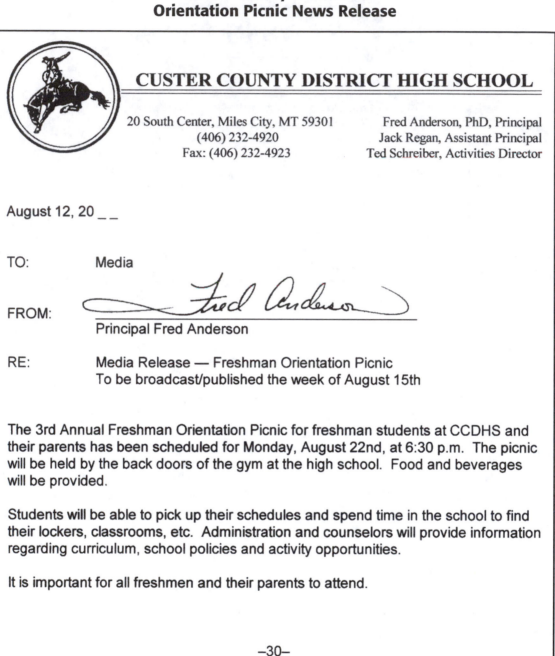

CUSTER COUNTY DISTRICT HIGH SCHOOL

20 South Center, Miles City, MT 59301   Fred Anderson, PhD, Principal
(406) 232-4920   Jack Regan, Assistant Principal
Fax: (406) 232-4923   Ted Schreiber, Activities Director

August 12, 20 _ _

TO: Media

FROM: *Fred Anderson*
             Principal Fred Anderson

RE: Media Release — Freshman Orientation Picnic
             To be broadcast/published the week of August 15th

The 3rd Annual Freshman Orientation Picnic for freshman students at CCDHS and
their parents has been scheduled for Monday, August 22nd, at 6:30 p.m. The picnic
will be held by the back doors of the gym at the high school. Food and beverages
will be provided.

Students will be able to pick up their schedules and spend time in the school to find
their lockers, classrooms, etc. Administration and counselors will provide information
regarding curriculum, school policies and activity opportunities.

It is important for all freshmen and their parents to attend.

—30—

term *press conference* is mentioned, and they are likely to attend. The main benefit to the school district, and school, of a press conference is that information is explained fully before it is written up and printed. This means the chances are reduced that information will be distorted or incorrect.

Radio and Television Interviews

Radio broadcasting serves a useful role in a public relations information system. Radio offers a wide range of publicity possibilities. Radio is a mobile medium, available to almost everyone and suited to mobile people—its flexibility is unmatched by any other medium. In some parts of the country, the local radio station may be the only medium available, other than the local newspaper, to share the school's messages.

Radio listener surveys indicate newscasts at the top or near the top of lists of programs preferred by most listeners. By providing news for the radio newscast, the school's public relations person can reach a wide variety of listening audiences. Care must be taken to write the news for radio—not copies of newspaper releases. For example, all difficult names and words must be phoneticized for the announcer. Radio news must be written for the ear, not the eye. It must be brief, informal, conversational, to the point, and, most important, accurate.

Radio and television stations are severely constrained by time. They have to cover a story in just about one minute, which is about 150 words. They must hit the highlights and get to the point immediately.

Radio has some special advantages over television. Radio allows the announcer to read from a prepared text because no one can see the person. (Care must be taken so the announcer doesn't sound like he or she is reading.) The person does not have to worry about what to wear. In some cases, radio stations allow "real" people to read the news about their organization or activity. Radio interviews can take a lot less time and preparation than television because of the phone-in interview. When you are pressed for time, be sure to ask the radio station if this approach can be used.

Television Interviews

How well you do in an interview will depend on what you do before the interview. Assuming the interview is not dealing with a crisis situation, the following suggestions should help. By researching the program and host(s) and by paying attention to formats, styles, and values of the interviewers, you should have an idea of how you will be treated when you are interviewed. If possible, try to get an idea of the information the interviewers may be seeking or the points they want to get across.

The goals for each interview must be clear and precise. You may want to write a complete list of points, known as key points, usually up to three, that you want to get across. Put the most important point first, and so on, down the line. Edit your list to its shortest form, and then commit that list to memory and stick to it.

The reasons for this procedure are to plant your priorities firmly in mind and to make it necessary to memorize only a few simple items, which should allow you to adapt to last-minute reductions of time.

In some cases, if possible, practice saying your main thoughts to someone who is willing to help you. You may also want to practice responding to potential questions the interviewer may ask you. As part of the mock interview, have a colleague ask you questions that a reporter might pose and then critique your responses. You might also want to record the practice session to replay and critique. Following this procedure should help you come across in a more relaxed, knowledgeable way. Never "wing" an interview.

In the event you might be confronted by the media in an unscheduled situation, always try to have an honest, positive comment ready to share. All interviews are not created equal. In a print article, for instance, the writer's decisions and opinions control the content. Readers don't see or hear you. Quotes used may be selective, partial, perhaps out of context, and even inaccurate. As you might expect, print interviews are the most risky regarding accuracy and content.

Television interviews reveal more of your personality, less of your message. Interviews that are broadcast benefit you most when they are live or unedited. The most effective interview is a live television interview because you can be seen and heard saying what you choose in context without the risk of having anything deleted.

With these comments as an introduction, the following five main points should assist you in having a successful television interview.

Knowing the Importance of Style

The personal style of each individual is apparent on television. Appearance is important because more than 70% of all communication is nonverbal. Appearance, then, will either enhance or detract from the message being shared. The rapport that is established with the interviewer lowers resistance to the ideas and comments that are being presented. So it is important to win the interest and support of the people you will be working with on television.

Using Gestures Effectively

Of equal importance are appropriate *body language* and *gestures*. It is important to keep gestures as natural as possible. Too many gestures can be distracting, whereas no gestures convey the message of inflexibility and cause one to appear stiff or wooden-like. Hand gestures should be natural but not overexaggerated.

Body language of many kinds can defeat the purpose of the interview. For example, a slouching posture distracts and does not inspire confidence. Tapping of feet or fingers, crossing arms, and looking at a watch all say that the person wants to be anywhere but here. One of the U.S. presidential candidates in the 1992 debates innocently looked at his watch to see what time it was, but unfortunately, many of the viewers interpreted his actions to mean he was bored and wanted to leave.

Maintain eye contact with the interviewer while you are responding. Use the reporter's first name. Ignore the several people who may be walking around off the set. Stay where you are until you are told you are off the air. Thank the interviewer and crew for making the interview possible.

Using Your Voice Effectively

A conversational tone is more widely accepted by audiences and interviewers. Most people don't react favorably to lectures. Keep your voice firm and well modulated. By speaking loudly enough, others will believe you because you will appear to believe what you have said.

Never, never, *never* read an answer to a question verbatim from your notes. It will appear stilted and will promote the audience's lack of confidence in the speaker and his or her educational expertise.

Excitement and enthusiasm, when added to vocal inflections, will add interest to the message being shared. A vocal monotone will virtually ensure that the attention of the audience will be lost.

Stop speaking when the main points have been made. By building up to a major point, the message will be delivered with maximum impact. It is better to know when to stop than to continue rambling on. Remember, sometimes, less is more if you stick to your key messages.

Using Speech With Impact

A general rule in radio and TV broadcasting is that you should be able to make your point or answer a question in 15 seconds. Get to the point quickly.

Leave professional jargon or educationese at home. People who do not understand special terms will tend to distrust those words and concepts.

If the questions being asked are stated negatively, do not repeat the negative but rather concentrate on making the responses upbeat and positive.

Use a solid, fact-based presentation to sell ideas rather than hard-sell tactics. Facts sell—vague generalizations don't!

Maintaining Your Self-Awareness

Always make an effort to be conscious of what you are doing—posture, voice, eye contact—every minute that you are on camera, because your total presentation style affects how well the message is getting across to the audience. If you know when you will be on television, you may want to set a VCR or DVR to record the interview for your review later.

Public Affairs Talk Shows

Cable television has opened up opportunities for public officials to share information with many people. Some cable companies have allocated weekly times for school districts, community colleges, and universities to present topical issues to the viewing area. Some general guidelines to consider when the opportunity arises to appear on a talk show or any other kind of television program are listed in the *16 Dos for Television Appearances* shown on the opposite page 207.

Remember that on television your body, face, voice, language, and overall personality make a statement. Seize the opportunity to make a favorable impression and gain new supporters for your school.

Public Service Announcements

A public service announcement (PSA) is a short spot similar to and scheduled in the same way as commercials. These announcements are aired free of charge by radio and television stations and are used to disseminate specific information in a short period of time.

How to Use PSAs

PSAs can be used to do any of the following:

♦ **Promote a school event.**

♦ **Highlight a school program.**

♦ **Inform the audience about an idea.**

♦ **Persuade the audience to accept an idea.**

♦ **Conduct a campaign to generate interest in or understanding of a school program or event.**

---

16 Dos for Television Appearances

- Dress neatly and in subdued colors.
- Sit up straight and do not squirm in the chair.
- Enunciate clearly; do not hurry.
- Never lie! Your credibility and reputation are yours forever.
- Strictly shun educational jargon.
- It is better to say something important more than once than several unimportant items.
- Avoid long, obtuse words and sentences. Keep your message simple.
- Know your ground; don't get sidetracked.
- Look directly at the camera when being introduced and at the host when speaking.
- Call reporters by their first names.
- Never lose your temper. The tougher the question, the shorter the answer and the calmer you need to be.
- Be upbeat, affirmative, and enthusiastic. Tell the good news.
- Stay positive; don't allow yourself to be put in a defensive position.
- Use the microphone effectively. Don't allow yourself to be caught off guard while the microphone is being attached. Don't say things you would never say with a microphone nearby simply because you believe it is not on. Even national political figures make this mistake.
- Try your best to be natural.
- Never speak "off the record."

How to Write a PSA

A PSA should be written just exactly the way it should be broadcast, because the announcer will most likely read the copy directly over the air. Like news releases, PSAs should contain pertinent facts, including who, what, where, when, why, and how. A conversational tone should be used, too. Where possible, important telephone numbers, dates, and contact persons should be repeated at the close of the announcement. Effective PSAs start with an interest-catching statement, followed by short sentences composed of familiar words. To help the station identify the length of the PSA, use this information as a guide to determine the length as you write:

10-second PSA—about 23 words

20-second PSA—46–50 words

30-second PSA—50–75 words

60-second PSA—140–150 words

By sending PSAs of various lengths to a radio or television station, greater flexibility will be offered and a better chance of having one or both used will be realized.

Television PSAs must be accompanied by visual material. For the most part, a short film, videotape, or one slide is enough for 10- or 20-second copy. Two or more slides, film, or videotape are needed for 30-second PSAs. Film or video tape must be used for 60-second television PSAs.

The PSA should be typed in all upper-case letters and double-spaced on one side of an 8.5″ × 11″ paper. Use a heading similar to the news release format. A sample PSA is shown here.

A Sample PSA

EAU GALLIE HIGH SCHOOL
1400 Commodore Boulevard
Melbourne, FL 32935

Tom Sawyer, Principal
Eau Gallie High School
Tel. No. 555-1496

USE ON OR BEFORE MARCH 1, 20_ _   TO RADIO OUTLETS

:10 SECONDS

ABE LINCOLN'S LOOK-ALIKE HOLDS A PRESS CONFERENCE AT EAU GALLIE HIGH SCHOOL, MARCH 15 AT 9 A.M. CALL 555-1496 FOR INFORMATION.

:20 SECONDS

DID ABE LINCOLN REALLY GROW HIS BEARD FOR A SPECIAL REASON? WHAT ARE THE DETAILS BEHIND HIS WRITING OF THE GETTYSBURG ADDRESS? BE THERE WHEN ABE'S LOOK-ALIKE, ACTOR SAM WEST, MEETS THE PRESS AT EAU GALLIE HIGH SCHOOL, MARCH 15 AT 9 A.M. FOR MORE INFORMATION, CALL 555-1496.

Dealing with Errors in Reported Stories

If you believe some information has been incorrectly quoted or reported, use a positive approach with the member of the media who reported the news. A personal contact should be made to provide the correct information to the person. Good reporters don't like errors in their work. If possible, reporters will update their information and offer a retraction. And, even if these things do not happen, the contact may motivate the reporters to be more careful with materials and promote accuracy in the future.

Three Basic Elements for Positive Media Relationships

A very simple PR effort can be conducted by a principal or by another employee who has the principal's full trust. It can improve the school's relations with the media almost overnight and maintain that relationship indefinitely if it contains three basic elements:

- ♦ Get to know the people who make a living covering the school personally. Just as important as that is allowing them to get to know the school's PR person; hopefully, that will be you. Invite them to visit the school, have lunch, and tour the building.
- ♦ Recognize that reporters earn their living by asking questions. Respond to their questions quickly and efficiently.
- ♦ Tell the truth.

Newspapers Report School Effectiveness

In Chapter 4, a discussion was presented about the new efforts many newspapers are making to report the effectiveness of the local schools to the local community and to anyone who has access to the World Wide Web. The expanded coverage of the reporting of a school's effectiveness should be a signal to school administrators and their staffs that a larger audience than ever has access to information about a school. Because of this fact, it is ever more important to develop a sincere, working relationship with the local media. If this is done properly, these key personnel can add to the interpretation of raw data to add other "points of pride" for the school.

> **All I know is what I read in the newspapers.**
> *– Will Rogers*

A Closing Thought

In this chapter, you were exposed to several major and important concepts about getting the positive, correct image of your school and its instructional program, faculty, staff, and student accomplishments shared with your school community. For that to happen, however, you must be proactive and honest, and work to provide quality learning opportunities for all of your students.

Effective relations with members of the media are an important part of any school's overall school–community relations plan. It must be cultivated, nourished, and constantly reviewed to get the best results. Those principals who are successful have learned the proper approaches to use. According to Wilcox (2001), a number of studies reveal that 55% to 97% of all news releases sent to the media outlets are never used. So the challenge is for you to develop skills that will help you create news releases that are among the 3% to 45% that are accepted. In addition to the ideas presented in this chapter, you are encouraged to monitor the types of news articles you read, see, and hear about in your own school district. Note how the five Ws and one H can be found in each of the stories.

Summary

The focus of this chapter has been on developing an effective relationship with the media. Why wait for a crisis to happen before you talk to the media? In fact, if you build credibility before a crisis, you'll have a less difficult time surviving it. Being proactive and contacting the media is a crucial step in establishing an effective school–community relations plan. The taxpayers want to know what they are receiving for their educational dollar. They want to know what their children are being taught in school. Those taxpayers who do not have children in school want to know how the neighborhood children are being prepared to meet the challenges of the future.

School principals need to create a good image for their school by focusing on what is *unique* and *positive* about their *school*, their *students,* and their *instructional programs.* Some principals carry with them a brief list of "six things I can say with pride about my school." Some examples might be "We have over 100 volunteers who provided 1,825 volunteer hours of work last year," or "Nearly 80% of our school's graduates go on to higher education," or "Our school's fourth graders' scores on the state's standardized tests exceeded the state's totals by 12 percentage points." These are samples of statements that indicate what is working in a school and come in handy when you are asked to make impromptu comments. How does the school reflect and enhance the community it serves? How does the school attempt to meet the special needs of the community? One effective conduit through which the answers to these and other questions progress is the media.

Most stories contain six basic facts, the five Ws and one H: who, what, when, where, why, and how. Your work with representatives of the press can be boiled down to six basic keys: accuracy, brevity, timeliness, neatness, courtesy, and interest. Consider the words of Rob Britt, now in his fourth year as principal of Carpenters Middle School in Bount County, Tennessee, as he responded to these statements from a reporter: "I see great publicity in the local newspaper about your school and its principal. I think you are making a real effort to get the word out." Rob replied, "We have to do these things. We, school systems in general, get bad press. We have to do a better job about telling the good news about what's going on in our schools. So far, we have won the battle of community support and community buy-in; the community here believes that this is a good school."

Case Problem

From the facts listed below, create a news story release.

- Current date is April 29.
- Gretchen Freeman.
- 12 years old.
- Beach Elementary School.
- Sixth grade.
- Winner of regional speech contest in Columbia, South Carolina, April 27.
- First sixth grader to win.
- More than 100 entrants, grades 5 through 8.
- Now eligible for Southeast United States finals, May 28.
- Received $500 savings bond from Bank One.
- Second year she competed in the contest.
- Plans to be a lawyer.
- 641 North Inglewood Drive.
- Oldest daughter of Drs. John and Nancy Freeman.
- You are the school contact person.

> **Good leadership includes teaching and learning, building relationships and influencing people, as opposed to exercising one's power.**
>
> **— Max DePree**

References and Suggested Readings

American Association of School Administrators (1998, Summer). *The leader's edge—Effective media relations,* Vol. 2, No. 3. Arlington, VA: Author.

Annenberg Institute on Public Engagement for Public Education. (1998). *Reasons for hope, voices for change.* Providence, RI: Author.

Blair, J. (2004). *Building bridges with the press: A guide for educators.* Bethesda, MD: Education Week Press.

Carter, A. H., & Jackson, P. *Public relations practices, managerial case studies and problems* (6th ed.) Upper Saddle River, NJ: Prentice Hall.

Greenbaum, S. (1986). *Educated public relations: School safety 101 with engineering consent.* Sacramento: National School Safety Center.

Ordovensky, P., & Marx, G. (1993). *Working with the news media.* Arlington, VA: American Association of School Administrators.

Potter, L. (1996). *How to work with the media.* Tips for Principals. Reston, VA: The National Association of Secondary School Principals.

Wadsworth, D. (1998). Images of education. *The American School Board Journal, 185*(5), 40–43.

Watson, A. (1998). The newspaper's responsibility. *Phi Delta Kappan, 79*(10), 728–734.

Wilcox, D. (2001). *Public relations writing and media techniques* (4th Ed.). New York: Longman.

8

Mentors, Volunteers, and Other Community Supporters

Why Involve Volunteers, Mentors, and Community Members in the Schools?

♦ Although the number of families with school-age children is decreasing, the number of senior citizens is increasing.

♦ Volunteers are excellent sources of knowledge and experiences that children and older students should benefit from as part of their learning.

♦ Many children are growing up in nontraditional family settings and the experiences with mature citizens could be beneficial to them.

♦ Many volunteers and mentors have indicated that they were rewarded from their experiences as much as the students were from having had time with a volunteer and/or a mentor.

In this era of reduced financial and human resources, school principals are constantly looking for ways to get support for their schools. One of the widest ranges of support may come from the volunteers who are available to help at the schools. School volunteers may come from every walk of life and from every part of the school district. They may be young, old, male, female, retired, working, professional, or just interesting people. Volunteers in the elementary schools can be high school students, college students, senior citizens, community members, and parents. According to a Gallup poll, nearly half of all teens and retirees spend at least four hours a week doing volunteer work. But some students are challenging the idea of mandatory volunteerism. Some school districts, like Bethlehem Pennsylvania, have developed requirements that each student must complete 60 hours of community service work before graduation (*Executive Educator*, 1994).

213

Volunteers at the middle/junior and high school levels are mainly parents of students, or community members, business partners, and retired citizens.

Mentors

Mentors serve as positive role models to students who need another adult in their lives to help them set goals, attend school regularly, realize the importance of a high school diploma, and get their lives on track. Mentors offer encouragement and a listening ear, help with homework, offer life advice, and serve as a role model. Mentoring programs are known by several titles. In Brevard County, Florida, and all of the 67 Florida counties, the school district's mentoring program is known as "Take Stock in Children Mentor Program." This statewide scholarship program targets students with a financial need and a desire to succeed. Mentors to the students encourage and guide students throughout high school as their role model, personal cheerleader, and, most of all, as a friend to the student. Mentors are expected to spend a minimum of 30 minutes a week at the schools during regular school hours. Students are expected to meet with their mentors each week, maintain at least a 2.5 grade point average (on a 4.0 scale), and stay away from drugs and alcohol. Those who succeed get a full scholarship to a community college and then go to a four-year state college or university. The program in Brevard County, Florida, is unique because it promotes long-term relationships and has one of the highest success rates in the state.

Mentors and volunteers in the state of Florida are required to complete a comprehensive application form that may include a criminal history check. A prior criminal record may result in disqualification for volunteering or mentoring.

The Brevard County School District conducts recruitment activities for citizens who might be considering becoming mentors. A successful approach used by the district is to offer a free luncheon at sponsoring restaurants. The restaurants are supporters of the district and also provide the meals for those attending the information sessions.

Some school districts, such as the Sacramento City Unified School District, provide monetary grants to support mentoring programs. The Juveniles at Risk program in Sacramento has seen three of four students go on to receive their GEDs. The impact the mentors have had on the lives of students has been significant and can be seen in the success of the students.

The parent resource person at Lovell Elementary School in Apopka, Florida, developed a mentoring plan at the school. She, and the community relations administrator for Sprint, developed a mentoring program between third-grade students and Sprint employees. With the assistance and support of the school's principal, Teresa Johnston, the program was developed for every at-risk third grader at the school. In addition, each of the five of the third-grade classrooms has been adopted by a department of Sprint. The mentors help the children with math facts and listen to them read. In addition, students share news about their classes and projects with their mentors via e-mail on a weekly basis. Students visit the Sprint facility to observe what their mentors do at work. Sprint will donate computers to the school. One computer will be given to parents, via a drawing at the end of the year, from those who participate in school meetings or events. Other computers will be donated to the school for students' use.

Volunteers

As the need to establish order, purpose, and a sense of direction in a volunteer program was determined, several members of the Southington, Connecticut, Public Schools community formed a committee that developed a *School Volunteer Program Handbook*. The 12-member committee, under the leadership of an elementary school principal, Dr. Tom Gramitt, met several times throughout a school year and produced the handbook, which was distributed to key members of each school's program. In addition to establishing the goals of a school volunteer program, the handbook contained information about identifying, selecting, assigning, orienting, and training the volunteers. It also included details about the legal coverage of volunteers, keeping track of the time contributed by each volunteer, how to terminate an unsuccessful volunteer, and giving volunteers recognition for their services. The committee recognized that a thoughtful evaluation of the volunteer program was needed by everyone involved—volunteers, teachers, support staff, and administrators.

The *Southington Volunteer Program Handbook* included samples of forms, letters, recognition materials, and a reference list of related articles and materials. The committee's efforts ensured that a strong volunteer program would be developed in the system's schools—and it did!

Volunteers can be recruited in a number of ways. One of the most commonly used techniques is an announcement, or request, in the principal's newsletter. Some elementary school principals recruit volunteers by distributing a sign-up sheet with students at the start of the school year. Other principals have recruited volunteers by making personal appeals at club meetings, PTO/PTA meetings, senior citizen centers, or grade-level meetings of parents. School district-level publications are also great recruiting devices for volunteers. Because these publications are generally distributed to all homeowners, the possibility exists to reach more potential volunteers. Even advertising in the local newspaper can bring positive results.

Dr. Patricia Ramsey, elementary principal at Orla Vista Elementary School in Orlando, Florida, includes a special request to parents to join the school's ADDitions School Volunteer program. Her initial request is embedded in her September message to parents in her newsletter to them. To aid potential volunteers, she provides a computer for them to sign up at the school's open house event. In addition, the name of the school's volunteer coordinator and contact information for her are included in another more detailed newsletter message.

Harriet Coleman, principal at Hunters Creek Middle School in Orlando, Florida, also includes an invitation for parents to become involved as members of the school's ADDitions program. She offers a few ways the person can help. "Volunteers support the work of teachers and school staff by providing an extra pair of hands in meeting the needs of students," she states. "You could be a classroom assistant, clerical assistant, or tutor. The opportunities for you to become involved are endless." Ms. Coleman's personal appeal at the school's open house always results in people signing up to help. She has the school's ADDitions coordinator available to meet with parents at the open house event.

Principal Lori Kinney of Mark Twain Elementary School in Centennial, Colorado, refers to the school's volunteers as VIPS—Volunteers in Public Schools. Specific ways that parents and others can get involved in the school are detailed in the parent–student handbook.

In some cases, people may respond to an appeal to volunteer in a school, but they don't know how they can help. The Southington Public Schools developed a 12-page *Southington School Volunteers* pamphlet, which is given to every potential volunteer. The purpose of the pamphlet was to acquaint the person with the program's goals and related procedures. Volunteers are encouraged to ask questions and to offer suggestions to enhance and improve the volunteer program.

Volunteers can be a valuable resource by helping with a variety of tasks in the school under the direction of a coordinating team. This responsibility should be delegated by the principal to a team of volunteer and parent coordinators. Teachers retain responsibility for programming and evaluation, whereas the volunteers provide a work force for projects and individual sessions.

The volunteer program is based on well-established volunteer management principles that combine decentralized management of volunteers with centralized coordination, In other words, all school staff members can be directly involved with volunteers, but a consistent schoolwide approach is ensured by two key types of leaders, the parent and staff coordinators. These coordinators see that staff members and volunteers receive the recognition and support required to operate the program successfully. This structure, along with careful attention to evaluation and planning, maintains quality and flexibility. What results is an effective, consistent program with a high degree of personal emphasis.

Before each school year ends, the teachers, support staff members, and administrators should review how the volunteers' services and talents supported the school's mission. Plans can be made to adapt those talents for the next school year. Perhaps two key questions can be asked in reviewing the volunteer program: "What kinds of needs do we have in the classrooms around the school?" and "What do we want to do that we can't do now?" The objectives of one school's volunteer program follow.

Objectives of the Apple Corps Program

- To help all children develop to their potential.
- To involve parents in their children's education.
- To stimulate parents' interest in their children's education and develop positive attitudes toward it.
- To use resource people from the community.
- To provide a wide variety of role models for students.
- To give teachers more time for planning, evaluating, motivating, and teaching to meet the students' individual needs more effectively.
- To acquaint the volunteer with the role and responsibility of the teachers.
- To acquaint the volunteer with the school's expectations of students, with the parent organization used at the school.
- To stimulate interest in the community to actively support public education.

– Rocky River, Ohio, Public Schools

The four goals of the Southington School Volunteer Program parallel those of the Beach School Objectives but are stated in a slightly different fashion.

Southington School Volunteer Program

1. To increase the educational attainment of children by assisting teachers so that they can provide more individual instruction by working directly with children in reinforcing instruction.

2. To enrich the curriculum, extend the horizons of children, and increase motivation for learning through the unique resources which volunteers can provide as they share their talents, abilities, and experiences.

3. To increase services to children through the use of volunteer help in media centers, offices, and with student activities.

4. To provide opportunities for interested community members to participate actively in the education process, thus strengthening school–community relations and public support of education.

– Southington, Connecticut,
School Volunteers Pamphlet, p. 2

An effectively functioning volunteer program produces benefits for the staff, the volunteers, the students, and the community. The benefits to each of the four groups are shown here.

Benefits of a Volunteer Program

To staff

- Better understanding of the community
- Better understanding of the children
- Increased familiarity with more parents
- More time for individual students
- More time for professional tasks
- Additional help for large projects

To volunteers

- Opportunities to contribute in meaningful ways
- Better understanding of the children
- Development of a closer relationship with staff members
- Opportunities to develop personal talents and skills
- Increased knowledge of the school's curricula, programs, and expectations
- Personal rewards from helping children learn
- Development of self-confidence

To students

- Wider contact with a variety of supportive adults
- Increased individual attention
- Broader variety of learning activities and aids
- Increased meeting of needs
- Developing a sense that education is important because several adults give of their time and talents

To community

- Stronger sense of togetherness
- Better understanding of a school's philosophy and policies
- Sense of pride and support for a school

The relationships among the participants in a school's volunteer program are found in the participant lines of communication.

Volunteer Program Participant Lines of Communication

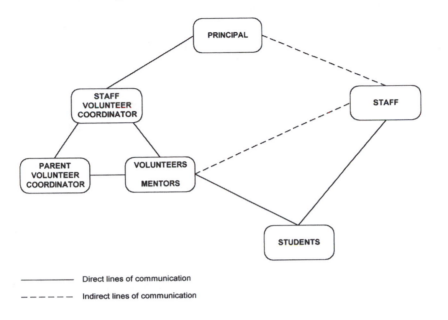

———————— Direct lines of communication

– – – – – – Indirect lines of communication

The Principal's Role and Responsibilities

The principal of a school has several key roles to play in the development of a successful volunteer program. First, the principal must foster an *open-door policy* in the school. That will send the signal that parents and members of the community are welcome in the school and are viewed as valuable resources to enhance the school's learning program. Second, the principal should set the tone for effective community relations with the school's staff. This can be done by sharing ways in which members of the community, serving as volunteers to the learning program, and can enhance the educational opportunities for students while supporting the teacher's role and responsibilities. The third responsibility of a principal is to allocate human and financial resources to support the volunteer program. A fourth role the principal must play is to plan the program with the leaders, introduce the program to the staff, and provide continuous support for the program throughout the school year. All of these call for *proactive* leadership from the principal.

The Teacher's Role and Responsibilities

Each teacher who wants to involve volunteers in the classroom must first identify the needs of the classroom. Teacher and student needs must be identified. The ways in which the volunteers can help, along with their responsibilities, must then be determined. Classroom needs must be communicated to the staff volunteer coordinator. Introducing the volunteers to the students, planning meaningful activities for the volunteers, and evaluating the volunteers' work are additional responsibilities of the teachers who use volunteers in the classrooms.

One caution that cannot be overstated: Volunteers need to be alerted to conflicts in the schedules they follow to help in the classrooms. For instance, if there will be assemblies, field trips, or testing activities on the scheduled times and days, that information needs to be shared, in writing, with the volunteers before the day of the change. In the event of a last-minute change of schedule, the volunteers should be telephoned with the information and invited to come to the school to help in another classroom or way. They should be given the opportunity to decline, though.

The Staff Volunteer Coordinator's Role and Responsibilities

This person should be a strong believer in and user of the school's volunteer program. One of the first responsibilities is to introduce and promote the volunteer program to the faculty and staff. Furthermore, the person has to be a supporter of effective community relations and be a provider of training in that area. One of the main responsibilities is obtaining volunteer requests from teachers and then, in conjunction with the parent volunteer coordinator, advertise the need for and request volunteers. After interviewing prospective volunteers, the coordinator matches and places the volunteers with teachers according to requests, skills, interests, and needs.

After checking with the teachers and volunteers to ensure that each placement and utilization plan is satisfactory, the volunteer coordinator needs to plan a time for each teacher and volunteer to meet and become familiar with one another. This time, usually 15 minutes, can be done before or after school hours or during the school day.

As the school year progresses, the staff volunteer coordinator serves as a communication link between staff members and volunteers regarding schedule changes or potential problems. Another ongoing role this person plays in the overall success of the volunteer program is in frequent contact with volunteers to provide positive feedback and to show interest in their efforts. Perhaps the most important task the staff volunteer coordinator, in conjunction with the parent volunteer coordinator, performs throughout the school year is to show appreciation to volunteers through thank-you notes, special functions, including recognition at the end of the school year, and perhaps a photo scrapbook album that records the volunteer activities for the year. Some schools are also including photos on the school's Web site of the volunteers working with students.

The Parent Volunteer Coordinator's Role and Responsibilities

The parent volunteer coordinator's primary role and responsibility is to assist the staff volunteer coordinator with organizing and implementing the volunteer program. Another important facet of this person's job is to create and maintain a positive feeling toward the program among the volunteers. Again, in conjunction with the staff, the volunteer coordinator schedules initial interviews with each potential volunteer, provides relevant information about the school's program to each volunteer, matches and schedules volunteers to meet each teacher's needs, confirms the schedule with each volunteer, and assists with the clerical training of each volunteer.

Other relevant and important tasks include regularly communicating with the volunteers to receive feedback and to provide encouragement and feedback. Another ongoing responsibility includes preparing materials for the volunteer program such as job descriptions, identification buttons, schedules, and handbooks, as well as updating volunteer hour records.

This person is a key in spreading the word about the usefulness of volunteering in the schools by presenting details to various community resources and agencies. Last, the appreciation shown to volunteers through a supportive attitude, positive notes, special functions, and the photo scrapbook are key functions of the parent volunteer coordinator.

In recent years, because of isolated incidents of child abuse, many states have passed legislation mandating that all adults who serve as volunteers or mentors, or who provide service to schools, but are not regular employees, must undergo criminal background checks and fingerprinting. To offset the costs of these expenses to the volunteers, many service organizations have either borne the total costs or assisted with them.

What Volunteers Can Do

One of the questions most frequently asked by potential volunteers is, "What can I do that would be useful?" A partial list of what a volunteer can do follows.

What a School Volunteer Can Do

- Assist students without evaluating them.
- Monitor student activities, drills, practice, or research.
- Tutor individual students.
- Listen to choral reading.
- Read stories to students.
- Assist in the media center.
- Assist with field day activities.
- Assist in the computer lab.
- Record tapes for a listening center.
- Work from home (typing, phoning, cutting of materials).
- Assist students in language experiences, especially English for speakers of other languages (ESOL) students.
- Provide clerical assistance in the office.
- Assist with special events, special arrangements, and field trips.
- Serve as club coordinator (crafts, stamp collecting, calligraphy).
- Share real-life experiences, that is, travel experiences and artifacts from the trips.
- Contribute other creative ideas not yet identified.

Two members of the Des Moines, Iowa, School Board pushed to have volunteers from each school contact the parents of the district's 32,000 students. Their goal was to increase parent involvement, leading to better student achievement. The volunteers, not teachers, would follow a script for the phone calls they will make during evening hours. Parents who work in the evening would be contacted at other convenient times. One board member, Connie Boesen, indicated the school board members were planning to contact parents who don't have telephones and parents who don't speak English by using home visits and interpreters.

One successful approach that has been adopted in many elementary schools is the Grandparent or Adopt-A-Grandparent program. Both students and grandparents can realize many benefits from either of these programs. For instance, the children can benefit from the experience and wisdom of the older people. The grandparents will see themselves as needed and capable of meeting the needs or interests of the students.

Another effective strategy to incorporate the talents, interests, and experiences of senior citizens is through their involvement as resource speakers in schools at all levels. Middle schools often sponsor career fair days as a way to involve currently employed workers and retired workers in sharing details about their jobs.

Ways Volunteers Can Help at the Secondary Level

Although most school volunteer services are used at the elementary school level, they can be effective workers at the secondary level. One-on-one communication can go a long way to keep students from failing or dropping out of school. In Milwaukee, Wisconsin, the One-on-One Teen Initiative is designed to promote educational achievement, improve possibilities for economic self-sufficiency and expand career options for students at risk of failing or dropping out of school. Each Milwaukee mentor develops a link with a selected teenager and helps that youngster by coaching, motivating, instructing, sharing, planning, listening, and caring. In addition, there are other ways volunteers can help students at the secondary level. Some ways this can be done are shown on page 224.

Eight Components of a Successful Volunteer Program

A review of several successful volunteer programs has resulted in the identification of eight key components:

- Identify needs
- Recruit volunteers
- Interview potential winners
- Match needs with abilities; develop schedules
- Train the volunteers
- Stress teamwork and retention
- Show appreciation and recognition
- Evaluate and make adjustments

Identify Needs

The needs of teach teacher who is interested in having the services of a volunteer in the classroom must be determined. As those needs are identified, each student for whom the teacher is responsible must be thought of as well, for each of them will have specific needs a volunteer might be able to meet. The needs of a teacher and the needs of each student should match the overall needs of the school. A sample volunteer request form, to be completed by interested teachers, is found on page 225.

Ways Volunteers Can Help at the Middle and High School Levels

- Assist students without evaluating them.
- Volunteers who are native speakers from other countries can give ESOL students extra practice.
- Volunteers can be available in guidance offices to help students with questions about careers or colleges or universities.
- Volunteers can serve as resource people for social studies units.
- Volunteers can help students use library resources and assist with research projects.
- Volunteers can help teachers gather resources for units of study.
- Volunteers can tape record textbooks so that students who have reading problems can listen to a cassette as they read their assignments.
- Volunteers can prepare tactile materials for visually impaired students, using large-print typewriters and Brailling machines.
- Volunteers can assist in science, math, and computer laboratories.
- Volunteers can assist in vocational classrooms and laboratories.
- Volunteers can accompany the school chorus and help build sets for school plays and performances.
- Volunteers can share collections or discuss careers, travels, hobbies, and other areas of special knowledge.
- Volunteers can assist with audio-visual equipment maintenance and the production of video cassettes and other A-V products.
- Volunteers can help students who were absent to make up missed work.
- Volunteers can help supervise students who are taking tests.
- Volunteers can demonstrate a variety of artistic abilities.
- Volunteers can assist in organizing a career exploration day or week.
- Volunteers can assist with clerical duties in the office or media center.

Sample Volunteer Request Form

VOLUNTEER REQUEST FORM

If you are interested in obtaining volunteer assistance, fill in this form and return it to the staff volunteer coordinator's mailbox at your earliest convenience.

TEACHER: _____   DATE: _____

GRADE/SUBJECT AREA: _____   ROOM: _____

Type of volunteer assistance needed: _____

_____

_____

_____

_____

Days and times volunteer assistance is requested:

	MON	TUES	WED	THURS	FRI
8:00 AM – 9:30 AM					
9:30 AM – 11:00 AM					
11:00 AM – 12:30 PM					
12:30 PM – 2:00 PM					
2:00 PM – 3:30 PM					

COMMENTS: _____

_____

_____

If the volunteer is not needed all year long, please indicate the time period.

_____

_____

Recruit Volunteers

The recruitment of interested volunteers is an ongoing process. After conducting a needs assessment of the school and individual teachers, the next component of the total program is the *recruitment* of volunteers. The recruitment of volunteers is the first of the 3 Rs of a volunteer program.

Recruitment 3Rs

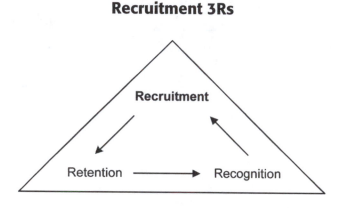

Some educators say the most effective recruiting is done by *satisfied, happy volunteers.* Some of the effective volunteer recruitment methods used by schools that have been mentioned earlier are the following:

Strategies to Recruit Volunteers

- School newsletter
- Staff recruitment
- Personal invitation
- School district newsletter
- Phone calls
- Open houses
- Invitation letter from the principal
- Word of mouth
- Local newsletters
- Community agencies
- Junior/senior high service options
- University/college students

Some important steps to follow in the recruitment of volunteers include these:

- *Identifying potential sources of volunteers* such as parents, senior citizens, and members of community organizations
- *Planning the recruitment* campaign to increase community awareness of the school volunteer program as well as to recruit volunteers

◆ *Coordinating the campaign with other school/community activities* to include back-to-school publications and activities, PTA meetings, and community meetings

◆ *Designing publicity materials* such as newsletter items, fliers, brochures, and posters

Another important consideration in the recruitment of volunteers is to *involve everyone in the recruitment effort.* Teachers can make personal contacts with parents, current volunteers can approach their friends and neighbors, and children can deliver notes to nonparent volunteers.

Sample information and recruitment letters from school principals used to recruit volunteers are shown below and on pages 228 and 229.

Oak Park Elementary Recruitment Letter

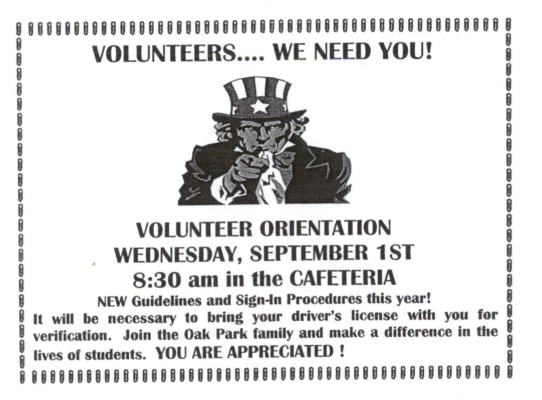

After the initial responses have been received from potential volunteers, some school principals send a follow-up letter to volunteers to determine the ways they can help. The follow-up letter and related materials used by the Southington, Connecticut schools and another school are shown on pages 230–233.

(Text continues on page 234.)

Urbin T. Kelley Recruitment Letter

URBIN T. KELLEY SCHOOL
501 Ridgewood Road

Dear Parents:

It's back to school again and we need you! We need you to assist in the classrooms, work in the media center, and to serve as resource speakers.

We welcome back volunteers from previous years and extend a hearty welcome to all new volunteers.

Come when you can, stay as long as you like, work where you're needed and help us make this school year the best yet!

If you can volunteer some time, please fill in the form below and return to school as soon as possible.

We're waiting for you!

Try it — you'll like it!

Many thanks,

Kelley School Staff

Name _____ Telephone Number _____

Days Available _____

Time Available _____

Preference _____

    Classroom _____

    Media Center _____

    Resource Speakers _____

    Other (clerical, typing, etc.) _____

Urbin T. Kelley School Staff Letter

•   FOLLOW-UP LETTER   •

Dear _____:

      Thank you for your interest in our School Volunteer Program.

      Attached please find a School Volunteer Registration Form and a
more detailed explanation of the kinds of volunteer services we are
seeking. We hope that you will want to join with us in the exciting and
challenging work of education.

      We would appreciate your returning the registration form to the
school at your earliest convenience.

      You are invited to a School Volunteer Orientation meeting to be
held on _____ from _____ in _____. Even if
you are undecided about committing yourself as a volunteer, you are still
invited to this meeting.

      Please feel free to phone me at the school if you have any
questions.

                               Sincerely,

                               _____

                               Principal

- -

I will be able to attend this meeting. [ ]

I will not be able to attend this meeting. [ ]

I am definitely interested but cannot make this meeting. [ ]

(We will phone you to make arrangements.)

Signature _____ Phone _____

Principal's Follow-up Letter

•   FOLLOW-UP LETTER   •

Listed below are some of the things that a volunteer could do. Please
check what you would like to do.

Would you like to:	Yes	No
1. Check attendance		
2. Do housekeeping chores		
3. Prepare art supplies, bulletin boards, supplementary materials, transparencies		
4. Check objective tests		
5. Record test scores and grades		
6. Discuss careers or hobbies		
7. Collect money		
8. Compute statistical information		
9. Reproduce materials		
10. Prepare teaching materials		
11. Administer remedial drill work such as flash cards		
12. Help individuals and small groups in independent study and follow up		
13. Assist with music, drama, art		
14. Tell and read stories to children		
15. Listen to children read		
16. Type student books for Young Authors Program		
17. Assist on field trips		
18. Be a room parent to correlate classroom social activities, etc., and handle notices and appointments		
19. Assist in learning centers		
20. Set up learning centers		
21. Help contact parents		
22. Work in health room or media center		

Follow-up Letter Checklist

Listed below are some of the things that a volunteer could do. Please check what you would like to do.

Would you like to:	Yes	No
23. Practice vocabulary with non-English-speaking students		
24. Make instructional games		
25. Play instructional games		
26. Help with book fairs		
27. Reinforce Dolch words		
28. Make props for plays		
29. Help children learn to type		
30. Teach children to sew, knit		
31. Help with cooking projects		
32. Set up experiments		
33. Visit a sick child at home		
34. Work with a handicapped child		
35. Help young children with walking on a balance beam, jumping rope, or skipping (motor skill problems)		
36. Reinforce learning of alphabet		
37. Reinforce recognition of numerals		
38. Drill recognition of color words		
39. Play a musical instrument		
40. Help students who play instruments		
41. Make puppets		
42. Help with handwriting practice		
43. Drill spelling words		

School Volunteer Registration Form

• SCHOOL VOLUNTEER REGISTRATION FORM •

Name _____   Date _____

Address _____   Phone _____

Child's Name _____   Homeroom # _____

Person to be notified in case of emergency:

Name _____

Address _____   Phone _____

In which grade level would you be most interested?

First Choice _____   Second Choice _____

In which areas would you like to work? (See Kinds of Volunteer Services attached)

Please number in order of preference if you would like to work in more than one area.

Classroom Volunteer   Resource Volunteer _____

   a. Tutorial Aide _____   Library Media Center Volunteer _____

   b. Teacher Helper _____   Computer Volunteer

Clerical Volunteer   a. Tutorial _____

   a. Classroom _____   b. Clerical _____

   b. Media _____

   c. Office _____

On which days can you work? _____

Hours available   A.M. _____   P.M. _____

List below any skills, talents, hobbies or vocational experiences which may be helpful, such as typing, sewing, photography or any experiences in working with children.

Oak Park Volunteer Sheet

Dear Parent,

     Oak Park has many special activities and projects throughout the 2004-2005 school year that require participation and help from parents and community. Please consider the opportunities listed below and check the appropriate program or programs in which you are interested. A teacher or volunteer coordinator will contact you with information concerning the items you checked.

     Thank you for becoming involved and making Oak Park a terrific school.

Kathy Smith
Academic Specialist,
Volunteer Coordinator

*****PLEASE PRINT*****

Name _____   Home Phone _____

Student Name _____   Cell Phone _____

Grade _____   Teacher _____   Work Phone _____

_____ Homeroom Parent	_____ Assist with Book Fair
_____ Assist with classroom parties	_____ Parent Teacher Organization
_____ Field Trip Chaperone **	_____ Teacher Appreciation Week
_____ Book Publishing	_____ Office/Library Helper
_____ Math Superstars	
_____ Assist with Vision and Hearing Screening	
_____ Mentor (work with a particular student throughout the year)	

_____ Homeroom Parent may have access to my phone numbers.

The County Volunteer Application **must be on file and approved prior to attending a field trip as a chaperone.

Interview Potential Volunteers

Once potential volunteers have been identified, the next step is to interview each volunteer who has not served at the school. The interview does not have to take a long time—15 minutes seems to be the consensus of those chairpersons who have performed them. The purpose of the interview is to provide the potential volunteer an opportunity to ask questions about the program, to visit the school setting, and to remove any uncertainties before getting involved in the program. Generally speaking, the staff and parent volunteer coordinators conduct the interviews. The interview responsibilities of the staff volunteer coordinator are listed here:

Interview Responsibilities of the Staff Volunteer Coordinator

- Help the volunteer feel at ease with an informal chat.
- Orient each volunteer to the school. Provide job descriptions (clerical assistant, classroom assistant, media assistant, computer assistant, or tutor) and briefly discuss each one.
- Discuss what each volunteer's interests are and the amount of time each is willing to spend in the school.
- Fill out the volunteer registration form.
- Introduce the file folder with schedules, emergency exits, and related procedures.
- Discuss the volunteer's code of ethics and need for confidentiality.
- Discuss identification procedures used at the school, such as wearing the identification badge, sign-in/sign-out procedures, and other specific procedures.

The code of ethics just mentioned (and shown on the facing page) is an important aspect of a successful volunteer, mentor, or community involvement program.

The second key person's responsibilities, those of the parent volunteer coordinator, for a successful interview are also shown on the facing page.

The value of the individual interview cannot be minimized as a school looks for volunteer help. The important points to remember are to ask the right questions, to allow ample time for each potential volunteer to answer every question thoroughly and thoughtfully, and for those conducting the interview to be effective listeners.

Volunteer's Code of Ethics

- Classroom work is always confidential and is to be kept between teacher and volunteer.
- A volunteer is an assistant; the teacher's judgment is final at all times.
- Volunteers should be prompt and dependable. The volunteer program will work well when all the people show up at all times.
- A volunteer sets an example by appearance and behavior.
- A volunteer does not compare one child to another, or one teacher to another.

Interview Responsibilities of the Parent Volunteer Coordinator

- Assist in helping make each volunteer feel at ease and comfortable.
- Support the need for confidentiality and regular attendance.
- Encourage each volunteer to think of ways the person can share other talents, interests, or skills with the students.
- Provide the tour of the school when needed.

Match Needs With Abilities and Develop Schedules

The goal of developing an effective volunteer program is met when the needs of the individual teachers, students, and the school are closely matched with the interests, abilities, and personalities of the volunteers. The schedules of teacher needs and volunteer availability need to be determined. The schedules should be shared and confirmed with teachers and volunteers and also be posted in the school's work area. Also, volunteers should have a time sheet to record the time they contribute to the school each time they volunteer. A sample form used by the Southington, Connecticut, Schools is shown next. Many schools and school districts use the information for annual reports of volunteer hours contributed to the school district. Also, many volunteers receive special recognition plaques, certificates, or other awards for the service they render to a school and the school district.

School Volunteer's Time Sheet

VOLUNTEER TIME SHEET

NAME _____   ADDRESS _____   PHONE _____

Please write the <u>NUMBER</u> of hours (to nearest 1/4 hour) in the appropriate column and <u>TOTAL</u> for the day. Thank you!

<u>EXAMPLE</u>:   If you spent 3 hours doing classroom work and 2½ hours in the Media Center, put 3 under CLASSROOM, and 2½ under MEDIA, and 5½ under TOTAL.

DATE	CLASSROOM	MEDIA	CLERICAL	RESOURCE	FIELD TRIP	OTHER	TOTAL

Train the Volunteers

Once the matches of volunteers and teachers have been made, the success of the program depends on how well the volunteers are prepared to meet the challenges and responsibilities of their assignments. Much of the success of the program can be traced to the relationships that will develop between the individual teachers and their volunteer(s). Some suggestions for teachers who work with volunteers to consider are the following:

- ◆ Make sure work assignments are understood and agreed to by the volunteers.
- ◆ Remember, the volunteers' job is to help children practice a skill, not to teach the students a new skill.
- ◆ Share classroom routines and rules with the volunteers.
- ◆ Introduce the volunteers to the students. Have the students wear name tags until the volunteers knows the students' names.
- ◆ All volunteers should have name tags or badges to wear whenever they are working with students. Most schools have the name tags returned to the office area when not in use. See examples of some name tags that have been used at some schools.
- ◆ Explain, demonstrate, or model to the volunteers what is to be done. Remember, modeling is the strongest form of showing someone how to do something. Put the directions in writing.
- ◆ Show the volunteers where materials are located.
- ◆ Have a place for the volunteers to work.
- ◆ Be organized. Use volunteers' time effectively.
- ◆ Do not discuss confidential school issues with volunteers.
- ◆ Give feedback to each volunteer.
- ◆ If a problem develops with a volunteer, discuss the problem with the staff coordinator and try to resolve it early.
- ◆ Notify the staff coordinator if you do not require the services of the volunteer, with enough warning to allow for cancellation or rescheduling. Nothing turns volunteers way from a school faster than not being used properly at the school.
- ◆ Be understanding if a volunteer is occasionally absent. Notify the staff coordinator of persistent absences.
- ◆ Show appreciation whenever the opportunity presents itself.

Volunteer Name Tags

Stress Teamwork and Retention

The second R of a successful volunteer program is the *retention* of the volunteers.

Retention 3 Rs

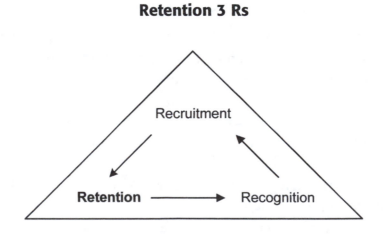

Volunteers continue to participate in a school's program if they feel their efforts and contributions do make a difference at the school. The individual teachers and support staff members can make that feeling become reality through their regular interactions with the volunteer. By realizing that each volunteer has specific needs that may be met through involvement in the school's volunteer program, a member of the professional staff can go a long way to enhance the personal beliefs of every volunteer. Some of the needs volunteers have are shown here:

- A feeling of personal worth
- A sense of belonging and need
- Contributing to an important cause
- A feeling of freedom to share ideas
- A sense of adequate training
- Ample opportunities to evaluate performance
- A sense of recognition
- Confidence in superiors
- A sense of pride in self and in the school
- A feeling of receiving honest communication

The attitude of the person who works closely with each volunteer—for the most part, that will be a classroom teacher—plays a large part in the success or failure of the volunteer program. The personal interactions of each faculty member with the assigned volunteer(s) are critical. The little things are often the ones that make the difference, including the following:

- Show an interest in the volunteer as a person.
- Make introductions to students and other faculty members.
- Give credit when it is warranted.
- Be available to talk with the volunteer.
- Say "we," not "I," whenever possible.
- Guide and direct the volunteer patiently and thoughtfully.
- Have students remember the volunteer on special days.
- Show appreciation continually.

Show Appreciation and Recognition

Although most volunteers don't serve a school to get recognized, it is a valuable responsibility each school *must* do at least once a year. The third of the 3 Rs of a volunteer program is *recognition.*

Recognition 3 Rs

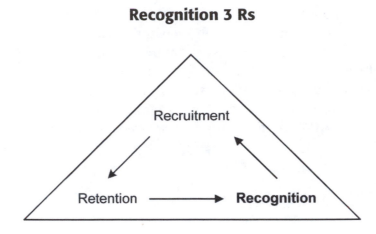

Retention and successful *recruitment* depend on the *recognition* that is given to *volunteers*. The success of a volunteer program takes place when volunteers develop a feeling of belonging. This feeling increases their desire to participate. A well-motivated volunteer derives satisfaction from helping the teachers, the students, and the school. Satisfied volunteers will spread good news about the school's volunteer program and help in the recruitment procedures.

A volunteer's pay is often a smile, some student-produced art work, a compliment from a child, or just a thank-you note from the faculty member. In addition to these informal day-to-day recognitions, there needs to be a planned program of formal recognition. Types of formal recognition used by the Southington, Connecticut, School District and other schools and districts include the following:

- Appreciation teas or similar events on an individual school or systemwide basis (see sample invitations)
- Articles in newsletters, newspapers, and in radio or television programs
- A school volunteer recognition week (usually in May of each school year)
- Thank-you notes from students and teachers (see samples)
- Letters of appreciation from the superintendent and principal (see samples)
- Certificates of service and appreciation
- Invitations to experienced volunteers to train new volunteers
- Sending volunteers to special conferences
- Letters of recommendation when volunteers request them

Principal Marilyn Sylvester of Longleaf Elementary School in Melbourne, Florida, expressed the school's gratitude for the many hours of volunteer service to her large elementary school at the school's Volunteer Recognition gathering. Ms. Sylvester identified the Volunteer of the Year as Kathi Wood. Ms. Wood received the special recognition because of the many hours of time she is at the school. Vicki Patterson, the elementary specialist at the school, said, "There is nothing she doesn't do for us. She is so incredible. She not only finds time for the children, but she recognizes when the staff is pressured and thinks of them too." The comments about Ms. Wood were featured in a newspaper article about the school's volunteer program.

Oak Park Volunteer Breakfast

> ## "Volunteers Take Time To Make A Difference"
>
> Dr. Betsy B. Butler requests the honor of your presence for a special breakfast for Oak Park volunteers.
>
> Date: 04/20/04
>
> Time: 8:30-9:30 am
>
> Oak Park Elementary
> Cafeteria
>
> RSVP by April 16, 2004
> to
> Kathy Smith, Elem. Spec.
> 269-3252 ext 3011
>
> WHERE EAGLES SOAR 03-04

A lasting memento of the volunteer's efforts at a school for each year can be recorded with photographs that become part of the school's photo album or scrapbook. Some schools also videotape or take digital photos of the volunteers while they are working with students or performing assigned tasks. Either way, a lasting record of the volunteers' contributions has been made. The digital photos can be added to a school's Web site to highlight the work of volunteers and used as a tool to recruit other volunteers, too.

(Text continues on page 243.)

Urbin T. Kelley Thank You Note

Urbin T. Kelley School
501 Ridgewood Road
Southington, CT   06489
Tel. # 628-3307

Dear Volunteers,

Our school year is coming to a close and with it another successful year with our School Volunteer Program.

This success is due to you and the hundreds of hours shared by so many generous volunteers — 172 volunteers and over 8,500 hours logged!

We send you our heartfelt thanks for your generous gifts of time, effort and concern for our children at Kelley School. The benefits are immeasurable.

We sincerely hope that you will consider sharing your time with us again next year.

Have a happy and restful summer.

The Staff at Kelley School

Oak Park Annual Vision and Hearing Screening

ANNUAL VISION and HEARING SCREENING

Last week we completed our school-wide vision and hearing student exams. This valuable program provides early detection and possible correction of problems that drastically effect a student's ability to learn. This process was quite successful in large part to the wonderful staff of Oak Park volunteers. Mrs. Smith would like to extend her sincere thanks to the following:

Mrs. Woloshin	**Mrs. Baxter**	**Mrs. Montgomery**
Mrs. Starr	**Mrs. Custer**	**Mrs. Smith**
Mrs. Logan	**Mrs. Tyson**	**Mrs. Strickland**
Mrs. Merrow	**Mrs. McNaughton**	**Mrs. Marple**
Mrs. Duggan	**Mrs. Bellemore**	**Mrs. Barett**

Mrs. Aranyos ... YOU'RE THE GREATEST!

Sample award certificates used by various schools follow.

(Text continues on page 248.)

School Volunteer Program Certificate of Recognition

School

SCHOOL VOLUNTEER PROGRAM

Certificate of Recognition

Name

Activity or Project

Very Special Volunteer Certificate

Making a point to say thank you!

---

is a

VERY SPECIAL VOLUNTEER

at

School

Date

Volusia County Volunteer of the Month Certificate

Teacher-Volunteer Recognition Certificate

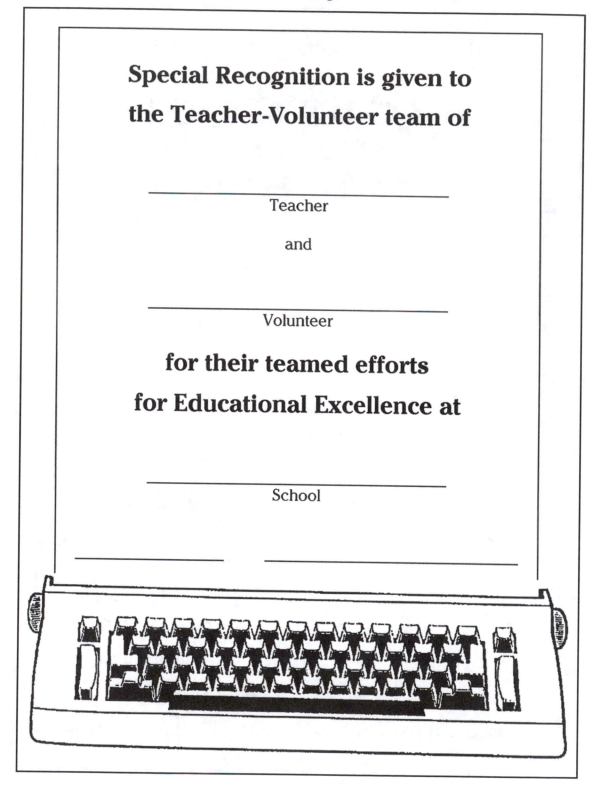

Special Recognition is given to

the Teacher-Volunteer team of

_____

Teacher

and

_____

Volunteer

for their teamed efforts

for Educational Excellence at

_____

School

Principal's Award for Excellence

Principal's AWARD For Excellence

To: _____

For: _____

*B*ecause of you our school is a better place to learn.

You have demonstrated through your actions

that one person can make a difference.

I applaud you for what you have accomplished

and look forward to hearing even more great things

about you in the future.

Given This _____ day of _____ _____

_____
Signature

Congratulations and best wishes!

Evaluate and Make Adjustments

The eighth and final component of an effective volunteer program centers on the evaluations of the program and adjustments that result from the evaluations. The most effective volunteer programs provide for evaluation and feedback from the teachers, the volunteers, and the students. Some schools use a suggestion box to receive anonymous ideas to improve the program. Other volunteer coordinators conduct individual interviews or hold small group meetings to discuss the program. The Southington, Connecticut, School District developed various forms to be used to evaluate the program. The volunteers evaluate the volunteer program using the Volunteer's Evaluation of School Volunteer Program form (p. 249).

Teachers or staff members evaluate the volunteer program (p. 251) and the volunteer assistance received (p. 250). Student evaluations are generally done through informal interviews with the teachers, the school volunteer coordinator, or school principal. The Southington program requires the school principal or staff volunteer coordinator to complete an evaluation form and annual report, which is a 20-question survey (pp. 252–253).

Other informal measures of the volunteer program's success can include:

- Some measurable indicators of success
  - The number of volunteers
  - The number of volunteer hours
  - The return rate of volunteers
  - The "dropout" rate
- Observations by the leadership team

If the volunteer program evaluation reveals it is not thriving, could it be that:

- You have not designed sufficiently meaningful jobs for the volunteers?
- Volunteer support and supervision is inadequate?
- There is staff resistance and nonsupport of volunteers?
- The volunteer incentive and motivation efforts need to be improved?
- The program has unrealistic goals—it is growing too quickly or too slowly?
- The interview and screening are ineffective because inappropriate people who will not last are admitted?
- Additional methods of recruitment need to be implemented?

(Text continues on page 254.)

Volunteer's Evaluation

VOLUNTEER'S EVALUATION OF SCHOOL VOLUNTEER PROGRAM

Thank you for your part in making the School Volunteer Program successful in our school. We would appreciate your answers to the following questions so that we can evaluate this year's program and improve the program for next year. You need not sign the questionnaire unless you want to.

1. How often did you serve?   _____

2. Describe briefly what you did as a volunteer: _____

    _____

3. Were you placed according to your interests and abilities?

    Yes _____ No _____   Comments _____

4. Did you meet with the teacher before starting your assignment?

    Yes _____ No _____

5. Did the teacher requesting your assistance prepare you for your assignment?

    Yes _____ No _____

6. Did the teacher inform the students of your role?

    Yes _____ No _____

7. Were needed materials provided for your use?

    Yes _____ No _____

8. Was a place provided for you to work? Yes _____ No _____

9. Did your principal and/or coordinator meet your needs in the areas of:

    Orientation _____   Information _____   Consultation _____

10. Were you made aware of the results of your work by:

    Principal and/or Coordinator _____   Teacher _____

    Other _____   No one _____

11. Are you interested in serving next year? Yes _____ No _____

12. Can you suggest ways in which we can improve the program?

    _____

    _____

School _____   Name _____
                                                      (optional)

Evaluation of Volunteer Program

TEACHER'S EVALUATION OF SCHOOL VOLUNTEER PROGRAM

Teacher's Name _____   School _____

Date _____

1. Have you used the services of a volunteer this year? _____

   If yes, was it: Regularly _____   Occasionally _____

2. How many volunteers did you utilize? _____

3. In what capacity?

   _____ Classroom Volunteer   _____ Computer Volunteer

   _____ Clerical Volunteer   _____ Media Center Volunteer

   _____ Resource Volunteer

4. How would you describe your rapport with the coordinator?

   Excellent _____   Good _____   Fair _____   Poor _____

5. In what ways have you benefited from utilization of volunteers?

   More planning time _____

   More time for individualization _____

   Improved classroom climate _____

   Preparation of classroom materials by volunteer _____

   Enrichment of existing program _____

   Other _____

6. What suggestions do you have to improve training of volunteers?

   Was on-the-job training provided for volunteers?

   Yes _____   No _____

   Should volunteers receive more training? Yes _____ No _____

   Other: Please specify _____

7. Do you plan to utilize volunteers next year?

   Yes _____   No _____

8. Do you have any additional comments? _____

   _____

Evaluation of Volunteer Assistance

TEACHER'S OR STAFF MEMBER'S EVALUATION OF VOLUNTEER ASSISTANCE

School _____   Volunteer _____

Teacher or Staff Member _____   Date _____

1. How often have you used the services of this volunteer this year?

   Regularly _____   Occasionally _____

2. Would you like to have this volunteer assigned to you next year?

   Yes _____   No _____

3. Does the volunteer have good rapport with adults?

   Yes _____   No _____

4. Does the volunteer have good rapport with students?

   Yes _____   No _____

5. To what extent has the volunteer increased your efficiency as a teacher in relationship to:

   a. Planning _____

   b. Pupils _____

   c. Professional Growth _____

6. Has the volunteer shown initiative in helping in the classroom?

   Yes _____   No _____

7. Do you feel the volunteer was given adequate training before his/her assignment?

   Yes _____   No _____

8. In what areas was he or she most helpful? _____

9. What are special strengths of this volunteer? _____

   _____

10. What skills or techniques were found most useful in his or her work?

    _____

11. Should the volunteer be encouraged to continue in the program?

    Yes _____   No _____   Why _____

12. What additional comments and suggestions can you make to improve the performance of this volunteer?

    _____

Evaluation Form and Annual Report
(p. 1)

SOUTHINGTON PUBLIC SCHOOLS

**PRINCIPAL OR SCHOOL VOLUNTEER COORDINATOR'S
EVALUATION FORM AND ANNUAL REPORT**

1. How many volunteers have participated in your program? _____

2. How many volunteers did you have to begin the year? _____

3. How many new volunteers were added to the program during the year? _____

4. How many volunteers dropped out of the program during the year? _____

5. How many volunteers wish to continue services next year?

    _____

6. How many staff members used volunteer help? _____

7. How many staff members have requested a continuation of volunteer services next year? _____

8. How many staff members do not wish continuation of volunteer services? _____

9. How many *new* requests for volunteer help have been received for next year? _____ (Do not include those from #7)

10. Were you able to obtain enough volunteers to fill all staff requests? Yes _____ No _____

11. How have volunteers been utilized within your school? Please list kinds of volunteers and numbers for each kind.

    _____

12. What has been the general reaction of the staff to volunteers?

    Good _____ Fair _____ Poor _____

    Comment _____

Evaluation Form and Annual Report
(p. 2)

13. Has volunteer service appreciably relieved staff of non-professional tasks? Yes _____ No _____

    Comment _____

14. Have volunteers established sound working relationships with staff? Yes _____ No _____

    Comment _____

15. Were volunteers given pre-service and on-the-job training?

    Yes _____ No _____

    Comment _____

16. Were volunteers given recognition for their services?

    Yes _____ No _____

    What _____

17. What is your reaction to the added responsibility of having volunteers in your school?

    Too much work _____ Great help _____

    Other (please explain) _____

18. Do you plan to continue the program next year?

    Yes _____ No _____ Undecided _____

19. What do you plan to do to improve the quality of the volunteer program next year?

    _____

    _____

20. How can the Assistant Superintendent for Curriculum & Instruction help in any phase of the volunteer program?

    _____

    _____

    _____

Summary

Successful school volunteer and mentor programs add much to the overall effectiveness of the school's instructional program. Knowledgeable and understanding volunteers and mentors are some of the school's strongest allies and spokespersons within the community. School personnel who follow the suggestions and ideas offered in this chapter have found many rewards for their volunteer programs. Dr. Tom Gramitt, retired principal of Kelley School in Southington, Connecticut, said, "Because of their involvement, parents and community members really feel like our school belongs to them. And, of course, it does."

The materials presented throughout this chapter have focused on how to involve parents and community members as volunteers and mentors in the learning program at each school. The vast amount of information presented can be restated as it is below.

Tips for Effective Volunteer and Mentor Programs

- Inform and get the commitment of the faculty and staff.
- Identify faculty and parent volunteer coordinators.
- Match volunteers' and mentors' talents and interests with school needs and jobs.
- Provide awareness sessions for faculty and staff.
- Provide training for volunteers and mentors.
- Find ways to involve as many volunteers and mentors as possible.
- Make volunteers and mentors feel welcome, needed, and appreciated.
- Maintain open lines of communication.
- Conduct an end-of-the-year evaluation and needs assessment.
- Show appreciation throughout the year and at the end of the year, too.

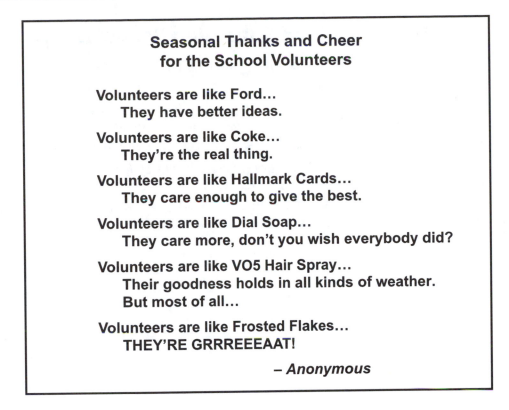

**Seasonal Thanks and Cheer
for the School Volunteers**

Volunteers are like Ford…
　They have better ideas.

Volunteers are like Coke…
　They're the real thing.

Volunteers are like Hallmark Cards…
　They care enough to give the best.

Volunteers are like Dial Soap…
　They care more, don't you wish everybody did?

Volunteers are like VO5 Hair Spray…
　Their goodness holds in all kinds of weather.
　But most of all…

Volunteers are like Frosted Flakes…
　THEY'RE GRRREEEAAT!

– Anonymous

The world has never been so rich in helpers as it is today, and consequently never have there been people so happy and blessed in their lives. Volunteers for human service seem to spring from the ground. It would be difficult to point out a more encouraging fact for the world's future.

– Minot Simmons

Case Problem

You have just been appointed to your first principalship. One of the goals you and the superintendent have agreed to accomplish during the school year is to improve the school's volunteer and mentoring program.

Develop an action plan to accomplish those goals. List the steps you would take, whom you would involve, and how you would evaluate the success of your efforts. If time permits, develop a recruitment item for your first newsletter to parents or for the school district's news bulletin. Use your creative talents to brainstorm ways you could reward and recognize the volunteers for their efforts.

References and Suggested Readings

_____ (1992). *The Forbes scrapbook of thoughts on the business of life.* Chicago: Triumph Books.

_____ (1994). Front lines. *The Executive Educator, 16*(6), 12.

Grammit, T. (1990). *School volunteer program handbook, Southington, CT.* Southington, CT.

Grammit, T. (1990). *Southington school volunteers: Working with children.* Southington, CT.

Underwood, E. (1974). *The Apple Corps: Beach School handbook for volunteer aides.* Rocky River, OH: Beach Elementary School.

Wisconsin State Department of Public Instruction (1991). *Families in education: Visions for the future* (No. 92054). Madison, WI: Author.

9

Crisis Planning and Management

The vast majority of schools in the United States are safe places for children to learn and grow. According to the *1999 Annual Report on School Safety* prepared by the U.S. Department of Education and U.S. Department of Justice (1999), most injuries that occur at school result from accidents, not violence, and most crime is theft, not violent crime. Although schools are still considered "safe," many of them have had to resort to metal detectors, photo identification name tags with bar coding, strategically located cameras, and school resource officers (SROs).

School district crises require special attention and special communication efforts. A crisis may include student disturbances, problems with employees, natural disasters (snowstorms, floods, tornadoes, or hurricanes), contagious illness outbreaks, manmade catastrophes (fire, bomb, kidnapping, shooting, or knifing), employee strikes, unexpected shutdowns of the school system or related services (power outage, disruption of water service, or transportation shutdown), and serious rumors. Some other specific examples of crisis situations that might occur at a school are:

- Gang-related violence
- Weapons
- Bomb threat
- Bullying
- Child protective order
- Death or suicide
- Armed person
- Hostage situation
- Arrests

- Fire and smoke damage
- Hazardous materials spills
- Power outage or gas leak
- Computer contamination
- Toxic mold
- Vandalism
- Robbery
- Medical emergency
- Lockdown

Each of these incidents requires an organized response from the educators at the school. It appears there are four basic steps to consider in handling an emergency situation.

> **Four Basic Steps in Handling an Emergency**
>
> ♦ Have a plan.
> ♦ Control the emergency or crisis.
> ♦ Communicate.
> ♦ Deal with the aftermath of the situation.

Many districts have added SROs to their schools. The SROs are charged with keeping the peace, mediating disputes, and handling traffic around the schools. They patrol the school's hallways and outdoor areas when students are present. The Georgia school systems of Gwinnett, Cobb, Fulton, and DeKalb Counties have had SROs in place for many years. These systems have their own police forces composed of sworn officers. The Atlanta Public Schools has a contract with the Atlanta Police Department to supply officers for its schools. In their dual role of investigator and confidant, they must use a great deal of common sense in working with school administrators, teachers, and involved students.

Have a Plan

Every school district, and every school within the district, needs to have a plan to guide the administrator and staff to respond in an orderly manner to a crisis. Without such a plan, when a crisis occurs, confusion and loss of credibility will likely result. More than likely, the situation will intensify if a plan has not been developed.

The key to an effective crisis management plan is structure. A crisis plan has to be simple, concise, and flexible. Although it can't answer all the questions that could arise, it should provide a framework to help guide the school through trouble. A comprehensive guidebook designed to help administrators prepare for, manage, and evaluate several site-based responses to various crisis situations, *A Critical Incident Planning and Development Guide,* was prepared by Larry Stevens (2002). The 183-page handbook contains valuable suggestions and scenarios to help the reader plan for critical incidents.

The crisis plan for a school must be easily understood, readily available, and practiced periodically. As the plan is discussed and planned, it is important that attention be given to the role of *all* staff members within the building, including secretaries, custodians, teachers, support staff, cafeteria workers, and volunteers and mentors. Ten basic questions should be considered at every level as a crisis plan is developed.

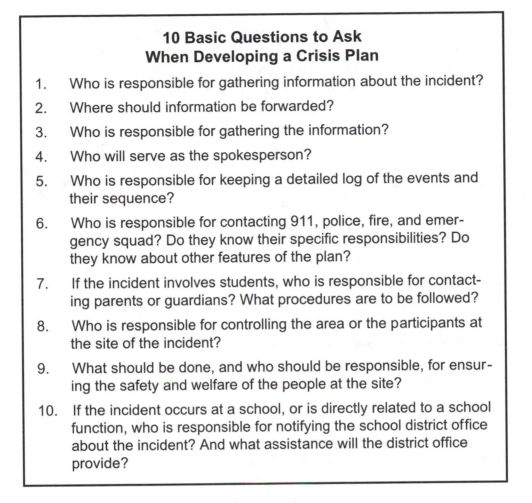

**10 Basic Questions to Ask
When Developing a Crisis Plan**

1. Who is responsible for gathering information about the incident?

2. Where should information be forwarded?

3. Who is responsible for gathering the information?

4. Who will serve as the spokesperson?

5. Who is responsible for keeping a detailed log of the events and their sequence?

6. Who is responsible for contacting 911, police, fire, and emergency squad? Do they know their specific responsibilities? Do they know about other features of the plan?

7. If the incident involves students, who is responsible for contacting parents or guardians? What procedures are to be followed?

8. Who is responsible for controlling the area or the participants at the site of the incident?

9. What should be done, and who should be responsible, for ensuring the safety and welfare of the people at the site?

10. If the incident occurs at a school, or is directly related to a school function, who is responsible for notifying the school district office about the incident? And what assistance will the district office provide?

Many school districts and individual schools have successfully used the services of a crisis team or committee. Once a situation has been designated as a crisis, a small group of people—ask for volunteers first—who have the knowledge and skills to act as troubleshooters and consultants are identified. At the school level, the crisis team might be composed of the principal, selected teachers, selected support personnel, nurse, custodian(s), and a secretary or recorder. If possible, a representative from the district office should be invited to serve on the team. At the high school level, one or more students could be invited to serve, too. In most cases, the members of the crisis team or committee move to serve in a new capacity as a member of the school's crisis response team. As Stevens (2002) pointed out, this team can meet with the principal to discuss a "possible response" to a crisis situation. This meeting would be a planning, or *what-if*, session. Another time to meet would be after a crisis situation, to develop plans to address the situation and to work with staff to help counsel people experiencing stress.

Once the team members have been selected and have agreed to serve, a meeting of the crisis team should be scheduled. The details of the plan and the roles and responsibilities of each member should be discussed *before* a crisis occurs.

The first task the crisis team or committee needs to tackle is to analyze the individual school's crisis needs. This can be done through a brainstorming session. Other faculty and staff members should also be given opportunities to share their ideas and concerns by responding to a survey. Their responses, and the frequency of the responses, will help the crisis team identify what other people feel could be crisis concerns. The use of Stevens's guide (2002) could serve as an organized, systematic method to organize a team, gather relevant data, and make relevant plans of action for all incidents.

Most school districts have been mandated by state law to develop districtwide and school-specific crisis plans. If that is the case, the major task will be to keep the information and procedures accurate and up to date.

All staff members should be involved in the planning (as they were by responding to the initial survey) and implementation of the crisis plan as well as in the practice of critical incident drills. A properly trained school staff is the best defense against a crisis situation. Stevens (2002) suggests that drills should be held periodically to streamline procedures and increase understanding of security measures.

For the most part, in a small school district the superintendent or his/her designee should be responsible for carrying out the details of the crisis plan. And, because the superintendent is ultimately responsible for what happens in a school district, the superintendent probably will want to be the spokesperson for the school district. In a larger school district, usually a person is employed to handle the details of implementing the crisis plan. In many cases, that person also acts as the spokesperson for the district. But whatever the size of the school district, the superintendent should be informed of proceedings and actions as they develop.

At the school level, and again depending on the size of the school and the number of other administrators available, the assignment of responsibilities will vary.

The crisis plan should contain the following items and information:

♦ The members of the crisis team or committee, with their current telephone numbers presented in a phone tree manner. In most cases, the principal is at the top of the responsibility tree.

♦ Thorough descriptions of what procedures are to be followed and who will perform them.

♦ A central point where all staff members who are not directly supervising students should report. This might be considered the crisis center; it needs to have a radio, telephone, and fax machine.

- A warning system that indicates the type of incident by letter or color, such as "A" means "hostage situation," or "Code Red" means "take cover or shelter-in-place."

- All possible tasks that the crisis team might be assigned. Each crisis team member should be assigned specific tasks but should know what all the possible tasks are. Classroom teachers should remain with their students and be responsible for them. All other people should be asked to help with answering phones, handling paperwork, or assisting wherever needed.

- Evacuation plans and procedures. Several evacuation routes should have been developed in the event one or more routes have been blocked. These plans and procedures should be part of an all school faculty discussion and possible walk through.

  I served as principal of several schools, and at least once a year at each school the custodian and I would block one of the designated exits that were used in a fire drill. Teachers were expected to have practiced what to do in that event with their students. The best procedure each faculty decided on to show the exit was blocked was for the lead students to hold up their hands above their heads. As other students saw those arms and hands raised, they did the same. No one was allowed to speak except the teachers, and when they saw the silent signal, they told their students to silently turn around and face in the opposite direction to hear new instructions.

- Communication plans and procedures should be in place and known to everyone. As part of the plan, a specific place to meet the media representatives away from the school site should be established. In some cases, a member of the crisis response team may be designated as the spokesperson to communicate with parents, relatives of school personnel, students, and the news media.

- Procedures for specific crisis situations. Each of the crisis situations mentioned earlier will identify areas that need to be more carefully addressed. The specific guidelines developed by the faculty and crisis team or committee should make dealing with that crisis easier.

- Frequent training and evaluations of the crisis plan. If all staff members are aware of expectations they have to do, and are aware of the crisis plan, they will have greater success in dealing with any and all crises. Stevens (2002) suggests having a training session at the start of the school year along with review sessions throughout the year. Of course, each member of the crisis team or committee should have a complete crisis procedure plan or, as Stevens refers to it, the CIP—crisis incidence plan.

♦ Plans and provisions to update information in the crisis plan should be made on a regular basis.

♦ TO GO boxes. According to Stevens, because principals are responsible for the security of their buildings, they should prepare TO GO boxes for any type of emergency. There should be at least two TO GO boxes at each school site. One box should be kept in the nurse's office, and one should be kept outside the school. Stevens suggests that the other one could be in the trunk of the principal's car. Someone should be assigned to keep the boxes current and stocked with necessary items. The TO GO boxes should contain the following items:

- Student rosters with emergency phone numbers and contacts

- Maps of the school building(s)—floor plans with room numbers and teachers' names, maps of gas and electrical shut-offs

- A copy of the crisis response plan

- Keys to all doors

- Flashlight with extra batteries

- Notebook and pen or pencil

- Self-sticking name tags and markers

- Teachers' phone chain

- Lists of students who need medication

- List of emergency numbers for gas, electric, and water companies, superintendent, and crisis services

- Cell phone (principal should have one at all times)

- First aid kit

- A few optional items: rubber gloves (blood pathogen protection), transistor radio and batteries, yellow caution tape, bull horn, and walkie talkies (Stevens, 2002, pp. 4–5)

Controlling the Crisis

Once a state of emergency or crisis has been declared, the crisis team is responsible for putting the crisis plan into effect. It is important to make sure the plan is operative and that these members of the crisis team assume their roles. One group of school district administrators suggests setting up a crisis headquarters to handle the details of the incident and ensuing activities (Kelly, Stimeling, & Kachur, 1989).

The value of the crisis plan will become evident once the crisis plan plays itself out. It will be important to remain calm in the face of turmoil, high emotion, and many rumors. By remaining calm, confidence in the school's ability to respond to the crisis will be evident, and those not involved in it will remain calm, too.

As the crisis unfolds, it must be constantly assessed, and priorities must be established. The most important decision school personnel must make regarding a crisis is the communications that will be developed.

Communicating

In that regard, the decision to plan an *offensive, proactive* or a *defensive, reactive* role with regard to the crisis must be made. With the offensive or proactive role, the school takes the initiative, provides the leadership and attempts to lead the crisis in an objective direction.

In the defensive, or reactive, role, a school district administrator or school principal has a number of choices to make. They include:

- Hope no one hears about the crisis (not likely!).
- Be reluctant to participate in it and hope the issue dies (the head in the sand technique; doesn't work!).
- Don't say anything unless someone wants to correct a fact (hear no evil, see no evil, speak no evil!).
- All of the above.
- None of the above.

When a crisis develops in a school district, saying a curt "no comment" to the news media is neither adequate nor appropriate. Rather, open and honest communication is necessary to reduce fears and dispel rumors. Tom Salter, a communication manager for the Alabama Department of Education, indicated that dispelling rumors is an important part of a communication plan in crisis situations. Quoting Winston Churchill, Salter (2003) said, "When the eagles are silent, the parrots begin to chatter. The only way to stop a rumor is to let the eagles scream." He suggested that the best way to do that is to keep the employees, parents, students, community leaders, and the public informed. Although face-to-face communication is the best strategy to use, Salter suggested posting information on the district's Web site as a means to inform large numbers of people. E-mail and fax messages will also reach other people. Wisely, he reminded readers that bus drivers, food service workers, and custodians must not be neglected.

With the offensive, or proactive, choice, the school administrator will be in a position to convey factual information, clarify the related issues, and lead the crisis dialogue. So, in a typical crisis, a school administrator should take the initiative and, with both their individual publics (internal, external, and key communicators) and the news media, use candor and honesty to convey their viewpoint (Harper, 1989).

Earlier, in Chapter 4, the importance and value of a network of key communicators was discussed. These valuable human links with the school community can disseminate factual, creditable information to the community. If the key communicators have been trained properly in advance, they can spread information and squelch rumors as they surface. The information can be conveyed to them initially and in follow-up conversations via a telephone tree. All of the facts that are known should be shared with each of the key communicators. The facts can also be shared with the key communicators via a fax machine—this method allows a written copy of the facts to be available for others to read, too.

In addition to the key communicators, all other channels of communicating with people during a crisis should be considered. Include in the communication efforts special faculty meetings, letters to parents, press releases, and special school board meetings. If possible, share information about the crisis with all of the members of the faculty and staff before any discussions are held with people outside the school(s). Not only does that tell them they are valued members of the school system, but it also expands the corps of well-informed representatives of the school system. This type of communication sharing can best be done at an emergency faculty and staff meeting held first thing in the morning or before people leave to go home at the end of the day.

At the individual school site, disturbing information about a crisis should be shared with students in individual classrooms rather than at a school assembly, because of the unpredictable reactions of the students. Internal communications about a crisis situation, when shared with students, should be prepared specifically for that purpose. That way all students will be ensured of getting the same, accurate information (Kelly et al., 1989).

Letters sent home to parents could be an effective, but slower, method of sharing information with the parents. In some cases, these letters can be used as summary statements after the crisis has passed.

Communications during a crisis are usually based on personal judgment. What is said or not said is a judgment call and will vary with every situation and community.

There is no one way to handle crisis communication with members of the media. If a school principal has communicated effectively with members of the media and the school community, levels of understanding and trust should be established. Well-established, good, productive relationships with local reporters will ensure more understanding and cooperation from the reporters when a crisis develops.

One of the primary considerations that must be dealt with in a crisis is distinguishing fact from rumor. The key communicator network can help with that, but an effort must be made to disseminate accurate information to the community as it is available. Rumors flourish in the absence of reliable information, so the best defense is to provide as much accurate information as possible to everyone. The job of gathering and verifying facts and channeling them through the members of the media and key communicators should be assigned to members of the crisis team.

The efforts of the media should not be controlled but rather enhanced through the sharing of as much accurate information as possible. Some school systems have included in their crisis plans places for the media to work as they prepare their stories.

In conclusion, the importance of establishing and maintaining the machinery of crisis communication before the crisis itself is an issue that cannot be emphasized enough.

Dealing with the Aftermath

Just as in any other action plan, a careful review of how everything went during the crisis should be done. Thus, no matter how smoothly everything went, by reviewing the plan of action you'll always be able to handle things better the next time a crisis occurs—and, unfortunately, another one will happen. The review of the crisis plan can occur during the crisis (done by a member of the crisis team) and must occur afterward.

As a result of a tornado alert and the ensuing confusion about what to do, the Richardson, Texas, Independent School District developed a notebook of procedures to handle crisis situations, including a flow chart and telephone lists. A committee of 30 people worked an entire school year to develop the Crisis Communication Notebook for distribution to each school in the district, the school board members, and key community organizations. A school district committee reviews the document annually.

In addition to reviewing the crisis plan, an *evaluation* of the plan should be conducted. A part of the evaluation should include an awareness and willingness to make changes in the plan if deemed necessary.

Also thoughts should be turned to identifying why the crisis occurred and what steps would be taken to prevent it from happening in the future. In some cases the prevention of a recurring crisis may be out of the control of the school, but the exercise of reviewing what was done as a result of, or in reaction to, the crisis situation should be conducted.

Another aspect of dealing with the aftermath of a crisis is working with the media to inform the community about what is being done as a follow-up to the situation. The relations previously developed with the media will have a great deal to do with the accuracy and thoroughness of the information shared by the media. So do the necessary groundwork and establish effective links with all aspects of the media as soon as possible. Maintain those relationships using the suggestions offered in Chapter 7.

An emotional reaction will often follow a crisis situation. Careful consideration should be given to determine the appropriate support services for the school staff, students, and parents to enable a return to normalcy. In recent years, many school districts have responded to the increases in crisis situations by developing crisis reaction teams. Members of these teams are school guidance counselors, psychologists, and other school personnel who have been trained to deal with the feelings and emotions of people who have been involved in a crisis.

A last suggestion is to extend thanks to the media, school personnel, parents, and the community for their cooperation and support during the crisis. The message can be delivered in person at gatherings of the groups, through a message in a school newsletter, or in a letter to the editor of the local newspaper.

Homeland Security Incident

In the fall of 2004, the United States Department of Education alerted school leaders to watch for people spying on their schools. This warning was based on the school siege in Russia where nearly 340 people were killed. That alert was coupled with a computer disk being found in Iraq with diagrams and photographs of some American schools. The information on the disk had apparently been downloaded from government Web sites. As a reminder, government officials urged school districts to improve the security of all buildings. Among the suggestions were installing locks on all doors and windows, having a single entry point into buildings, and ensuring that school bus drivers can be contacted in an emergency.

Schools as Emergency Shelters

During the fall semester of the 2004–2005 school year, many Florida school districts experienced the wrath of hurricanes. Because of the severe nature of the hurricanes, many citizens who lived in coastal areas were encouraged to evacuate their residences and move to shelters provided throughout the school districts. Many of those designated places were schools in the districts. Although Red Cross workers and others were assigned to the sites, the schools' principals were expected to be there, too. Although they volunteered for the duty, they had to be trained in helping where needed. Some of the schools were designated as "special needs" shelters to accommodate people of all ages with certain medical conditions. As a way of saying thanks to the people who helped her during the hurricanes, Dr. Betsy Butler, principal of Oak Park Elementary School in Titusville, Florida, wrote a letter of sincere thanks to the superintendent of schools, Dr. Richard DiPatri, for the help she received from many people. In her letter, those individuals were specifically identified so that their supervisors could later acknowledge the work they did. Each of the supervisors was sent a copy of the letter to the superintendent.

Elementary principal Carl Brown of Manatee Elementary School was the shelter manager for his school for the more than 850 people who came there. Mr. Brown and his volunteer supporters wore T-shirts that contained the message, "I stayed at the Manatee Hilton." To help those who were at the school, Brown also organized a talent show in which 15 or 16 acts entertained. Mr. Brown used a crisis situation to its best advantage by adding humor and a lighter approach to shelter operation.

Once the storms had passed and the shelters residents left, the schools had to be cleaned and readied for the return of teachers, students, and support staff.

> **If you fail to plan, you plan to fail.**

Summary

Throughout this chapter, the importance of developing a crisis plan before a catastrophe occurs has been stressed. Without such a plan, a school and the school system are in constant jeopardy. When a crisis erupts, the flurry of events will consume the time for reflection or deliberation. Don't rely on time being available to make spontaneous decisions—it probably won't be. Remember, a crisis situation could be a time for a major mistake to be made that could jeopardize a professional career and the reputation of a school or school system.

There are several ways to get a message across to the public during a crisis. Among them are the following:

- Prepare a short, concise message worded from the school district's superintendent and delivered by the superintendent or designated spokesperson.
- Issue a press release that includes the who, what, where, when, and why of the situation presented.
- Grant interviews or hold a press conference to meet reporters so they can get the quotes or sound bites they need.
- Develop a special link to the school district's home page for crisis-related situations. This can become the site for the facts and could also help to reduce the impact of rumors. In addition to the official statements from the school district, press releases can be added to the link.
- Write a letter to district residents to calm people's fears, to squelch rumors, and to direct parents and others to the appropriate school personnel.

Although no crisis plan can cover all possible contingencies, the discussion and suggestions presented in this chapter can improve the likelihood that you and your schools will survive a crisis without any long-term, lasting effects. With a thoughtful plan in place, a school and/or school district will be prepared to meet the challenges of effectively communicating with the media and ultimately the public during and after a crisis situation.

Case Problem

Since being reassigned over the summer months to be the principal at Sunburst Elementary School, Ellen Fleming has encountered one problem after another. Renovations to the building had begun with completion dates before the students arrived in August. As that date approached, Ms. Fleming realized that students and teachers would be coexisting with construction workers, noise, dust, and dirt. She knew it wouldn't be long before parents realized that their children, along with the school staff, were working in an unsafe situation.

Parents protested at the school, many attended school board meetings to confront the school board and superintendent, and some even withdrew their children from the school. Corrections and improvements were made to the school site, and everything seemed to be under control.

About two weeks after the December holiday break, Ms. Fleming arrived at school to find asbestos hazard signs and tape posted around part of the construction site. When parents arrived to drop off their children, they saw the newly posted signs. Word spread rapidly, and more than 125 students were withdrawn from the school.

Bob Blumberg, the school district's director of environmental services, said, "Principal Fleming knew in general what was happening at the school." However, he admitted that she had not been notified about the signs by the time parents began dropping off children at the school. Mr. Blumberg added, "From now on, we will try to notify Ms. Fleming by seven in the morning if there is anything done on asbestos abatement at the school the night before. We need to improve our communication—that's where the problem is."

Molly Merritt, a five-year member of Sunburst's school improvement committee, responded, "Ninety percent of these problems could be avoided if the county office would let the people know what is going on. They don't put children number one—they put the budget as number one. If that were not true, they would not have children on a construction site—this is an absolute disaster area! I have a real serious lack of trust."

Later that morning, Ms. Fleming received a telephone call from the newly hired school superintendent. She was being summoned to an afternoon strategy session. She was told to bring suggestions about how the school district should confront the new problem at Sunburst. What suggestions would you take to the meeting if you were Ms. Fleming?

> **Character is not made in a crisis—it is only exhibited.**
> *— Robert Freeman*

References and Suggested Readings

Blair, J. (2004). *Building Bridges with the Press: A Guide for Educators*. Bethesda, MD: Education Week Press.

Carter, A. H., & Jackson, P. *Public Relations Practices, Managerial Case Studies and Problems* (6th ed.). Upper Saddle River, NJ: Prentice Hall.

Harper, S. (1989). *School Crisis Prevention and Response*. NSSC Resource Paper. Malibu, CA: National School Safety Center.

Kelly, D., Stimeling, W., & Kachur, D. (1989). Before worst comes to worst, have your crisis plan ready. *The Executive Educator, 11*(1), 22–23.

Learning First Alliance (2001). *Every Child Learning: Safe and Supportive Schools* [Brochure]. Baltimore, MD: Author.

National School Safety Center, 4165 Thousand Oaks Blvd., Suite 290, Westlake Village, CA 91362.

Norris, J. (2004). *Safe Schools Initiative*. Group Dynamics & Strategy Training Associates, Inc. Available at norris_j@hcde.org

Salter, T. (2003). Nipping the rumormonger. *The School Administrator, 60*(7), 40.

Stevens, L. J. (2002). *A Critical Incident Planning and Development Guide: An Administrative Handbook*. Lanham, MD: Scarecrow Press.

U.S. Department of Education and U.S. Department of Justice. (1999). *1999 Annual Report on School Safety*. Washington, DC: Authors.

10

Assessing the Effectiveness of Your School–Community Relations Plan

One of the main characteristics of an effective school–community relations plan is the fact that it must include two-way communication. Earlier in this book (Chapter 2), an introductory discussion was presented about the types of two-way communication to use in a school–community relations plan.

This chapter refocuses attention on the topic and presents several methods used by school principals to receive that all-important feedback for the school. Among the strategies and techniques to use are: citizen, parent, and student groups of all kinds; key communicators; visits to and use of the school by parents and the public; questionnaires, direct interviews, and informal opinion surveys; parent-teacher meetings and visits; school board activities; use of the community power structure; and other miscellaneous techniques.

Citizen, Parent, and Student Groups of All Kinds

Most schools have developed *citizen advisory committees* as decisions are made about the school. The feedback from members of the committee (teachers, parents, community members and/or business partners, and perhaps students) can be very valuable. The leaders and members of the *parent–teacher organization* (either PTA, PTO, or PTSO) can provide relevant information about the effectiveness of the school's instructional program. *Small group meetings* of invited parents, held either in the school or in the homes of students, have proven to be effective. This approach is effective because the small number of participants (no more than 20) allows more active participation by those attending. A sample of a request form used at an elementary school follows.

Beach School Coffee with the Principal

Beach Elementary School
Rocky River, Ohio

COFFEE WITH THE PRINCIPAL

I am interested in hosting a coffee _____

    Check one: Day _____

                      Evening _____

    Which day of the week? _____

I am interested in attending a coffee _____

    Check one: Day _____

                      Evening _____

    Which day of the week? _____

I have already attended a coffee, but if numbers permit,
I am interested in attending again _____

    Check one: Day _____

                      Evening _____

    Which day of the week? _____

Name _____   Phone Number _____

You will be contacted by your host or hostess as to the specific date.

▸ **PLEASE RETURN TO YOUR CHILD'S TEACHER** ◂

Other meetings, such as *focus groups,* arranged as the need to have them is identified, can be sources of additional information.

Newsletters sent from the principal, a classroom teacher, or the school district can include brief feedback requests on a monthly basis or at the end of the year. Several survey forms used at the elementary school level, but adaptable for use in middle in high schools, follow.

(Text continues on page 289.)

Gotsch Parent Newsletter Survey

PARENT NEWSLETTER SURVEY

I would appreciate your taking time to answer these few questions regarding the Gotsch Principally Speaking newsletter. Please return this survey to the Gotsch office by May 13th.

1.   What do you LIKE about Principally Speaking?

    _____

    _____

    _____

    _____

2.   What TOPICS would you like to see in next year's editions?

    _____

    _____

    _____

    _____

3.   General suggestions and/or comments regarding the newsletter:

    _____

    _____

    _____

    _____

THANK YOU FOR YOUR INPUT!

PAM SYLVARA, PRINCIPAL

Grant Street Elementary Report Card
(p. 1)

GRANT STREET ELEMENTARY REPORT CARD

School evaluation is an ongoing process. We have just completed our self-study this school year and, from that assessment, have established school goals. These goals will be our guide to future school improvement for all aspects of our program. Along with our goals we need continual input from the parents affiliated with Grant Street Elementary.

Two years ago, parents completed a report card on our progress as a school. We received a tremendous amount of constructive data and incorporated that information into our self-study. Since evaluation is ongoing, it is time for another **Grant Street Report Card**!

In filling out this survey, please generalize from your own knowledge, your child's experiences, and what you hear about the school. We understand that everyone has a different knowledge base, but that is what makes this tool so powerful and helpful. Be assured that all ratings and comments will be carefully reviewed and will become the foundation for future school goals.

Directions: Circle the response which most clearly represents your feelings.

1. GRANT STREET ELEMENTARY has an orderly environment.
    A. Strongly agree   B. Agree   E. No opinion
    B. Disagree   D. Strongly disagree

2. The curriculum, instruction, materials, and methods meet your child's needs.
    A. Strongly agree   B. Agree   E. No opinion
    B. Disagree   D. Strongly disagree

3. GRANT STREET ELEMENTARY is organized effectively.
    A. Strongly agree   B. Agree   E. No opinion
    B. Disagree   D. Strongly disagree

4. My child looks forward to going to GRANT STREET ELEMENTARY each day.
    A. Strongly agree   B. Agree   E. No opinion
    B. Disagree   D. Strongly disagree

5. GRANT STREET ELEMENTARY is helping teach children to be responsible citizens.
    A. Strongly agree   B. Agree   E. No opinion
    B. Disagree   D. Strongly disagree

6. School rules and regulations affecting students at GRANT STREET ELEMENTARY, both in school and on the playground, are reasonable.
    A. Strongly agree   B. Agree   E. No opinion
    B. Disagree   D. Strongly disagree

7. Teachers at GRANT STREET ELEMENTARY care about students.
    A. Strongly agree   B. Agree   E. No opinion
    B. Disagree   D. Strongly disagree

8. The administrative operation at GRANT STREET ELEMENTARY is good.
    A. Strongly agree   B. Agree   E. No opinion
    B. Disagree   D. Strongly disagree

Grant Street Elementary Report Card
(p. 2)

9. GRANT STREET ELEMENTARY students are challenged academically and staff has high expectations for student success.
    A.   Strongly agree   B.   Agree   E.   No opinion
    B.   Disagree   D.   Strongly disagree

10. The homework assigned GRANT STREET ELEMENTARY students seems appropriate to the grade level.
    A.   Strongly agree   B.   Agree   E.   No opinion
    B.   Disagree   D.   Strongly disagree

11. Parents receive adequate information regarding their student's progress and happenings at school.
    A.   Strongly agree   B.   Agree   E.   No opinion
    B.   Disagree   D.   Strongly disagree

12. Food service and bus service are good for GRANT STREET ELEMENTARY students.
    A.   Strongly agree   B.   Agree   E.   No opinion
    B.   Disagree   D.   Strongly disagree

13. Changing the students' school day schedule at GRANT STREET ELEMENTARY to begin at 8:00 AM and dismiss at 2:00 PM to reduce student travel time on buses is reasonable.
    A.   Strongly agree   B.   Agree   E.   No opinion
    B.   Disagree   D.   Strongly disagree

14. If you were a staff member at GRANT STREET ELEMENTARY, what would you change?

    _____

    _____

    _____

    _____

15. Additional comments.

    _____

    _____

    _____

    _____

Overall, how do you feel about the quality of education your child receives at GRANT STREET ELEMENTARY:

A   B   C   D   F

Please return this report card to school by June 1, 1989. A returned report card is good for one pencil inscribed with "Grant Street Elementary" on it!

Baturyn "A Few Minutes Please…"
(p. 1)

A FEW MINUTES PLEASE . . .

That's all it will take to answer these questions. In order to receive parent input into school programs and policies, we need your help.

Please take the necessary time, now, to fill in this question-naire and have your child return it to school.

Please fill out one form for each child.

1. Students are given the grades A, B, C, D, and F to denote the quality of their work. If this school was graded in the same way, what grade would you give Baturyn — A, B, C, D, or F?

    _____

    Comments: _____

    _____

2. What do you think are the biggest problems with which Baturyn School must deal?

    _____

    _____

3. What things does your child like most about Baturyn School?

    _____

    _____

    _____

4. What things does your child like least about Baturyn School?

    _____

    _____

    _____

5. What things do you like most about Baturyn School?

    _____

    _____

    _____

Baturyn "A Few Minutes Please…"
(p. 2)

6. What things do you like least about Baturyn School?

    _____

    _____

    _____

7. Do you feel we should continue to recognize student excellence in citizenship through Proshu Awards?

    _____

    _____

    _____

    _____

8. Do you think the school curriculum at Baturyn needs to be changed to meet today's needs or do you think it already meets today's needs?

    _____

    If you feel the school curriculum needs to be changed, then in what ways do you feel it needs to be changed?

    _____

    _____

    _____

    _____

9. Here's an idea to improve Baturyn School: _____

    _____

    _____

    _____

10. Additional comments you wish to add would be appreciated. _____

    _____

    _____

    _____

    _____

    Many Thanks!
    Principal

Port Orange 2001–2002
Parent Questionnaire (p. 1 of 5)

PORT ORANGE ELEMENTARY SCHOOL'S
2001–02 PARENT OPINIONNAIRE

In order to help us evaluate our school program this year and to plan for next year, we need to know what you think and how you feel about Port Orange Elementary. Please share your thoughts with us by completing this survey and returning it to school by **April 24, 2002.**

The comments on each form will be read and considered so please communicate openly with us. We want to hear both the pros and the cons because that helps us make necessary changes. You do not need to sign your name, but you may if you like. **COMPLETE ONLY ONE QUESTIONNAIRE PER FAMILY. WHEN PUTTING COMMENTS, PLEASE PRINT OR WRITE LEGIBLY.**

1. Indicate the number of children you have in each grade.

    _____ K,   _____ 1,   _____ 2,   _____ 3,   _____ 4,   _____ 5

2. If you are satisfied with the instruction provided in the following areas, check **Yes**. If you are not, mark **No**. If you don't have enough information to make a judgment, mark **Don't Know**. Please check only the columns in which you have children. **RESPOND TO ONLY THOSE ITEMS THAT APPLY.**

Area/Grade	Kindergarten			Grades 1 - 2			Grades 3 - 5		
	Yes	No	Don't Know	Yes	No	Don't Know	Yes	No	Don't Know
Reading									
Mathematics									
Phonemic Awareness									
Creative Writing									
Spelling									
English/Grammar									
Science/Health									
Social Studies									
Art									
Music									
Physical Education									

3. In general, how would you rate the education your child has received this year?

	Excellent	Good	Fair	Poor
Kindergarten				
Grade 1				
Grade 2				
Grade 3				
Grade 4				
Grade 5				
Resource ESE				
Resource Gifted (K-1)				
Art				
Music				
Phys. Ed				

COMMENTS:
_____
_____
_____
_____
_____
_____
_____
_____
_____
_____

STUDENT CONDUCT/DISCIPLINE

4. How would you rate the handling of student conduct in the following areas?

	Appropriate/ Fair	Inappropriate/ Unfair	Not Observed	Please Comment
Classroom				
Special Area				
Lunchroom				
Administration				
Bus				
Before School				

Port Orange 2001–2002
Parent Questionnaire (p. 2 of 5)

COMMUNICATION WITH SCHOOL PERSONNEL

5. In general, how would you rate your **communication** with the following?

	No Contact	Excellent	Good	Fair	Poor	COMMENTS:
Your Child's Homeroom Teacher						
The Principal, Mr. Ronca						
The Asst. Principal, Mrs. Fisher						
The Office Staff						
The Clinic Asst., Mrs. Emerson						
The Media Specialist, Mrs. Britton						
The Elem. Resource Teacher, Mrs. Presnell						
The Guidance Counselor, Ms. DelGreco						
The Gifted Resource Tchr., Ms. Morris						
The Art Teacher, Ms. Mathewson						
The Music Teacher, Mrs. Harris						
The Phys. Ed. Teacher, Mr. Kinsey						
The Speech Teacher, Mrs. Hawver						
The Cafeteria Manager, Mrs. Budd						

6. Please respond to the following by checking **YES** or **NO**.

		YES	NO
a.	Do you feel free to schedule a conference with your child's teacher?		
b.	Do you like the report card conferences at the end of the first & third* grading periods? * Conferences for the third grading period are required only for students experiencing difficulty.		
c.	Do you think your child received the appropriate **amount** of homework?		
d.	Do you think your child received the appropriate **quantity** of homework?		
e.	Have you been adequately informed about your child's progress in school this year?		

7. How often do you see your child's graded work?

_____ Daily   COMMENTS: _____
_____ Weekly   _____
_____ Other   _____

8. Please respond to the following by checking **YES** or **NO**.

		YES	NO	Please comment if you answered "no" to any portion of #8.
a.	When you have come to school, have you been treated with courtesy and respect by the office staff?			
b.	Was the Parent-Student Handbook (K-2 School Rules Booklet / 3-5 Agenda) helpful to you?			
c.	Does Tiger Tales provide you with adequate news about the school and its activities?			
d.	Was the addition of the Tiger Bulletin this year helpful to you?			

9. What information should be added to the following:
Parent-Student Handbook: _____
_____

(Weekly) Tiger Bulletin: _____
_____

(Monthly Newsletter) Tiger Tales: _____
_____

Port Orange 2001–2002
Parent Questionnaire (p. 3 of 5)

STUDENT SERVICES AND/OR PROGRAMS

10. Please rate the following areas if you have first-hand knowledge of them or if your child has commented on any of them.

	No Information	Excellent	Good	Fair	Poor	COMMENTS:
Media Center						_____
Lunchroom						_____
Gifted Resource (K-1)						_____
Gifted Self-Contained (2-5)						_____
Guidance						_____
Exceptional Student Education-Resource & Consultation						_____
Exceptional Student Education-Self-contained						_____
Elementary Resource Services						_____
Speech						_____
Clinic						_____
Accelerated Reader Program						_____
Math Superstars/Sunshine Math						_____
Computer Lab						_____
Literacy Coaches						_____
After School Tutoring						_____

SCHOOL CLIMATE AND SCHOOL ACTIVITIES

Please answer the following questions by checking YES or NO.	YES	NO
11. Is your child happy at Port Orange Elementary?		
12. **Does your child feel safe** at Port Orange Elementary?		
13. **Do you feel your child is safe** at Port Orange Elementary?		

COMMENTS: If your answer to any of these questions is "No," please suggest what we can do to improve.

_____

_____

SCHOOL ACTIVITIES

Please respond to these questions by checking YES or NO.	YES	NO	If your child participates in any of the activities in #15, please comment on the quality of the programs or give suggestions for improvement.
14. Does the school provide adequate activities for your child during the school day? (assembly programs, field trips, speakers, etc.)?			_____
		YES	_____
15. Please put a check if your child participates in any of the following:			_____
a. Florida Future Educators (FFEA)			_____
b. Student Government (SGA)			_____
c. Safety Patrol			_____
d. Peer Mediation			_____
e. After school band			_____
f. Other			_____

Port Orange 2001–2002
Parent Questionnaire (p. 4 of 5)

EXTENDED DAY

Please answer *if* your child is in the Extended Day After School Program.	YES	NO
a. Do you feel that the program is well planned?		
b. Does your child like the daily activities that are provided?		
c. Do you feel there is adequate supervision?		
d. Are you treated with courtesy and respect by Extended Day staff?		
e. Do you feel your child is safe in this program?		
f. Is there adequate communication between you and the Extended Day staff?		
g. Are there any activities that you would like to have provided that we do not currently have? If so, please list in the comments section.		

COMMENTS: _____

_____

COMPUTER INFORMATION

Please respond by checking **YES** or **NO**.	YES	NO
17. Do you have a computer in your home with Internet access?		
18. Does your child have regular access to a home computer?		
19. Does your child use *KnowZone* or *FCAT Explorer* outside the school setting?		

PARENT ACTIVITIES

20. What topics or programs would you like to have considered for future PTA meetings?

_____

_____

_____

21. Please put an **X** by each topic which you would be interested in having presented or discussed.

	Self-esteen		study skills		communicating with my child
	Divorce		helping my gifted child		helping my exceptional child
	Discipline		parenting skills		remaining positive in troubled times
	Family violence		motivation		dealing with societal violence/gangs
	Goal setting		school safety		teasing/bullying/acceptance of others
	Grief		substance abuse		anger management
	Gun safety		dealing with head lice		helping my ADD/ADHD child
	Homework help		FCAT information		preparing for middle school

22. Please indicate if you would be interested in the following:

	YES	NO
Getting my G.E.D.		
Improving my reading skills		
Taking classes to learn to speak English		
Taking classes to learn to speak another language (Specify which language)		
Improving computer skills		

If you answered YES to any of the above, please contact Mrs. Peggy White in the school office.
We'll try to provide these classes through our Community Education Program.

Port Orange 2001–2002
Parent Questionnaire (p. 5 of 5)

23. I would like to see Port Orange Elementary consider the following:

	YES	NO
Offering more after school extra-curricular activities/clubs Suggestions:		
Creating a self-contained Kindergarten and/or 1st grade gifted classroom		
Other suggestions:		

24. Please give us your input on the **drop-off and pick-up areas** of the school:

_____
_____
_____
_____
_____

25. What do you think are the **greatest strengths** of our school?

_____
_____
_____
_____
_____

26. What do you think we need to **improve** most?

_____
_____
_____
_____
_____

THE SCHOOL ADVISORY COMMITTEE IS AWARE THAT THIS IS A LONG SURVEY, BUT WE TRULY VALUE YOUR INPUT AS WE WORK TOWARD A SUCCESSFUL 2002-03 SCHOOL YEAR.

REMEMBER THAT WE WOULD LIKE AT LEAST ONE SURVEY PER FAMILY RETURNED TO SCHOOL NO LATER THAN WEDNESDAY, APRIL 24, 2002.

THANK YOU FOR TAKING THE TIME TO SHARE YOUR THOUGHTS.

West Newton Times to Remember

TIMES TO REMEMBER
MARCH
  9 – ISTEP/CTBS TESTING BEGINS
  11 – NO SCHOOL—PARENT TEACHER CONFERENCES IN P.M.
  13 – SPIRIT DAY
  14 – WEST NEWTON CRAFT FAIR

Dear Parents,

As we continually assess and evaluate our programs, we would like your help. Please take a few minutes to fill out this survey and return it to your child's homeroom teacher by March 16. We thank you for your help and input as we begin to plan for the 92-93 school year.

                                    Sincerely,
                                    Janet Larch
- -

1. What do we do that makes your child successful? _____

_____

_____

2. What can be done to improve success for all students? _____

_____

_____

3. As you think about the structure of the professional teaching team, what do they do

that makes them successful? _____

_____

_____

4. What can our team do to improve? _____

_____

_____

West Newton Elementary School, West Newton, Indiana

New Hope Parent Survey
(p. 1)

NEW HOPE ELEMENTARY — PARENT SURVEY

We would like our parents to evaluate our progress this year by completing this evaluation and returning it to NEW HOPE via your child (or through the mail). It is very important to us as a staff that we continually improve our means and methods of providing a quality educational program for your children. PLEASE RETURN TO SCHOOL.

CURRICULUM AND INSTRUCTION

	EXCELLENT	GOOD	AVERAGE	UNSATISFACTORY	NO OPINION
The curriculum in relation to your child's individual educational needs is:	☐	☐	☐	☐	☐
The learning materials in relation to your child's educational needs are:	☐	☐	☐	☐	☐
The instructional staff in meeting your child's educational needs are:	☐	☐	☐	☐	☐
The instructional methods in meeting your child's educational needs are:	☐	☐	☐	☐	☐
The manner in which New Hope is organized is:	☐	☐	☐	☐	☐
The number of students in your child's class (pupil-teacher ratio) is:	☐	☐	☐	☐	☐

PROGRESS REPORTS

	EXCELLENT	GOOD	AVERAGE	UNSATISFACTORY	NO OPINION
The student report cards are:	☐	☐	☐	☐	☐
Parent-Teacher Conferences are:	☐	☐	☐	☐	☐

GUIDANCE AND COUNSELING

	EXCELLENT	GOOD	AVERAGE	UNSATISFACTORY	NO OPINION
New Hope's efforts in helping your child become a well adjusted human being are:	☐	☐	☐	☐	☐

ATTITUDE

	EXCELLENT	GOOD	AVERAGE	UNSATISFACTORY	NO OPINION
Your child's enthusiasm for school is:	☐	☐	☐	☐	☐

DISCIPLINE

	EXCELLENT	GOOD	AVERAGE	UNSATISFACTORY	NO OPINION
Classroom rules, routines and management are:	☐	☐	☐	☐	☐
Playground rules, routines and management are:	☐	☐	☐	☐	☐
School-wide rules and management are:	☐	☐	☐	☐	☐

COMMUNICATION:

	EXCELLENT	GOOD	AVERAGE	UNSATISFACTORY	NO OPINION
The exchange of information between school and home is:	☐	☐	☐	☐	☐

ADMINISTRATION

	EXCELLENT	GOOD	AVERAGE	UNSATISFACTORY	NO OPINION
The administration of New Hope is:	☐	☐	☐	☐	☐

FACILITIES

	EXCELLENT	GOOD	AVERAGE	UNSATISFACTORY	NO OPINION
The maintenance of the building and grounds is:	☐	☐	☐	☐	☐

FOOD SERVICE (Hot Lunch)

	EXCELLENT	GOOD	AVERAGE	UNSATISFACTORY	NO OPINION
The lunch program is:	☐	☐	☐	☐	☐

New Hope Parent Survey
(p. 2)

<u>COMMENTS</u>

(Please check one response under each question.)

What do you appreciate most about New Hope Elementary?

_____ The class size and student/teacher ratio

_____ The course of study and special programs (Chapter I, Special Education)

_____ The care and concern shown by teachers, principal, and staff

_____ Good communication between home and school

_____ School and classroom newsletters

_____ Assemblies and Special Programs

_____ Math and reading incentives

_____ No opinion

_____ Other (please specify) _____

_____

What do you believe is the most pressing problem facing New Hope Elementary?

_____ Overcrowding and lack of space

_____ Discipline

_____ Busing and behavior on the bus

_____ Lack of communication between school and home

_____ No opinion

_____ Other (please specify) _____

_____

Are there areas of the school program that should receive less emphasis?

_____ Too much competition and competitive programs

_____ Too many contests and rewards

_____ The school-wide discipline program

_____ Marks and grades

_____ None, it's great as it is

_____ No opinion

_____ Other (please specify) _____

Additional comments you would like to make for our consideration in the improvement of your school:

_____

_____

_____

Your Name (Optional) _____

Grade level(s) of your child(ren) _____

PLEASE RETURN TO SCHOOL. THANK YOU!

Hawley Parent Survey
(p. 1 of 3)

PARENT SURVEY
HAWLEY ELEMENTARY SCHOOL

– –

We are seeking parental input regarding your impressions and perceptions of Hawley Elementary School (HES). Please take a few minutes to complete this one-page survey and send it back to your child's teacher.

Results of this survey will be shared in the June newsletter.

PLEASE MARK ONE:	**Excellent**	**Good**	**Fair**	**No Opinion**
1. HES has an orderly environment.				
2. My child looks forward to going to school every day.				
3. HES is helping to teach children to be responsible citizens.				
4. Students at Hawley Elementary are generally respectful of each other.				
5. The morale of the students at Hawley Elementary is good.				
6. School rules and regulations affecting students are reasonable.				
7. Teachers at HES care about students.				
8. Hawley Elementary staff have high expectations for students.				
9. Hawley Elementary students are challenged academically.				
10. The homework assigned students seems appropriate to grade level.				
11. HES teachers help students develop critical-thinking skills.				
12. Basic skills are taught well at Hawley Elementary.				
13. Parents receive adequate information regarding students' progress and happenings at school.				
14. Overall, how do you feel about the quality of education your child receives at Hawley Elementary?				
Grade(s) your Child(ren) are in:				

Hawley Parent Survey
(p. 2 of 3)

PARENT SURVEY
HAWLEY ELEMENTARY SCHOOL

- -

R E S U L T S

- -

Fifty-six (56) parent surveys were returned out of a possible total of nearly 300. Thank you to those parents who took a few minutes to complete the survey.

PLEASE MARK ONE:	Excellent	Good	Fair	No Opinion
1. HES has an orderly environment.	28	27	1	0
2. My child looks forward to going to school every day.	25	25	6	0
3. HES is helping to teach children to be responsible citizens.	20	32	4	0
4. Students at Hawley Elementary are generally respectful of each other.	7	30	19	0
5. The morale of the students at Hawley Elementary is good.	14	36	6	0
6. School rules and regulations affecting students are reasonable.	26	29	1	0
7. Teachers at HES care about students.	34	21	1	0
8. Hawley Elementary staff have high expectations for students.	30	25	1	0
9. Hawley Elementary students are challenged academically.	28	27	1	0
10. The homework assigned students seems appropriate to grade level.	17	35	3	1
11. HES teachers help students develop critical-thinking skills.	15	35	6	0
12. Basic skills are taught well at Hawley Elementary.	32	23	1	0
13. Parents receive adequate information regarding students' progress and happenings at school.	28	21	7	0
14. Overall, how do you feel about the quality of education your child receives at Hawley Elementary?	36	19	1	0

Hawley Parent Survey
(p. 3 of 3)

PARENT SURVEY COMMENTS

The following comments were received on the "Parent Surveys." We thank those parents for expressing some of their views related to the survey.

Each "--" and the comments below it represent one parent. Ten (10) parents responded.

— —

-- I am unhappy about the large class sizes in some of the upper grades.
-- I think some people's children are very mean to others — they have clubs and tell other children not to play with some because they are not in the club.
   Should not be able to tell children not to wear shorts if there is no dress code. We can't wear a dress to Phy. Ed.
   Should have more homework if students aren't doing well.
-- Need midquarter reports from every teacher. Please don't make 2 sections of 3rd Grade.
-- Kids are very mean to others and don't care about others' feelings.
-- I feel my child has had very excellent teachers so far.
-- Being open enrollment I haven't been exposed to all teachers, but the ones I have — I'm extremely pleased.
   I'm pleased that Hawley's music department is tops.
   Science is advanced, but good to expose them to high tech terminology.
   Pleased with tutoring & important for peers to help classmates.
   Your monthly Nugget Newsflash is well organized and accurate!
   Overall — I am extremely HAPPY!
   Hawley should be extremely pleased with their schools — which seems to have been standard for many years. Former students and ex-teachers have high praise. GOOD JOB GUYS!
-- I especially appreciate the midquarter grades from 3rd Grade teachers.
-- I would like to see more parents' involvement and opportunity to volunteer my services.
-- Please keep both conferences each year!
-- I am concerned about some children who seem to be "left out" and called names because of being overweight, lacking in personal cleanliness or not wearing the best clothes.

* *

This represents the last newsletter for the school year.

The next newsletter will be mailed to all families with elementary students on or about August 20.

If you hear of families who are <u>moving away</u> or <u>moving into</u> Hawley this summer please give us a call.

ENJOY THE SUMMER AHEAD! DON'T FORGET ABOUT <u>READING</u> DURING THE SUMMER.

SEE YOU ALL IN THE FALL!

Pam Sylvara, former Gotsch School principal, encouraged parents to give her feedback about her newsletter, *Principally Speaking*. In Chapter 5, a clip or return slip was included that I used with all of my newsletters to verify that parents had received the newsletter.

The principal of Hawley Elementary School in Hawley, Minnesota, used the parent survey to obtain information from the parents of students. The information was requested in May of a school year, and the results of the parental input were reported back to the parents in the June parents' newsletter. The results of that survey and the comments shared by the parents are shown. This immediate feedback and sharing of information is an effective technique to show parents that their input was received, evaluated, and shared with everyone. Notice also that the principal has informed parents that they have received their last newsletter for that school year and told them when they can expect the first newsletter for the following school year.

If the superintendent and school board members receive the principal's newsletter on a regular basis, they can see the survey results firsthand and be aware of the parents' concerns, likes, and dislikes. In some cases, if parents express concerns about the physical conditions at a school, the board members and superintendent can begin to deal with their concerns before the parents raise their concerns to them.

Prior to making changes to one school, the Minnetonka, Minnesota, School District provided parents an opportunity to give input through survey forms that were included with the principals' newsletters. The survey form used to obtain the information is shown on page 291.

Theodore Roosevelt School, a preK–8 school in Cocoa, Florida, included the Theodore Roosevelt School Critique sheet (p. 291) with a newsletter. This "official form for problems, suggestions, and solutions" is also available in the school's office.

Some school principals seek information from students, too. In some cases this is done when the student leaves the school, in an exit interview, or graduates. When Martin Kane was the principal at Roosevelt High School in Kent, Ohio, he distributed a copy of the Roosevelt High School Spring Survey form (pp. 292–293) to all 9th, 10th, and 11th grade students. Because the students did not have to identify themselves, they could be very honest with their responses. Mr. Kane used the input from the students to evaluate the instructional program and make adjustments as needed.

(Text continues on page 294.)

Middle Years' Communications Survey

MIDDLE YEARS' COMMUNICATIONS SURVEY

In the fall of 1993, Minnetonka School District will open two middle schools for sixth, seventh and eighth graders. (See <u>Anchor</u> articles, pages 3 and 6.) Numerous committees are working on various aspects of the transition. We want to do our best to keep you informed as we plan these two schools.

Please take a moment to fill out this questionnaire and send it back to the office in your child's school. The following topics and others will be discussed in newsletters and other publications. We would like to know your questions about these or other areas.

Middle School Schedules	Extracurricular activities and enrichment
Student conduct and discipline	Teacher and student placement
Student support services	Reporting to parents
Curriculum	Facilities
Social aspects of school	Boundaries
Transportation and parent option	Other

Your questions: (Please continue on the back if necessary)

_____

_____

_____

What are good ways for you to find out about middle level education? (Put + below.) Also, which of the following media would not be good information methods for you? (Mark with a 0).

+ or 0

_____   Newsletter
_____   Parent education breakfasts at school
_____   Parent education evening meetings at school
_____   District wide multi-faceted information events at school
_____   Local Cable TV
_____   Videos for free checkout
_____   Speakers
_____   Other (Please explain.)

Thanks for your help. Please return this survey to your child's school by May 22.

Theodore Roosevelt School Critique

Theodore Roosevelt School Critique
Official Form for Problems, Suggestions, and Solutions

Please describe the problem:

_____
_____
_____
_____
_____

Your suggested solution:

_____
_____
_____
_____
_____

Your offer to volunteer or help correct the problem:

_____
_____
_____
_____
_____

Today's date: _____

Would you like us to contact you? ☐ *yes*   ☐ *no*

Your name (optional): _____

Address: _____ *Phone:* _____

--------- OFFICE USE ---------

Logged in: (date) _____ (number) _____ Assigned to: (staff member) _____

Suggestor contacted:
(1st call) _____ (2nd call) _____ (3rd call) _____ (note sent) _____

Resolution: (date) _____ (action) _____
_____
_____
_____

Suggestor notified of resolution:
(1st call) _____ (2nd call) _____ (3rd call) _____ (note sent) _____

Roosevelt High School Survey
(p. 1)

ROOSEVELT HIGH SCHOOL SPRING SURVEY

1. Grade in school this year?   9   10   11   (Please circle one.)

2. Your approximate grade point average this year?   3.5-4,   3.0-3.49,   2.5-2.99
   2.-2.49,   1.5-1.99,   1.-1.49,   below 1.   (Please circle one.)

3. About how many times did you meet with a counselor during the school year?
   _____ registering for classes   _____ schedule change(s)
   _____ career information or O.I.S.   _____ testing or test information
   _____ assistance for college/financial aid _____ other related information
   _____ personal concerns   _____ other reasons of any kind
   _____ never met with a counselor (Check, if appropriate.)

4. What is your counselor's name: _____

5. To what extent has the guidance and/or counseling you have received been helpful to you?
   (Please check one.)
   _____ extremely helpful   _____ helpful
   _____ of some help   _____ very little help
   _____ no help   _____ no help requested

6. To what extent do you feel the need for more personal attention on such matters as selecting
   courses, going to college, or getting a job? (Please check one.)
   _____ I would like to be able to talk to someone more often than I can now.
   _____ Someone is usually available when I need to discuss such matters.
   _____ Someone is always available when I need to discuss such matters.

7. How would you describe the academic standards or expectations set by your teachers this
   school year? (Please check one.)
   _____ much too difficult   _____ somewhat easy
   _____ somewhat difficult   _____ much too easy
   _____ about right

8. How satisfied are you this year with your own personal academic achievement? (Please check
   one.)
   _____ thoroughly dissatisfied   _____ somewhat dissatisfied
   _____ satisfied   _____ thoroughly satisfied

9. Check the English section you were in this year:
   _____ General   _____ College Preparatory   _____ Advanced
   In your general, college preparatory, or advanced English class this year, how often were you
   asked to write a paragraph, theme, or composition as a writing assignment in class, as a
   homework assignment, as part of a literature exam, or as part of a journal? (Please check
   one. Also, please be accurate.)
   _____ once per day   _____ once every other week
   _____ once per week   _____ once per month

Roosevelt High School Survey
(p. 2)

10. On an average over the entire school year, how much homework were you expected to do each night this year? (Please check one.)

    _____ less than 30 minutes   _____ between two and three hours

    _____ between 30 minutes and one hour   _____ between three and four hours

    _____ between one hour and two hours   _____ more than four hours

11. Assign a letter grade to Roosevelt High School's performance this year. (Please check one.)

    _____ A   _____ B   _____ C   _____ D   _____ F

    Why do you feel this way?

12. Do you enjoy attending school? (Please check one.)

    _____ Yes   _____ Sometimes   _____ No

13. Do you feel the adults at Roosevelt High School are friendly? (Please check one.)

    _____ Yes   _____ Usually   _____ No

14. Do you think discipline is handled fairly by administrators? (Please check one.)

    _____ Yes   _____ Usually   _____ No

15. Have you been sent to the office for discipline this year? _____ How many times: _____

16. Do you feel that the courses you have taken this year have been worthwhile? (Please check one.)

    _____ Yes   _____ Some of them   _____ No

17. Do you feel you can get extra help at Roosevelt if you ask for it? (Please check one.)

    _____ Yes   _____ Usually   _____ No

18. Do you think Student Council gets worthwhile things done at school? (Please check one.)

    _____ Yes   _____ Sometimes   _____ No

19. Do you feel that you are being adequately prepared for whatever you plan to do beyond high school? (Please check one.)

    _____ Yes   _____ No

20. List the things that you like most about Roosevelt High. List those things you feel are its strengths: _____

    _____

    _____

    _____

21. What suggestions do you have for improving Roosevelt High School's academic program?

    _____

    _____

    _____

22. Any other suggestions for improving Roosevelt High School.

Information can be requested from elementary school students, too. One intermediate level elementary school teacher, Lenore Stoia, invited her students and their parents to grade her (pp. 295–296). She also sought input from them. Ms. Stoia looped with her students—that is, she was promoted to the next grade with them. (See question 5 on the parents' survey, page 297.) A Report Card to a Special Teacher (p. 298) can be used with intermediate-level elementary students.

By providing an opportunity for employees of the school district to express their opinions and make suggestions (pp. 299–302), the Edmonton, Alberta, Canada, Public Schools demonstrates an awareness of an important concept: Employees will work harder and take responsibility for the organization to a greater degree if they have been allowed to give their input. Note the questions that were asked and the creative method used to get the names of the employees who responded.

The superintendent of the Affton, Missouri, School District sought information from the citizens of the community. One type of survey used is the Community Education Interest Survey (pp. 303–308), which requested information from community members about programs in which they would like to participate.

Another superintendent used a Parent Report Card (p. 309) as one source of information for a self-study the district was completing.

Visits to and Use of the School by Parents and the Public

When citizens, parents, and others visit a school, this provides opportunities to get feedback about the school's instructional program. Some school principals plan opportunities for groups to visit the school, have lunch with the students, or observe school assemblies. Earlier in this book, suggestions were made about getting senior citizens involved in volunteering and mentoring at a school.

Open houses and *back-to-school nights* are two excellent opportunities for parents to visit the school and leave their opinions or suggestions about what they felt or observed. Some school principals invite civic organizations to meet in their schools. These meetings provide opportunities for citizens to see the school in action and give verbal or written feedback.

(Text continues on page 310.)

Ms. Stoia's Student Survey
(p. 1 of 2)

Student Survey

I have spent the year teaching you and grading you. Now it is your turn to grade me. On the line, please give me a grade of A, B, C, D, F. You do not have to put your name on this, but please be honest.

1. Miss Stoia enjoys teaching. ____

2. Miss Stoia cares about me. ____

3. Miss Stoia lets me know if I am behaving right or wrong. ____

4. Miss Stoia is fair when children misbehave. ____

5. Miss Stoia chooses books and things that will help me learn. ____

6. Miss Stoia knows a lot about what she is teaching us. ____

7. Miss Stoia talks and writes so I can understand. ____

8. Miss Stoia uses more than one way to help me learn. ____

9. Miss Stoia is ready to start a new activity as soon as we finish one. ____

10. Miss Stoia makes our classroom look nice. ____

11. Miss Stoia works with small and large groups and individual children. ____

12. Miss Stoia is polite and nice. ____

13. Miss Stoia explains things so I can understand them. ____

14. Miss Stoia makes me feel safe when I am in school. ____

15. Miss Stoia rewards children who behave well. ____

16. Miss Stoia rewards children who make good grades. ____

**Ms. Stoia's Student Survey
(p. 2 of 2)**

Please answer the following questions in your own words.

1. What was your favorite thing we did this year?

2. What was your least favorite thing we did this year?

3. What did you think of your rewards (Breakfast club, tickets, table points, etc.) and consequences?

4. What could I have done differently?

Please list any other comments that you have.

Be sure to return this by May 7.

Ms. Stoia's End-of-the-Year Teacher Evaluation

End of the Year Teacher Evaluation

Dear Parents,
       As a professional educator, I am continually looking for ways to make myself a stronger teacher. Please take the time to fill out this evaluation. Feel free to comment on any topics. Please return this to me in the envelope provided.
                    Thanks for your help,
                    Miss Stoia

1. Please tell me how you feel as a parent about communication between school and home.

2. Please list any things that you feel would have helped you more.

3. Please list your feelings on my rewards/consequences (tickets, treasure box, honor roll lunch, breakfast club, etc.)

4. Please list any things that I did not do that you as a parent feel would have made this year better.

5. If your child was with me for 2 years, do you feel this helped them? Why or why not?

6. Additional comments:

                Thanks for your help! I appreciate it!

Report Card to a Special Teacher

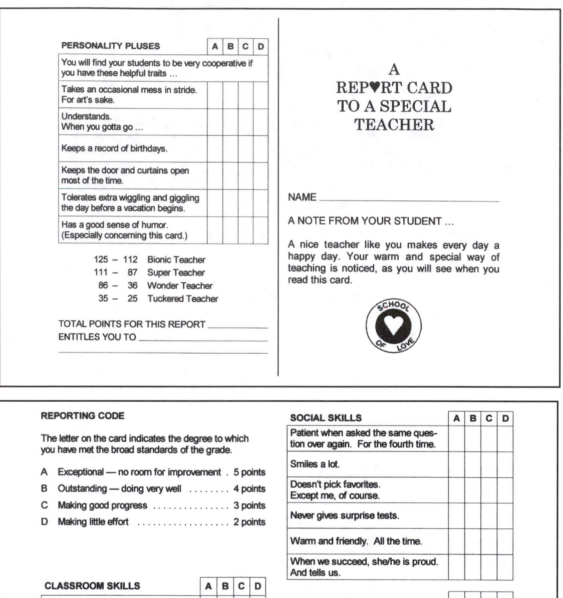

PERSONALITY PLUSES

	A	B	C	D
You will find your students to be very cooperative if you have these helpful traits …				
Takes an occasional mess in stride. For art's sake.				
Understands. When you gotta go …				
Keeps a record of birthdays.				
Keeps the door and curtains open most of the time.				
Tolerates extra wiggling and giggling the day before a vacation begins.				
Has a good sense of humor. (Especially concerning this card.)				

125 – 112   Bionic Teacher
111 – 87   Super Teacher
86 – 36   Wonder Teacher
35 – 25   Tuckered Teacher

TOTAL POINTS FOR THIS REPORT _____
ENTITLES YOU TO _____

A
REP♥RT CARD
TO A SPECIAL
TEACHER

NAME _____

A NOTE FROM YOUR STUDENT …

A nice teacher like you makes every day a happy day. Your warm and special way of teaching is noticed, as you will see when you read this card.

SCHOOL OF LOVE

REPORTING CODE

The letter on the card indicates the degree to which you have met the broad standards of the grade.

A   Exceptional — no room for improvement . 5 points
B   Outstanding — doing very well …… 4 points
C   Making good progress …………… 3 points
D   Making little effort ……………… 2 points

CLASSROOM SKILLS

	A	B	C	D
Writes neatly on the chalkboard. Without drawing guidelines.				
Pronounces names correctly. And remembers them.				
Keeps her (his) desk neat and clean.				
Carries a tune. In tune.				
Decorates the bulletin board and room cheerfully. For every holiday.				
Graces papers with stamps, stars, or nice comments.				

SOCIAL SKILLS

	A	B	C	D
Patient when asked the same question over again. For the fourth time.				
Smiles a lot.				
Doesn't pick favorites. Except me, of course.				
Never gives surprise tests.				
Warm and friendly. All the time.				
When we succeed, she/he is proud. And tells us.				

EXTRA CREDIT CLUES

	A	B	C	D
Reads good books to class. School books don't count.				
Tells long stories. Especially when we're supposed to be working.				
Assigns 1/2 hour or less homework. Per week.				
Allows (a little) time for us to do our own thing.				
Lets us take turns erasing the blackboard.				
Knows jokes and riddles.				

Staff Bulletin Survey
(p. 1 of 4)

The Staff Bulletin wants to know:

What's on your mind ?

Return your completed survey to the Communications-Community Relations branch by June 15 and be eligible to win a $25 Continuing Education gift certificate.

Draw date: June 15

Submit your responses in confidence. Put completed surveys "on the truck."

Thank you for letting us know what's on your mind!

Optional:

_____

_____
Name

_____
Telephone

Communications-Community Relations
2nd Floor
Centre for Education

Staff Bulletin Survey
(p. 2 of 4)

I   **What is your current position?** [check one]

1 _____ Principal or Assistant Principal
2 _____ Teaching Staff
3 _____ Support Staff
4 _____ Maintenance Staff
5 _____ Custodial Staff
6 _____ Community Members
7 _____ Retired Staff
8 _____ Key Communicator
9 _____ Central Services Administration
10 _____ Other [describe] _____

II   **What sources do you rely on for information regarding Edmonton Public Schools?**

List in order of first to the last source:

_____

_____

III   **What sources provide the information you require in these areas?**

1 professional development, inservices, workshops, opportunities for involvement
    a _____   b _____
    first source   second source

2 organizational planning or operational planning
    a _____   b _____
    first source   second source

3 board news
    a _____   b _____
    first source   second source

4 personnel policies and procedures
    a _____   b _____
    first source   second source

5 educational issues of provincial, national, or international significance
    a _____   b _____
    first source   second source

6 district events
    a _____   b _____
    first source   second source

7 programs or activities outside my department, branch, school
    a _____   b _____
    first source   second source

8 staff, school, and student initiatives and accomplishments
    a _____   b _____
    first source   second source

9 Other [specify] _____
    a _____   b _____
    first source   second source

Staff Bulletin Survey
(p. 3 of 4)

IV   The *Staff Bulletin* reports on many issues which are included in the sections listed below. For each section, check the response that most accurately describes how often you read it.

	Regularly	Occasionally	Seldom	Never
1 Viewpoint				
2 Board Highlights				
3 Olive Elliott				
4 Labour Relations				
5 Archivist's Corner				
6 Curriculum				
7 In Memoriam				
8 Bulletin Board				
9 Other Features				

V   How would you rate the *Staff Bulletin* in the following areas?

	Very Good	Good	Poor	Very Poor
1 usefulness of extra, single topic *Staff Bulletins* [e.g., budget, appointments, leadership]				
2 four column format				
3 frequency of publication				
4 use of colour				
5 size of print				
6 location of sections within the *Staff Bulletin*				
7 current feature writers				
8 variety in submissions selected for publication by the editorial committee				
9 submissions chosen are interesting				
10 submissions chosen are relevant				
11 opportunity exists to submit school or department items				
12 opportunity exists to submit own views on items				

Staff Bulletin Survey
(p. 4 of 4)

Please attach additional pages if you require more space for your comments.

VI   What would you like to change, delete, or add to the *Staff Bulletin*?

_____

_____

_____

_____

_____

_____

_____

_____

_____

_____

VII   Please make any additional suggestions regarding the *Staff Bulletin* here.

_____

_____

_____

_____

_____

_____

_____

_____

_____

_____

_____

Thank you from the Communications-Community Relations branch!

EDMONTON PUBLIC SCHOOLS

**Communication Education Interest Survey
(p. 1 of 6)**

COMMUNITY EDUCATION INTEREST SURVEY

▸ PLEASE HELP US — FILL OUT AND RETURN ◂

Community education is a concept being expanded in the Affton School District. We hope to promote lifelong learning through maximum use of community resources.

Community education is making our schools and facilities available to everyone, not just to school-age children during class hours. Whenever space is available, why not use the facilities for games, crafts, adult classes, recreation, or service to the community?

Your comments, together with those of your neighbors, will be used to plan programs in your school community.

This survey has been designed so you will be able to complete it in approximately 15 minutes. We appreciate your contributions to this effort.

Here is an opportunity for you to have input into our long-range planning.

1. There are _____ people residing in your household.

2. They are in the following age categories. List number in each category and star (*) your own age group.
   [ ] 0-5   [ ] 16-21   [ ] 36-45
   [ ] 6-11   [ ] 22-25   [ ] 46-54
   [ ] 12-15   [ ] 26-35   [ ] 55 and over

3. Are you interested in community education?
   [ ] Yes   [ ] No

4. Have you ever participated in a community education program in our district?
   [ ] Yes   [ ] No
   In another school district?
   [ ] Yes   [ ] No

5. Do you regularly read a newspaper?
   [ ] Yes [ ] No
   If so, which one(s):
   [ ] Post-Dispatch
   [ ] South County Journal
   [ ] Gravois/Watson Times
   [ ] South County News
   [ ] Other

6. Child-parent-school related subjects (please check if interested):
   [ ] Doing volunteer work at school
   [ ] Understanding your child's math program
   [ ] Understanding your child's reading program
   [ ] Understanding your child's science program
   [ ] Other

7. How many in your family would be interested in attending classes for credit at the following levels:
   [ ] Undergraduate College
   [ ] Post Graduate College
   [ ] Adult Basic Education
   Are you interested in a high school diploma?
   [ ] Yes   [ ] No
   Are you interested in college credit extension courses?
   [ ] Yes   [ ] No

Communication Education Interest Survey
(p. 2 of 6)

8. Some **RECREATIONAL ACTIVITIES** are listed below. Please check areas of interest by age category for each member of your family.

	6-12	13-17	18+	65+
Backpacking (Camping)				
Basketball				
Bridge, Chess				
Exercise				
Football				
Gymnastics				
Handball				
Self-Defense				
Wrestling				
Soccer				
Softball				
Summer Day Camp				
Swimming				
Tennis				
Track				
Baseball				
Jogging				
Karate				

9. Some **EDUCATIONAL ACTIVITIES** are listed below. Please check the areas of interest by age category for each member of your family.

	6-12	13-17	18+	65+
Government				
Local				
State				
National				
History				
American				
Missouri				
Science				
Earth Science				
Life Science				

EDUCATIONAL ACTIVITIES cont.

	6-12	13-17	18+	65+
Mathematics				
Algebra				
General				
Geometry & Metric				
Foreign Language				
French				
Italian				
German				
Spanish				
Business Practices				
Bookkeeping				
Shorthand				
Typing				
Consumer Survival				
Consumer Law				
Income Tax				
Insurance				
Legal Aid				
Purchasing				
Saving				
Small Claims				
Wills & Probate				
English				
Creative Writing				
Journalism				

10. Some **COMPUTER EDUCATION** subjects are listed below. Please check areas of interest for a possible course offering.

	6-12	13-17	18+	65+
General knowledge/skills for microcomputers				
Programming				
Basic				
Pascal				
Logo				

Communication Education Interest Survey
(p. 3 of 6)

COMPUTER EDUCATION cont.

	6-12	13-17	18+	65+
Word Processing				
Spreadsheets				
Data Bases				

Other _____

Do you own a computer? If so, what type?

_____

Does your child have an interest in a summer computer camp?
[ ] Yes   [ ] No

11. Some *FINE ARTS* subjects are listed below. Please check areas of interest by age category for each member of your family.

Arts & Crafts	6-12	13-17	18+	65+
Art History				
Ceramics				
Decoupage				
Drawing				
Flower Arranging				
Graphic Arts				
Jewelry Making				
Leather-Craft				
Needlepoint				
Painting				
Photography				
Rug Making				
Sculpture				
Stained Glass				
Stitchery				
Weaving				

Other _____

Music	6-12	13-17	18+	65+
Group Instrumental				
Private Instruction				
Group Singing				
Private Singing				
Band for Pleasure				
Orchestra for Pleasure				
Instrumental Music				
Music Appreciation				
Voice				

What instrument? _____

What style of instrumental music? (Please check)
[ ] Classical   [ ] Folk
[ ] Jazz   [ ] Pop
[ ] Rock   [ ] Chamber

What kind of voice? (Please check)
[ ] Classical   [ ] Folk
[ ] Jazz   [ ] Pop
[ ] Rock   [ ] Barber Shop
[ ] Madrigal

Other _____

Dance	6-12	13-17	18+	65+
Ballet				
Ballroom Dancing				
Belly Dancing				
Creative Dance				
Folk Dance				
Modern Dance				
Rhythmic Aerobics				
Rock				
Square Dancing				

Other _____

Communication Education Interest Survey
(p. 4 of 6)

FINE ARTS cont.

Theatre Arts

	6-12	13-17	18+	65+
Acting				
Backstage				
Clowning				
Pantomime				
Plays				
Skits or Readings				
Speech				
Drama Workshop				

Other _____

12. Some **GENERAL SKILLS** are listed below. Please check areas of interest for a possible course offering.

	6-12	13-17	18+	65+
Bike Repair				
Cooking				
Dressmaking				
First Aid				
Gardening				
General Household Repair				
Interior Decoration				
Knitting				
Metal Shop				
Pet Care				
Radio (Ham, C.B.)				
Sewing				
Upholstery				
Woodworking				

Other _____

13. Some possible **HEALTH SUBJECTS** are listed below. Please check areas of interest for a one or two hour class.

How to select and use:

[ ] Clinics
[ ] Doctors
[ ] Mental Health Facilities
[ ] Family Planning
[ ] Health Care Society
    (American Cancer Soc.,
    Visiting Nurses Assn., etc.)

Other _____

Seminar Areas:

[ ] Health Care for Children
[ ] Health Care for Men
[ ] Health Care for Women
[ ] Health Care for Elderly
[ ] Heart Disease
[ ] Medicare
[ ] Nutrition
[ ] Parent-Child Relationships
[ ] Medical Terminology
[ ] The Cost of Medical Care . . .
    What is Involved

14. Would you or anyone you know be interested in instructing any of the previously mentioned or other classes or activities? Please list them below.

Person   Activity

_____   _____

_____   _____

_____   _____

Communication Education Interest Survey
(p. 5 of 6)

15. What are some of the problems in the Affton community with which you are concerned?

_____

_____

_____

_____

_____

_____

_____

_____

16. If you feel there has been an area we have not covered in this survey and you would like to add your own ideas and feelings, please do so.

_____

_____

_____

_____

_____

_____

_____

17. Does the principal wage earner of this household work in Affton?

[ ] Yes   [ ] No

18. Affton is considering expanding the use of volunteer help in our schools. Would you assist as a volunteer in the classroom, or in special programs? If so, please give name:

_____

and telephone number _____

19. How often do you use the following community facilities?

School Facilities	Frequently	Occasionally	Never
Classrooms			
Gym			
Auditorium			
Libraries			
Playground areas			
Swimming pools			
Tennis courts			
Ball fields			

20. What day(s) of the week would be best for you or members of your family to attend activities?

	Mon	Tue	Wed	Thu	Fri	Sat
Pre-School						
Children						
Teens						
Adults						

21. What time of the day would be best for you or members of your family to attend activities?

	6-9 a.m.	12 noon	12-3 p.m.	3-6 p.m.	6-8 p.m.	8-10 p.m.
Pre-School						
Children						
Teens						
Adults						

Please return by mail or drop off at your nearest Affton school. Thank you.

Communication Education Interest Survey
(p. 6 of 6)

Fold here

Place
Stamp
Here

COMMUNITY EDUCATION SURVEY
AFFTON SCHOOL DISTRICT
8701 MACKENZIE ROAD
ST. LOUIS, MO 63123

SCHOOL - HOME - COMMUNITY GROWING TOGETHER . . . BUILDING FOR THE FUTURE

Jackson County Parent Report Card

What do you appreciate most about Jackson County Schools?

_____

_____

What is the most pressing problem facing the Jackson County Schools?

_____

_____

Are there areas of the school program that should receive less emphasis?

_____

_____

Additional comments you would like to make for our consideration in the improvement of our schools:

_____

_____

Grade level of student: _____

Number of children you have in Jackson County Schools

_____

Comments on this card apply to my child attending

_____ School
(name of school)

Please have your student return this Parent Report Card to his or her teacher or principal, of if you prefer, return the completed card directly to:
   Timothy A. Wheeler, Superintendent of Schools
   P.O. Box 279
   Jefferson, Georgia 30549

THANK YOU!

Parent Report Card

Dear Parent:

A school system should constantly try to improve the quality of education its students receive. In Jackson County, we want to continually improve our schools. Our goal is to assure that each student is receiving the finest opportunity to develop his or her abilities. We know that parents in Jackson County desire the best possible education for their children.

Periodically, we give you a formal report of your student's progress in the educational program. This year, we would like to ask you to send us a report card on our progress, as you see us. Your evaluation comments, and constructive criticism will help us build an even better school system in the future.

I assure you, on behalf of the staff and Board of Education, that your comments will be carefully reviewed.

This year, our schools are undergoing a "self-study" to determine what we are doing well and what we might do better. Your continued help and cooperation are major strengths of our school system and are very much appreciated.

Sincerely,
Timothy A. Wheeler
Superintendent

P.S.: Please fill out a card for each child you have in a Jackson County School.

HOW WOULD YOU RATE JACKSON COUNTY SCHOOLS PERFORMANCE IN THE FOLLOWING AREAS?

E = Excellent; G = Good; A = Average; U = Unsatisfactory; N = No Opinion

	E	G	A	U	N
Curriculum and Instruction					
Curriculum in relation to your child's individual needs					
Learning materials in relation to your child's needs					
Instructional staff in meeting your child's needs					
Instructional methods in meeting your child's needs					
The manner in which your child's school is organized					
Number of students in your child's class (pupil-teacher ratio)					
Progress Reports					
Your child's reporting system					
Parent-Teacher Conferences					
Guidance and Counseling					
Your school's efforts in helping your child become a well adjusted human being					
Attitude					
Your child's enthusiasm for school					
Extracurricular Activities					

	E	G	A	U	N
Discipline In Your School					
Citizenship					
Your school's efforts in promoting good citizenship					
Rules and Regulations					
The exchange of information between school and home					
Administration					
How do you feel about the operation of your school?					
How do you feel about the operation of your school district?					
Facilities					
Your school building as a good place to learn					
The maintenance of your school building					
Bus Service					
Do you use it? Yes _____ No _____					
Food Service					
Finances					
The district's efforts in getting the most for your educational tax dollar					

Questionnaires, Direct Interviews, and Informal Opinion Surveys

These methods were discussed earlier in this chapter. Student interviews were identified as an effective means of getting information about a school. The *exit interview* of employees is equally as effective in obtaining feedback from departing employees. Having used this approach myself when I was a school principal, I found the employees willing to be open and honest with their comments, and for the most part they wanted to see the school continue to improve.

Parent–Teacher Meetings and Visits

Parent–teacher conferences are the most readily available way to obtain information and are excellent opportunities to listen carefully to what the clients of a school are thinking and feeling. Another effective method in gathering data from parents is through *telephone conversations* with them. If those telephone calls are made at breakfast time before the students leave for school and/or at the dinner hour, and positive comments are also shared about a student, the door will be opened for honest comments to be made—either then or in a follow-up message. Years ago, teachers made *visits* to the homes of their students. Recently, however, more care and caution have been exercised because of safety concerns. If it is felt there are no safety issues to be wary of, this can be a very effective method to obtain feedback. School systems that use the home visit strategy have two school personnel travel together and visit with parents/guardians.

School Board Activities

School board meetings are excellent sources of feedback. Most superintendents and school board provide a specified amount of time at each school board meeting for parents and other citizens to share their thoughts and comments. Pam Sylvara, former principal at Gotsch Intermediate School in St. Louis, Missouri, included the invitation to readers of her monthly newsletter to go to a school board meeting.

BOARD OPEN FORUMS
You Are Invited.

You are invited to attend the monthly Board Open Forums conducted by the Affton School Board. Please plan on attending these meetings which are held the second Monday of each month at 7:00 p.m. at Rogers Middle School cafeteria.

The Board will address questions and concerns from the floor.

Many school districts expect school principals to make formal presentations at school board meetings about their school's instructional programs. In recent years, many school principals, at all levels, have enlisted students from the school to share information about their school's instructional program. These presentations not only serve the purpose of sharing information but also provide opportunities to answer questions from school board members or other members of the audience about the school's instructional program.

Use of the Community Power Structure

An effective technique used by the former superintendent of schools in Rocky River, Ohio, Dr. Gorden Rodeen, included regular monthly *breakfast meetings with ministers* of the churches and all of the school principals in the school district. The meetings rotated among the churches in the district and, while the food was delicious at each site, the dialogue shared each month focused all members present on a concern someone had. With all of these dedicated professionals collaborating on possible solutions, several effective strategies usually surfaced. All of us who participated in those meetings felt ownership of the problems but also felt a sense of pride when they were resolved. The power of many helped to solve the problems of the community.

Another effective approach to get a school's message into the community is to share information at the *meetings of real estate sales associates*. Again, by being proactive, a school principal can highlight the instructional program at a school and also provide firsthand answers to questions from the sales associates. Because these people interact with potential future residents of a community, they will carry the message about the effectiveness of a school's program and their impressions of the person who is the school's leader.

Key Communicators

Key communicators have been identified as members of the community who hold positions or occupations that allow them to obtain information from the community to share with school district leaders. They are also counted on to share important information with members of the community in an attempt to quell rumors and share accurate details. They have a finger on the pulse of the community.

Miscellaneous Techniques

Bob Ziegler, retired principal at New Hope Elementary School in New Hope, Minnesota, scheduled evening hours for parents to contact him each month. He announced those hours in his monthly newsletter, and he remained in his office to either meet with parents in person or answer their questions during telephone conversations. When not busy talking with parents, he was able to catch up on tasks that were normally done at home after school hours.

Modern technology has also provided new opportunities for parents to communicate with school principals. One telephone program, Parent Connections, uses voice mailboxes where parents can receive messages from school personnel and leave messages for those personnel.

The Macomb, Michigan, Intermediate School District's MOST program (Macomb Online for Students and Teachers) is powered by Blackboard software and is available in all of the district's schools. Teachers can set up as many sites on Blackboard as they wish. Students can use the site to check homework assignments, schedules, and other classroom information. Teachers and students can interact in real time via instant messaging. Frank Miracola, the school district's interactive learning consultant, said that in one month 3,500 students and teachers accessed about 470 courses through the online system.

Many high school teachers, like Anita Stafford, Jessica Nelson, Brian Read, and Don Ciaravino, all of whom teach in districts near the Detroit area, are willing to converse online with their students. As Mr. Read said, "I have found that a lot of students say a whole lot more than they would in class." Ms. Stafford's reason for being available to students is strong, too. She said, "I would rather have an upset student call me than to have them feel anxiety in class over the same problem. It's almost like tutoring so that they don't feel awkward in class." But perhaps Mr. Ciaravino expressed it best. "I want the students to know I am always available for them," he said. "Too many teachers shut the door on their kids at the end of the say or even at the end of the school year."

What parents wouldn't support these teachers with their needs? Although I would imagine the teachers did not think of the public relations value their efforts have, can't you?

School district *hotlines* are useful in providing information to community members. Many of these programs also have provisions for the users of the program to leave information for school district personnel. Radio and television programs with call-in formats, as well as public access channels, provide additional opportunities for citizens to interact with key school personnel.

Community-sponsored *holiday gatherings* provide other opportunities for school personnel to share information and to receive data about what people are thinking. By participating in a July 4 community festival, a school principal who was new to the community got soaked several times in a dunk tank activity. In addition to showing he was a good sport for participating in the event, he was able to be in a good place to meet several people and hear what was on their minds.

Because members of the media have been a source of help in featuring a school's instructional program and personnel, they should also be involved in the evaluation of the school–community relations plan. A request should be made for suggestions for improving communications and news releases, as well as for specific new program ideas.

Communications Checklist

Each school principal can and should do an annual review of the school's communications plan. Five basic steps, if conducted properly, should yield details about the plan.

Communications Checklist—Five Steps

Step 1. Identify exactly what is to be communicated.

Step 2. Identify the different publics who will receive the communication.

Step 3. Have several persons read and react to written copy to see if they understand what you meant to say.

Step 4. Develop a format suitable for the particular information intended to be communicated.

Step 5. If time permits, put the communication aside until the next day and read it again before printing and distributing.

Four other considerations a principal should have as the school–community relations plan is developed are the content of communication, the format of communication, the legibility of communication, and the activities related to communication. Each is discussed in more detail. A checkmark placed before each item could indicate that adequate care and provisions have been made to meet the topic.

Content of Communication

☐ Content is accurate in terms of facts and information to be communicated in written form.

☐ Content is of a readability level for the public/publics who will receive the communication.

☐ Content has been checked for accuracy of spelling and grammatical usage.

Format of Communication

☐ The layout attracts the attention of the proposed reader and makes one want to read what is written.

☐ There is a balance in terms of word text and pictures, thoughtful use of white space, graphs, or other methods of breaking up long copy.

☐ Important words, ideas, or special points are emphasized for those who only skim or quickly read a communication.

Legibility of Communication

☐ Original has been checked for legibility (clear, readable master) prior to reproduction.

☐ The first few copies that are made are rechecked for errors.

☐ Finished copies have been skimmed to ensure that none are blurred or blank.

Activities Related to Communication

☐ Appropriate steps have been taken to alert the various publics to what type(s) of school communication will be sent to each public.

☐ Communications going home have been sent on days appropriate to the content and purpose.

☐ Communications going home from an elementary school are attached to regularly planned home communication such as the report card. At the middle school level, the communication has been mailed early enough to communicate important details. (Accurate mailing labels are maintained; bulk mailing permits have been purchased and used.)

☐ Students have been made aware of the content of communications and well help parents and others to understand the communications.

☐ The school has selected a masthead, special symbol, logo, or format that is readily identifiable, "attention getting," and alerts the various publics that this is a school communication and is important to read.

If your school communication passes the checklist items listed above, your communication efforts should be effective.

Any discussion of receiving feedback about a school initiative, and especially a school–community relations plan, must include mention of the importance of listening. Listening is a major part of communicating. Setting standards for effective listening to occur should be a top consideration. Some effective listening standards to consider are the following:

Standards of Effective Listening

- Learn to and want to listen.
- Be mentally present; don't daydream.
- Allow the speaker to express complete thoughts without interrupting.
- Write down the most important details, major facts, and key phrases of the message.
- Control distractions and avoid distractions when listening.
- Have an open mind. Refrain from turning off the speaker even if the message is dull or the speaker is not liked.
- Express a genuine interest in the other individual's conversation. Expect excellence.

We learn to listen and we listen to learn.

– Anonymous (cited in Dale, 1984)

A Closing Thought

An essential part of an effective school–community relations plan is the feedback loop where members of the internal and external publics are provided opportunities to share thoughts, information, and offer suggestions. When the surveys of public opinion are reviewed, it seems that four main points surface. The public supports (a) safety and order, (b) back to basics, (c) higher standards, and (d) traditional tracking. If these are strong parts of your school's program and have been identified through surveys you conduct, then you might be wise to emphasize them in your school–community relations plan.

Summary

The need to receive input from the various publics who are involved with a school–community relations plan cannot be ignored. This chapter has focused on several sound approaches to getting that feedback. As in any situation, each of these techniques should be reviewed, modified, and made relevant for use at a local school level. The most important concept to keep in mind is that feedback is needed and provisions to receive it should be a built-in strategy of a school's overall plan.

Case Problem

As you assumed the principalship of Stoney Summit Middle School, you became aware of some needs relating to the school–community relations plan previously used. The concerns centered around the lack of input received from the various publics. Using the information presented in this chapter, prepare an outline of how you would receive input from the various publics. Or, to carry it a step further, develop a survey that could be used at your school.

> **Feedback is the breakfast of champions.**
>
> *– Madeline Hunter*

References and Suggested Readings

Carroll, S. R., & Carroll, D. (2000). *EdMarketing: How smart schools set and keep community support.* Bloomington, IN: National Educational Service.

Carter, A. H., & Jackson, P. *Public Relations Practices, Managerial Case Studies and Problems* (6th ed.). Upper Saddle River, NJ: Prentice Hall.

Dale, E. (1984). *The educator's quotebook.* Bloomington, IN: Phi Delta Kappa Educational Foundation.

Fink, A. (2003). *The survey kit* (2nd Ed.). Thousand Oaks, CA: Sage Publications.

11

Future Focus

Public relations, as part of a school's community relations plan, and in spite of increased emphasis on it, is still not one of most educators' strong suits. Journalists and other members of the media continue to express the view that many educators are overly defensive and guarded in their relationships. But the record can be set straight with honesty, initiative, and a desire to get a school's story shared.

Because the percentage of families who have children attending public schools varies (from 25% to 37%) with different study results, a serious effort must be maintained to interest, inform, involve, and listen to the parents and other community members. Parents and others who are informed about and interested in their neighborhood school can be the strongest advocates of the school. One definite way to accomplish this task is through students who are motivated and excited about their school. Students who carry positive news and reactions about a school can create a contagious atmosphere about the school.

A significant portion of the population does not have reasons to be involved with or interested in a school. Therefore, the *proactive* efforts of a school principal in sharing information about the school can make the difference in gaining their support. But the public's appetite for more information relates to only one aspect of communication. Although it is essential to tell the public about a school, it is also incumbent on a principal to listen to the public's response to information and, after serious examination, to use the feedback to improve future communication.

The topic of effective school–community relations has evolved over the years, and it still is evolving. Polls continue to indicate that the school's publics—internal and external—want more information about the schools. Whatever the reasons for a school's failure to communicate—lack of skills, unawareness of the information needs, or interpretation of interest as opposition—the result has been a credibility gap that may explain many school–community problems.

A strong, effective instructional program that focuses on the needs of the students at a school is an essential ingredient of an effective school–community relations plan. Several research studies have confirmed the impact such a learning program has on the image of a school and the support it receives from everyone involved with the school.

> **Think of the glass as always half full,
> and never half empty.**

Marketing Your School:
Flaunt What You Do Best!

Charter schools, vouchers, high standards, and accountability are changing education like cable changed television. Through a series of 16 case studies, the Economic Policy Institute looked to see if there were any practices of private schools that public schools could, and should, adopt. Their conclusion was that marketing was the answer. Initially these schools had to develop a rationale for their being. Rather than attempting to be all things to all people, many schools have presented themselves as being dedicated to high academic standards, parental choice and satisfaction, and character development. The key is to evaluate what your school offers and articulate what your school is doing good for students. Once that is determined and you are sure of your strengths, make your presence in the community known. The message you create will help drive your communication efforts. For example, "There's no better place to learn than (your school's name)." Have your communication efforts reinforce your reputation and the reputation of the school in the community, and establish your position in your school district.

Reaching All Audiences
With a Variety of Methods

In this day and age, school principals can no longer rely solely on newsletters as the means of sharing good news, concerns, and information about their schools. With the explosion of the Internet and other modes of interactive communication, there is little excuse not to multiply those efforts to touch base with parents and other citizens. The real challenge now is how to mix the diversity of communication methods for the greatest impact. So, it seems that the initial step is to identify the communication tools and techniques most widely accepted and preferred by your school's community. To obtain that information, parents and other community residents could be asked in the school improvement survey, "What are your two main sources of information about our school?"

The school should have a Web site that is up to date and regularly maintained. The value of an effective Web site is in its potential for communicating with everyone from students to parents, prospective parents, the community at large, and alumni. Although most schools will continue to communicate through the media and school newsletters, other methods might be considered. Perhaps publications could be posted online if a high percentage of residents have access to computers and the Internet. As mentioned earlier in this book, some school principals have used the impact of communicating with others through *list servers* they have developed. Those principals have the ability to send periodic notices or messages that could include links to the school's latest publications and to the district's or school's Web site in general. A part of an effective school–community relations plan is the regular evaluation of all aspects of the plan. Periodic visits to measure the traffic on the Web can give some indication of how frequently online information is accessed and downloaded.

Many school systems have seized the opportunity to showcase schools and their instructional programs on public access television channels. The programming for television should involve students in the preparation and presentation of the school's successful programs, new academic initiatives, and successes.

Brady Keys, Jr., former member of the Pittsburgh Steelers, in conjunction with the educational software firm EPOS, launched Helping Involve Parents (HIP). The interactive program allows parents and teachers to form their own communications network via the Internet or on the telephone. The program, which allows parents to view homework assignments, class schedules, and student performance, is widely used in many schools in New York City.

June Million, NAESP's (National Association of Elementary School Principals) director of public information, reported that many elementary school principals had strong ties with a local high school. These relationships are good for the elementary students and also for the high school students. One Tennessee elementary principal and the high school baseball coach formed "Baseball Buddies." Thirty-three of the high school students visited their adopted classroom for 20 minutes a week. Each week they spent their time in the classrooms talking about the importance of studying, the harmful effects of drugs, what is important about school, or other appropriate topics. The elementary students built rapport with their player and got T-shirts with their player's number on them; and some even started going to the games. Each grade level was highlighted at every home game. Benefits to the high school students included improved self-esteem, because they were viewed as role models—for some of them, for the first time in their lives.

Another principal, Jill Eaton, started a yearlong, for-credit high school course at her high school. She and the high school principal arranged for students to use their first period as one-on-one tutors at the elementary school while also earning Carnegie Unit credits. The high school program participation has grown in numbers each year.

Making CDs and DVDs is getting easier to do each year. Several school principals have realized the value of each of these as a means of marketing their schools. Following the strategies that cities, businesses, and corporations have used, school systems and schools are beginning to see the impact of these interactive methods of selling the schools. The disks can feature video clips of teachers and students in action. Some elementary and middle school principals are planning to develop a separate CD or DVD for each grade or subject area. These media can contain highlights from a particular school year. The production of multiple copies can serve the same purpose as other fund-raisers the schools might use.

The Totowa, New Jersey, School District, like many others around the country, developed a Public Education Foundation to provide enrichment programs for the district's students outside the scope of the regular curriculum. The planners of the foundation wanted to encourage members of the business community to share their vision and to provide fiscal support for the foundation's programs. They have been successful in getting that needed support to the benefit of many students.

Establish a Key Communicator Program

Earlier in this book, the value of people who are in positions of advocacy for the school has been presented. The technique is the single most powerful, almost no-cost, ongoing two-way communications approach to school officials.

Summary

Educators, especially principals, need to court the school staff, parents, nonparents, community and business members, and the media. It is the principal's responsibility— or rather *duty*—to see that these internal and external publics and the school work together to serve and inform the community. Some chief assets of a school principal in accomplishing this important task are the following:

♦ A sense of honesty and trust—Reputations are built on this!

♦ Empathy—Try to imagine what the reporter goes through to meet deadlines and get stories reported.

♦ Accuracy—Remember the five Ws.

♦ Timing—Proactive is always better than reactive.

♦ Imagination coupled with vision—Dare to be different.

♦ A good disposition—Honey attracts more attention than vinegar!

Carroll and Carroll (2000, p. 129) suggest that using the following nine strategies will increase the effectiveness and quality of your marketing communication program:

1. Seize all opportunities that communicate quality to the customer.

2. Use word-of-mouth marketing to spread good news about your school system.

3. Use repetition to make your message memorable.
4. Develop a solid relationship with the media.
5. Name an EdMarketing coordinator.
6. Issue press releases and PSAs (public service announcements).
7. Start building an arsenal in writing and in pictures.
8. Develop your marketing communications with senior citizens in mind.
9. Develop and maintain a Web site.

A wise school principal should use the information from research projects, professional readings, firsthand experiences, and polls to learn about successful school–community relations plans. Developing a school–community relations plan that will meet the needs of a particular school is the next step in the process. The collective wisdom, creativity, and involvement of everyone at a school can lead to success at the school.

Good luck! Be on the lookout for creative ways to tell your school's story. Seek input from many sources, analyze and react to the input received, and modify the plan accordingly. You can begin the process of sharing, marketing, your school by identifying six "I can say with pride about our school" statements. Share these statements with parents and others who need to know about the school. These can be shared in newsletters, too, and also become large posters placed around the school. The principal's leadership will get the process started.

I believe that school principals who take seriously their responsibility to have a school–community relations plan are generally more successful principals. Accept the challenge to build your school's reputation by creating and supporting an effective instructional program. Recognize, respect, and acknowledge the contributions of every member of the school's internal and external publics. Maintain a number-one priority to motivate students to like and respect their school and everyone affiliated with it. That will happen if students are respected, too. Use the talents and good intentions of the media while you pay careful attention to input received from evaluations of the plan. Always seek to improve the plan.

Hopefully, as you read these paragraphs you will gained a new or renewed respect for and awareness of the need to have a school–community relations plan. Take and use ideas that you feel can become effective strategies at your school. Better yet, use ideas from this book as a foundation to create your own new techniques. Have fun, get lots of people motivated and involved, and watch their positive reactions.

Consider the words John Nagle wrote in 1968 and realize how loudly his message rings in our ears today.

> **The simple fact is that an American public school district is dependent on its public for support, financial and otherwise, that it commits educational hari-kari [*sic*] when it neglects the public, isolates itself from the community, leaves its citizenry either misinformed or completely uninformed.**
>
> *– John Nagle (1968)*

The potential for positive, and negative, public relations never ends.

References and Suggested Readings

Blair, J. (2004). *Building Bridges with the Press: A Guide for Educators.* Bethesda, MD: Education Week Press.

Carroll, S. R., & Carroll, D. (2000). *EdMarketing: How Smart Schools Get and Keep Community Support.* Bloomington, IN: National Educational Service.

Nagle, J. M. (1968). How to tell what your public really things. *The American School Board Journal, 156*(6), 8–11.